ROYAL COMMISSION ON
THE NATIONAL HEALTH SERVICE

The Working of the National Health Service

Research Paper Number 1

LONDON: HER MAJESTY'S STATIONERY OFFICE

ISBN 0 11 730110 8

Foreword by the Chairman

1. The Royal Commission on the National Health Service was appointed in May 1976 with the following terms of reference:

"To consider in the interests both of the patients and of those who work in the National Health Service the best use and management of the financial and manpower resources of the National Health Service."

The terms of reference cover the NHS in England, Scotland and Wales as well as the parallel services in Northern Ireland.

2. In October 1976 we published a booklet entitled "The Task of the Commission" which was offered as a guide to those who wished to submit evidence to us. We have received an immense amount of written evidence from a wide range of organisations and individuals, both within and without the NHS. We have been able to discuss their views with only a small number of those who have submitted evidence to us so far, though we shall be taking more oral evidence during the remainder of the period of our existence. We have been both heartened and impressed by the response to our earlier publication and the views expressed have influenced our discussions.

3. Much of the evidence we received was prepared in the immediate aftermath of health service reorganisation and concentrated on its effects. A common allegation is that the present structure of the NHS leads to delays in getting decisions made and consequently to frustration and inefficiency. We considered that the truth or otherwise of this claim was fundamental to our remit, and early in 1977 we commissioned Professor Maurice Kogan of Brunel University Department of Government to test it. This report—"The Working of the National Health Service"—is the result of the studies undertaken by him and his team. We are publishing it in order to stimulate and inform public discussion of the issues with which it deals.

4. The views expressed in the report are, of course, those of the author and his team alone and not of the Royal Commission.

A. W. Merrison
June 1978

The Working of the National Health Service

A Study for
The Royal Commission on the National Health Service
by a Team from
the Department of Government,
Brunel University

January 1978

Membership of the Team

This report is the result of work by a team working between March and December 1977.

Members of the team were largely drawn from, or associated with, the Department of Government, Brunel University. They were Maurice Kogan, Barbara Goodwin, Mary Henkel, Nancy Korman and Tim Packwood who are all members of staff of the Department of Government. They were joined by Tony Bush, Senior Lecturer in Public Administration at Luton College of Higher Education and Valerie Heyes, Principal Lecturer in Applied Social Studies at Croydon College of Design and Technology, both of whom had previously received higher degrees within the Department. Linda Ash and Janice Tester, student members of the Department, worked with the team on their work placement projects.

The team was also helped in part of its study of a Northern Ireland area by Chris Brown, lecturer in Management Studies, Ulster College, and by Helen Simons of the London University Institute of Education in work on the case study on hospital closures.

Successive drafts of the Field Interview Survey were written by Nancy Korman and Maurice Kogan. Individual authors are indicated on each of the case studies. It should be noted, however, that most members of the team participated actively at all points in the inquiry and the Report is the collective product and responsibility of all of the principal members.

For the most part, the team worked in small groups convened by different individual members who took responsibility for collating and administering parts of the study. The convenors were Tony Bush (West Midlands), Maurice Kogan (Grampian and Southern (NI)), Nancy Korman (North East Thames), Tim Packwood (Oxford) and Barbara Goodwin (Gwent).

The typing and general administration of the study was undertaken by Sally Marshall. To her particularly, but also to many other members of university administration, the Team wish to record appreciation.

Contents

PART I
The Scope and Methods of the Study

2

Terms of Reference

1. This report results from an invitation by the Royal Commission on the National Health Service to study the decision making processes in the re-organised service. Our terms of reference were to "test some of the evidence presented to the Royal Commission which suggests that the present organisation and working assumptions of the NHS lead to delays in getting decisions made and consequently to frustration and inefficiency".

2. We began with a rapid survey of the main literature on reorganisation (listed in the Appendix) in order to get some notion of its objectives which might be regarded as some of the criteria against which the working of the national health service could be judged, and to make a preliminary assessment of the main issues for assessment. At this stage these presented themselves as the development of consensus decision making; the number of tiers for the management and administration of the health service; the place of advisory committees; the accountability lines established from sector to district, area, region and department; and the integration of the hitherto separate three parts of the health service.

3. We then undertook a pilot study, based on interviews with 38 role holders in one English region, area and district, the main purpose of which was to identify the main issues felt to be faced by those working within the reorganised health service, which then could be put to the larger sample. The pilot study made it possible to identify the problems and achievements which derived from reorganisation itself and those which might emerge in any form of organisation created for the health service. A report on the pilot study was submitted in July 1977.

4. The issues clarified in the pilot study were carried forward into the substantive Field Interview Survey. We worked with NHS staff, health authority members, community health council members and staff, within six geographical areas of England, Northern Ireland, Scotland and Wales as follows:

Oxford Region
Oxfordshire Area (Teaching)
Berkshire Area
West Berkshire District

West Midlands Region
Coventry Area
Warwickshire Area
Rugby District

North East Thames Region
City and East London Area (Teaching)
Newham District

Grampian Board, Scotland
South Grampian (Teaching) District
North Grampian District

Gwent Area, Wales
South District, Gwent
North District, Gwent

Southern Board, Northern Ireland
Craigavon and Banbridge District
Newry and Mourne District

5. In addition, some interviews were conducted within the DHSS, the Northern Ireland Department of Health and Social Services (DHSS (NI)), the Scottish Home and Health Department (SHHD) and Common Services Agency (CSA), and the Welsh Office. In all, 482 interviews were conducted with 519 interviewees, excluding those participating in the four case studies.

6. The whole study consisted of four main elements:

(a) a pilot study undertaken within the Oxford region reported to the Royal Commission in July 1977;

(b) a Field Interview Survey which is the main source of our data. A list of roles studied will be found at the beginning of Part II of the report;

(c) case studies which attempt to describe and evaluate a range of decision making processes in more detail than proved possible in the Field Interview Survey. Detailed reports of the Case Studies can be found in Part III;

(d) conclusions derived from the Field Interview Survey and the case studies. In Part IV we attempt to interpret our findings and to draw out the main implications for policy.

7. The members of the research team felt that they were able to develop clear impressions of the structure and decision making processes within the health service. It was not, however, possible fully to explore and evaluate so large a range of issues, over so wide a geographical coverage, within the ten months available. Whilst there was time for a great deal of field work, the more reflective reading and reiterative meetings essential for deeper analysis and verification were not possible. We did, however, return both the Field Interview Survey and the case studies in draft to those with whom we worked, with a request that they make them available to all who participated in the hope that misinterpretations or errors would be corrected. 69 comments were received on the Field Interview Survey and 31 on the four case studies. We are extremely grateful to all of the authorities and individuals involved for the time spent with us in interviews, the access given to often sensitive materials, and the time spent in commenting on our first drafts.

8. The Field Interview Survey conveys the opinions of a reasonably representative range of workers within the health service and the Northern Ireland social services, members of authorities, of central government departments, and of the community health councils in England and Wales, the district committees in Northern Ireland and the local health councils in Scotland. The methods used in the Field Interview Survey are discussed in the Introduction to Part II of this report.

9. What is essentially a collation of perceptions of decision making has been corroborated by four more detailed analyses of specific decisions. The case studies deal with selected managerial processes since in the time available it would not have been possible to undertake a process analysis in all of the subject areas where the commission asked us to work. A somewhat more

detailed account of relations between health and local authority services, based on one English area, forms part of Section 7 of the Field Interview Survey. The four case studies were chosen so as to illustrate, as far as possible, the way in which detailed decision making is affected by some of the larger components of NHS structure. Between them they attempt to illustrate the types of decisions and relationships resulting from a planning system, the role of members of an authority as revealed in area board enquiries, public participation as exemplified by cases of hospital closure, and the role of clinicians in management as exemplified by the allocation of responsibilities in bio-medical engineering. Another factor determining choice of case was the availability of an issue which could be quickly researched. We emphasise that at no point did we fail to receive maximum co-operation in choosing case studies but some were, for a variety of reasons, more accessible to the research team than were others.

The Context Within Which the Study Took Place

10. The study is mainly concerned with reporting perceptions of the effects of reorganisation. But although the interviews and case studies were concerned with reorganisation, participants referred to factors which are not necessarily associated with changes introduced in 1973 in Northern Ireland and in 1974 in England, Scotland and Wales. The new structures attempted to enable particular priorities to be emphasised but in so doing have to take account of longstanding local characteristics, the more recent movements in social thought, and the well established ways in which different professional groups have worked within the NHS.

11. In at least two areas, for example, local politics are important to health administration and this was thought to affect the roles of chairmen and members in relation to those of officers and the community health councils. Elsewhere, geography and demographic patterns are central, for some areas have diffused populations with no natural centre for administration while others are dominated by one large town in which there might be a major concentration of health resources. Different authorities inherited different commitments and the means for meeting them.

12. The NHS has also inherited longstanding assumptions which jostle with more recent movements of social thought. Thus clinicians, particularly doctors, have always been able to get on with their work irrespective of the system which they may dislike or find frustrating. But national health service managers are expected to ensure that massive resources are used universally and equitably. The discretion of highly trained and professional individuals remains the starting point of health care but the introduction of systematic planning systems, the organisation for relating health and local authority functions, the general intention to depend on rational analysis of needs and services on the large scale, now more obviously contrast with the assumption that individual practitioners should be able to act autonomously on behalf of the patient. These changing assumptions about structure do not, of course, pre-empt the issue as to whether decision making in itself has deteriorated in the first years of reorganisation.

5

13. Moreover, the services reorganised in 1973 and 1974 are working in a vastly different atmosphere from those of 1946. The less prestigious working groups not only expect better conditions but also a say in the larger policy issues such as whether there should be pay beds which also, however, affect the status of individual practitioners. Differential concepts of status, salaries and authority are less easily accepted throughout the whole of the British employment system. The attempts to strengthen decision making by consensus, industrial democracy and social engineering, all might conflict with the principles of individual prescription and relationships with individual patients which were so explicitly embodied into the pre-reorganised service and which still constitute the basis of medical status and power. Many of these changes, however, cannot be attributed to reorganisation. They derive largely from the changed political, industrial and social climate of Britain in the 1970's.

14. The research team met interviewees in many different parts of the United Kingdom. The structures for England are different in many respects from those created in Northen Ireland, Scotland and Wales. There are, too, cultural differences in respect of the place accorded to health services in the different countries. Yet in spite of the differences confirmed by reorganisation and of the longer standing traditions in each country, the team found that organisational characteristics, and decision making processes, were remarkably similar wherever they went.

PART II

Findings from the
Field Interview Survey

Glossary

ADAC	Area Dental Advisory Committee
AEG	Area Executive Group
AET	Area Executive Team
AHA	Area Health Authority
AHB	Area Health Board
AMAC	Area Medical Advisory Committee (also called Area Medical Committee)
AMO	Area Medical Officer
AMT	Area Management Team
ANMAC	Area Nursing and Midwifery Advisory Committee
ANO	Area Nursing Officer
ATO	Area Team of Officers
CSA	Central Services Agency or Common Services Agency
CHC	Community Health Council (known as Local Health Council and District Committee in Scotland and Northern Ireland respectively)
DET	District Executive Team
DHSS	Department of Health and Social Security
DHSS (NI)	Department of Health and Social Services (Northern Ireland)
DMC	District Medical Committee
DMT	District Management Team
DAMO	District Administrative Medical Officer
DANO	District Administrative Nursing Officer
FPC	Family Practitioner Committee
FPS	Family Practitioner Services
HCPT	Health Care Planning Team
JCC	Joint Consultative Committee
JCPT	Joint Consultative Planning Team
LHC	Local Health Committee
LMC	Local Medical Committee
MDA	Multi District Area
NHS	National Health Service
RHA	Regional Health Authority
RMAC	Regional Medical Advisory Committee
RNMAC	Regional Nursing and Midwifery Advisory Committee
RMO	Regional Medical Officer
RNO	Regional Nursing Officer

RTO	Regional Team of Officers
SDA	Single District Area
SHHD	Scottish Home and Health Department
SSD	Social Services Department
WO	Welsh Office

List of Roles Interviewed

Region

(58 interviewees in 56 interviews)

3 Regional Administrators (in 4 interviews)
3 Regional Nursing Officers (in 4 interviews)
3 Regional Medical Officers
3 Regional Works Officers
3 Regional Treasurers
2 Regional Capital Services/Development Officers
2 Regional Pharmaceutical Officers
2 Regional Personnel Officers
1 Regional Supplies Officer
1 Regional Scientific Administrative Officer
1 Regional Education and Training Officer
1 Regional Ambulance Officer
1 Regional Architect
2 Specialists in Community Medicine (in 3 interviews)
4 Regional Nurses
1 Consultant
1 Principal Assistant Regional Treasurer
2 General Administrators, Service Planning
1 General Administrator, Capital Services
1 General Administrator
3 Works Specialist Staff

3 Chairmen, RHA ⎫
9 Members, RHA   ⎬ (in 7 interviews)
2 Chairmen, Regional Medical Advisory Committee
2 Chairmen, Regional Nursing and Midwifery Advisory Committee
1 Chairman, Regional Scientific Advisory Committee

Single District Area

(79 interviewees in 72 interviews)

2 Area Administrators
2 Area Medical Officers
2 Area Nursing Officers
2 Area Treasurers
3 Consultants, AMT
3 GPs, AMT
1 University Representative, AMT

2 Area Works Officers
2 Area Dental Officers
2 Area Personnel Officers
1 Area Planning Officer
1 Area Pharmaceutical Officer
1 Area Chief Ambulance Officer
1 Area Health Education Officer
2 Administrators, FPS
3 Specialists in Community Medicine
2 Area Nurses
1 Physiotherapist
1 Community Dentist
2 Consultants
1 GP
2 Junior Doctors
3 Divisional Nursing Officers
3 Senior Nursing Officers
1 Nursing Officer
2 Ward Sisters
1 Health Visitor
1 Chief Physicist
3 Sector Administrators
2 Unit Administrators
1 Administrator, Planning
1 Administrator, Support Services
1 Administrator, Health Services
2 Financial Specialist Staff
2 Works Special Staff
1 District Catering Manager
1 Porter

3 Chairmen, AHA ⎫
5 Members, AHA ⎬ (in 6 interviews)
                  ⎭
7 CHC—Chairmen, Secretaries, Members (in 2 interviews)

Some of the interviewees above held more than one role and we list below the additions:
Chairman, Cogwheel Executive Committee
Chairman, Therapeutic Advisory Committee

*Multi-District Area**

(156 interviewees in 142 interviews)

5 Area Administrators (in 6 interviews)
6 Area Nursing Officers
5 Area Medical Officers
5 Area Treasurers
4 Area Supplies Officers
5 Area Works Officers
6 Area Dental Officers

---

* Includes equivalent roles in Northern Ireland, Scotland and Wales.

13

5 Area Pharmaceutical Officers
4 Area Personnel Officers
2 Area Chief Ambulance Officers
1 Area Transport Officer
1 Area Records Officer
1 Area Health Education Officer
4 Administrators, Family Practitioner Services
12 Specialists in Community Medicine
11 Area Nurses
1 Speech Therapist
1 Physiotherapist
1 Chief Work Study Officer
1 Chief Internal Auditor
1 Administrator, Primary Care Services
7 Administrators, Planning
3 Administrators, Personnel
4 Administrators, Support Services
5 Works Specialist Staff
2 Financial Specialist Staff
2 CSSD Managers
2 Directors of Nurse Education
1 Director of Social Services
3 Assistant Directors of Social Services
1 Principal Psychologist

6 Chairmen, AHA ⎫
22 Members, AHA ⎬ (in 14 interviews)
6 Chairmen, AMAC ⎭
6 Chairmen, ANMAC (in 4 interviews)
1 Chairman, ADAC
1 Chairman, APhAC
1 Chairman, Area Staff Consultative Committee
1 Chairman, Area Consultative Committee of Paramedics

Some of the above interviewees held more than one role, and the following list indicates additions:
District Nursing Officer
Divisional Nursing Officer
District Nurse
Professor of Pathology
3 Consultants
GP
2 GP Pharmacists
Representatives, NUPE and COHSE—Chairman, West Midlands District Health Committee

*District**

(205 interviewees in 195 interviews)
8 District Administrators

---

* Includes equivalent roles in Northern Ireland, Scottish and Welsh districts.

5 District Finance Officers
8 District Nursing Officers
6 District Community Physicians
6 Consultants, DMT
4 GPs, DMT
3 District Works Officers
3 District Dental Officers
3 District Pharmaceutical Officers
2 District Supplies Officers
3 District Personnel Officers
4 District Catering Managers
3 District Domestic Services Managers
1 District Transport Officer
2 District Social Services Officers
2 General Administrators
2 Administrators, Personnel
2 Administrators, Planning
4 Administrators, Community Services
5 Administrators, Support Services
6 Sector Administrators
7 Unit Administrators
4 Financial Specialist Staff
3 Works Specialist Staff
2 Laundry Managers
13 Consultants
7 GPs
5 Junior Doctors
3 Community Doctors
1 Community Dentist
1 General Dental Practitioner
2 Unit Medical Administrators
4 Specialists in Community Medicine
2 Pharmacists
2 Physiotherapists
2 Radiographers
1 Occupational Therapist
1 Speech Therapist
6 Divisional Nursing Officers
7 Senior Nursing Officers
6 Nursing Officers
6 Ward Sisters
4 District Nurses
4 Health Visitors
1 Community Psychiatric Nurse
1 Staff Nurse
1 School Nurse
2 Nurse Auxiliaries
1 Community Midwife
1 Dean of Medicine Faculty
1 Senior Technician

1 Co-ordinator of Voluntary Services
3 Porters
18 CHC: Chairmen, Secretaries, Members (in 8 interviews)

Some of the above interviewees held more than one role. The following list includes additions:

Chairman, Area Dental Advisory Committee
3 Chairmen, Area Medical Advisory Committee
Chairman, Local Medical Committee
Chairman, District Therapeutic Professions Advisory
Committee
Chairman, Medical Executive Committee
Secretary, GP Sub-Committee of Area Medical Advisory Committee
Chairman, Staff Side, Joint Consultative Staff Committee
Secretary, District Consultative Committee
Chairman, Area Association of Health Service Unions
Branch President, NALGO
Branch Secretary, NUPE
Branch Secretary, COHSE
President, District Branch of Health Visitors Association
Representative, RCN

Central Departments and Agencies

The total number of interviews with a total of 21 individuals/groups was 17, excluding preliminary discussions about the project. The numbers of different individuals seen were:
10 Administrative Staff
5 Medical Staff
3 Nursing Staff
1 Social Work Staff
3 Central Service Agency (Scotland)

Introduction and Methods

1. The Field Interview Survey was intended to gather the opinions of a widely representative range of workers, members of authorities, of central government departments and community health councils within the health service.

2. The main instruments of enquiry were interviews for which we allowed an hour and a half in each case. Many, in fact, exceeded that time—three and three quarter hours was the maximum—whilst a few took less than an hour. The researchers kept to a general schedule based on the issues revealed as most relevant from our pilot study, but did not attempt to apply a questionnaire which would restrict respondents in expressing their own view of the impact of reorganisation and nature of decision making in the health service.

3. Each interview was written out in full, usually in typescript, and was available, on file, to the whole research team. Two members of the research team then went through every interview note and collated findings independently of the field interviewers. The whole draft was then seen by other members of the research team and amplifications and corrections made.

4. The material was then put to those interviewed, for comments. Most of those who replied confirmed the general tenor of the report. Many referred, however, to particular findings and where these comments have clarified or extended the findings already noted, they have been drafted in. Where they challenge the findings, but were out of line with the rest of the data, they have been referred to as a minority view.

5. Not all interviewees discussed all of the issues elucidated by our Pilot Study. Some questions could not be answered from the particular experience of the interviewee. We felt it more important to get full statements of views rather than to administer mechanistically a question and answer session. As a result, inevitably, answers emerged with different levels of clarity and comprehensiveness. Because of the circumstances of particular interviews, or of the time available for interviews, not all of the questions could be put by the member of the team conducting the interview. For the same reasons, most respondents replied with a high level of generality. We have indicated the main views on each issue as well as minority expressions which either added specifically to particular points or presented a particular interpretation of an issue. That particular interviewees did not make a specific comment does not, of course, mean that they would not agree with it; it was often a problem for the interviewer not to put words in the mouth of the interviewee in order to make comments more precise. For the most part, however, interviewees were questioned on the whole range of issues embodied in this report.

6. The report that follows is, therefore, a summary of the views of the 519 participants in the Field Interview Survey.

7. In each section of the survey report, we give the context within which participants' views should be considered. We then analyse the main views expressed. A brief summary of the findings is then given. We then add the research team's own interpretations of the material analysed in the section.

1. Reorganisation: Objectives and Impact

Context

1.1 The main objectives of reorganisation, as stated in the official documents* leading to reorganisation, were: a fully integrated health service bringing together all members of health care professions; the provision of health needs locally; the co-ordination of health and local authority services, and, in Northern Ireland, their integration; comprehensive planning of health services; administrative support systems for professional practioners; participation of doctors and dentists in decision making; uniform standards of care; rapid implementation of innovations; clear and flexible career structures for staff; effective education and training of health service personnel.

Report

The Main Objective as Stated in the Interviews: Integration

1.2 Almost half of all interviewees specifically cited *integration* as the main objective of reorganisation. In addition, those who did not mention it specifically as an objective frequently commented on the degree of integration achieved, so that it was apparent they assumed it as an objective. At all levels, integration of hospital and community services was noted by administrators, professional managers and practitioners as a gain to the health service. The nursing staff spoke most frequently about the integration of community and hospital nursing services (although this was favourably mentioned by others as well); for many this is now seen as a reality, an accomplishment of reorganisation. The success here was related to comments about a better service being offered to patients because of continuity of care. For staff in supporting services the unification of function had been an important gain and they mentioned it even when the changes were not particularly associated with reorganisation. Changes referred to included the bringing together of different professional groups concerned with buildings and maintenance; the unifying of the different branches of pharmacy and dentistry; the creation of a personnel function; advantageous adjustments to supplies organisation. Services for children were singled out by some community medicine specialists at the area level as having improved because of integration. A union official spoke of the benefit of dealing with one employing authority whereas previously unions had to deal with the local health authority as well as with the RHB and HMCs.

1.3 Integration was seen as successful at all levels of teams of officers; it enabled chief officers to co-ordinate related activities and enhanced control and more comprehensive planning of work. A district nursing officer cited her ability so to plan cuts in nursing establishment that community and long-stay services were least affected. Pharmaceutical officers at district, area and region spoke of being able to offer better services to community clinics. An

---

* Management Arrangements for the Reorganised NHS, DHSS, 1972.
The Management Arrangements for the Reorganised NHS in Wales, Welsh Office, 1972.
An Integrated Service: The Reorganisation of Health and Social Services in Northern Ireland, February 1972.
The SHHD did not issue guidance in a single document, but through circulars and other memoranda on particular aspects of reorganisation.

area records officer reported giving help to general practitioners and clinics in record keeping and in gaining access to the more comprehensive information now available for planning. A regional management services officer pointed out the use now made of his services by DMTs and ATOs and not only by hospitals as prior to reorganisation. There was a widespread feeling that community services had benefited in many ways from the more specialised services now available to them.

1.4 There were disappointments that integration had not been carried as far as was hoped:

(a) at all levels there was mention of the continued independence of general practitioners; a "bipartite" service was a phrase often used (an area medical officer said general practice had been "encapsulated, not integrated"). This criticism was echoed in Scotland and Northern Ireland where the administration of family practitioner services was more closely integrated with other parts of the health service. However, attitudes towards general practitioner independence varied. One GP remarked that they guarded their independence all the more having observed the "increasing dictation to hospital clinicians". Their independence enabled them to act more effectively in hospital dominated committees. Some nurses and consultants, too, were glad that general practitioners remained independent;

(b) health and personal social services had not yet found ways of relating services, although some exceptions were noted. This is true as well in Northern Ireland where unification under one Authority was a major objective of reorganisation. (See Section 7);

(c) dental officers thought that in general terms their profession had acquired a structure for an integrated service. Two dentists mentioned an improvement in service for handicapped children. But other dentists pointed out that further integration was frustrated by legal restrictions on, for example, cross referrals between community and general practitioner dental services and on access to school dental services, which are unavailable to handicapped children over the age of 16;

(d) the feelings about integration of teaching and non-teaching hospitals were mixed. In some areas it was thought that teaching hospitals still dominated, and a few thought they should revert to a separate management structure. In other areas respondents noted that although teaching hospitals might have suffered from reorganisation, the teaching area had benefited as a whole from sharing in its services. These views may be linked with the more general feeling that hospitals still tended to dominate the health service.

Other Objectives

1.5 *The use of resources*—more efficiently, more fairly and through a good planning system—was the second most frequently mentioned objective, cited by 65 respondents. Views about its achievement varied. Some clinicians stated that administration absorbed too much money and staff. A more general point was that in most areas planning as such was embryonic. There were staff, however, who thought that services which had been neglected or underfunded in the past were now doing better—examples were given in supporting services and in psychiatry (although evidence about this field was contradictory)—and that there had been a general shift of resources to community services. In addition geographical areas which had been underfunded were now thought to be receiving more attention and more money. Although some of these developments were in evidence before reorganisation, many respondents pointed out how they had been enhanced by the new structure.

1.6 *Giving professionals a voice in management* was noted by 30 respondents as an objective. Nurses, both managerial and clinical, in particular felt that they had gained considerably from having a formal and recognised role as team members and this was a view held not just by DNOs, ANOs or RNOs (or their equivalents in Scotland, Wales and Northern Ireland) but by nurses of all ranks. Nursing as a profession was seen to have raised its status through obtaining team membership and chief officer posts. Other professional groups also felt they had gained by having a member of their own profession heading their service: dentists, pharmacists, paramedical professions, specifically speech and occupational therapists. While some had not attained chief officer level, they nonetheless felt it a benefit to have a professional head of their own even if they participated in managerial team meetings through the administrator, a community specialist or through a limited right of access. The impact of clinicians in management was the subject of mixed comments: consultants generally felt that they had lost influence; others considered that the existence of teams of officers with two or three medical members indicated a gain in medical influence.

1.7 *Better co-ordination of health and local authority services* was cited by only 24 interviewees as an objective and, of these, half were from Northern Ireland (9 from the area level) even though housing and education were not local authority services there. Of the English respondents, 7 were from the areas. This theme will be discussed in Section 7 but its development was seen to be quite slow.

1.8 Other objectives were mentioned by small numbers of interviewees: *better patient care*, either directly or indirectly through better management of services, was cited by 18; *improved decision making* by 15, *better career development and career structures* by 13, *development of greater expertise in management* by 12, and *greater responsiveness to local needs* and *more public participation* by 8 each.

1.9 Of the almost 400 respondents who spoke of the objectives of reorganisation, only 54 mentioned two objectives, a further 18 cited three objectives and six mentioned four or more objectives (usually by referring to the Grey Book). Some interviewees did not reply to the question on objectives because they had joined the NHS after reorganisation, or felt that their work was too far removed from the central functions of health service provision. Others responded in terms of the impact rather than objectives. In some cases, for the reasons given above, the question was not put. But answers to other questions contained indirect statements about objectives and their implementation.

General Views on Impact of Reorganisation
1.10 There were many comments about the management structure and management procedures which will be reviewed in more detail in Section 13.

In terms of the impact of reorganisation on the health service, it should be noted that the majority of comments made were negative. It took longer to make decisions, consultation was "rampant", the structure was top heavy and bureaucratic, it was difficult to locate where decisions were made and who had sufficient authority to make them. The size of the organisations created in 1973 and 1974, whilst seen by some to be necessary to make use of limited expertise, was thought to decrease identification between staff and the institutions they served. People felt comfortable in the working unit but lost and unrecognised in the larger organisational settings. An area pharmaceutical officer said that reorganisation had destroyed the allegiance of hospital staff which was the source of efficiency within the NHS. Two interviewees implied that the health service had had to work hard to get through the period of reorganisation at all.

1.11 But not all comments were disparaging. A regional officer said that decisions were now made more openly and that people were required to justify their choices. Others thought that the management structure was better able to control expenditure. The chairman of an RNMAC thought that a wider section of the public was now involved in the NHS than under the old structure. Several interviewees, but in no particular pattern, thought that communication and working relations between professional groups were beginning to improve.

1.12 Many interviewees commented that reorganisation had little or no impact on the services received by patients, and that better patient care was or should have been a major objective. Nurses tended to think that there was now more continuity of care, while other staff groups perhaps noticed no change. Among consultants and general practitioners the consensus was that nothing had improved for the patient and some thought that services had deteriorated. The main cause of deterioration, according to these respondents, was an increase in administration which they thought costly and inefficient (see below, paragraphs 13.7 and 13.18).

1.13 It was stated that many other factors impinged on the health service besides reorganisation. Perhaps the most important one was economic cuts which came almost immediately after reorganisation and eroded expectations that more funds would be available for developments. The smaller amounts of new monies had increased competition among professional groups for whatever funds were available and added to difficulties of redeployment of existing funds. (It is worth noting that there was a strong minority opinion that the health service was not under-funded but made poor use of its resources due to various pressures. Some pointed out that financial stringency compelled decision makers to consider difficult and unpopular issues which in times of growth could easily be avoided. In default of a fully developed planning system, financial stringency might be one of the few disciplines compelling a thorough consideration of priorities.) Professional attitudes were seen as a stumbling block to more rapid integration of services. Several staff groups had only recently been reorganised prior to 1974, for example, nursing and supplies organisation in England, Wales and Scotland and pharmaceutical officers. They felt that they had been faced with too many changes. Changes in industrial relations and unionisation of health service employees, public apathy towards large organisations, uncertainty about the future of the NHS structure all contributed to feelings of stress during this period and had little to do with reorganisation itself.

1.14 Another factor still uppermost in interviewees' minds was the way in which reorganisation was carried out, including the sequence of staff appointments at different levels, and the need to match the timing of reorganisation with changes in local authority structure. Many staff members resented the way in which they, and others, were treated, and the uncertainty that they had continued to feel since, as a result of persistent reviews and reappraisals of the service, had not made this easy to forget. Interviewees thought that there should be some pronouncement about the future of the structure. If certainty could be established, staff could then concentrate on learning how to make the management system work for the good of the patient. The implications of this will be discussed in the section on morale. (See Section 14).

Summary

1.15 At all levels and among all groups, the objective of *integration* stood out as the major aim of reorganisation. This was seen in terms of bringing together different disciplinary working groups (such as nursing, medical, supplies, pharmacy, works and personnel), of bringing together hospital and community services, and of integrating management structures for the health services. Some staff in all authorities could see worthwhile beginnings; others emphasised, however, that integration was already taking place irrespective of reorganisation. The *better use of resources* through planning was seen as the next most important objective, and again, some interviewees were able to point to achievements. *Participation by professionals in management* was next in frequency of mention, with nurses as a group seeing this as an important gain for their professional standing. *Co-ordination of health and local authority services* was cited by a smaller number of respondents, especially in Northern Ireland. Other objectives were also mentioned: *better patient care; improved decision making; better career structures; development of greater expertise in management; greater responsiveness to local needs* and *participation by the public.* Judged by the frequency with which these objectives were mentioned, they were seen to be less important than others, and the degree to which they could be found embodied in the health services at present varied.

Comment by the Research Team

1.16 Asking interviewees to say what they thought were the objectives of the reorganisation posed a difficult task for them; more likely than not they responded with what they liked and disliked about the new management arrangements. But the fact that over half either said or implied that reorganisation had made little difference to patient care (implying that it had not actually improved patient care) points to the difficulty of talking about good management in the health services; management is needed to support professional workers in providing services, but there seems to be little sympathy for the sheer complexity of this task. It also points to a basic management problem, that of providing the practitioner with what is needed to treat his patients while simultaneously ensuring the overall wellbeing and equitable distribution of resources of an organisation. Management and practitioners "pull" in different directions.

1.17 Many interviewees commented that the reorganised structure was just settling down and that improvements were gradually coming about in its functioning. This comment, we think, reflects the magnitude of change with which health service employees have had to cope. Reorganisation attempted so many things at once. Not all began with reorganisation but all were expected to improve with it. Clearer accountability, more participation of staff in management, provision of national priorities and standards, and more equitable and efficient use of resources may not live comfortably with greater public involvement, multidisciplinary working and responsiveness to local needs. All of these are manifested in at least one aspect of the new management arrangements and it is somewhat surprising that less than one ninth of interviewees cited more than one objective. The difficulties experienced by NHS staff in attempting to cope with changes of this kind should say something to those who undertake to reorganise large scale organisations. It is probable that the effort involved in reorganisation was severely underestimated.

1.18 The disappointments expressed about reorganisation may say as much about unrealistic expectations as they do about what is happening. That little good has been achieved for the patient and that the NHS management seems to practitioners to be oriented more towards resource allocations, than towards patient care, are feelings about reorganisation, but they are not necessarily facts. A tighter and more integrated managerial system may be a prerequisite for a more integrated service for patients but, at this stage, many staff felt they were paying too high a cost. The health services are now required to encompass wider concepts of health which entail reassessments for both the public and professional practitioners.

2. Structure: (i) The Central Departments

Context

2.1 The earlier documents on reorganisation emphasised the strategic role of the central departments. They assumed that there would be strong and viable health authorities freed from detailed control and expected to be fully accountable for planning and administering services for themselves, although within national frameworks.

Report

Views of Those Within Departments

2.2 The research team was not able to interview numbers of participants comparable to those at the regional, area, district and operational levels of the health service itself and what follows is based on interviews with 14 members of the four central departments.

2.3 The relationship between the four central departments and the health services must vary if only because the DHSS relates to 14 regional health authorities, who themselves work with 90 area health authorities, whilst the SHHD works with 15 health boards, the Northern Ireland Department of

Health and Social Services with four and the Welsh Office with eight area authorities. In all cases, the central departments wield considerable authority. They determine the revenue flows to the health authorities, and the major capital projects that may be undertaken, although degrees of control vary as between the different central departments. They approve each consultant post to be established by health authorities. They are partners in salary and condition negotiations and have, in effect, a veto over what might be agreed between the employers and the employees. These characteristics are common to the relationships between the central departments and health authorities in all four countries. It is, perhaps, in the planning systems that some of the larger differences between the countries might be observed, and it is there, too, that larger uncertainties of role and perspective can be identified.

2.4 Planning systems (considered more fully in Section 12)* have got underway in England and Wales under the guidelines published in 1976. In contrast, the Scottish Home and Health Department, although it possesses a planning unit, has not formally inaugurated a planning system. Both the English and the Scottish departments are concerned to build up adequate planning technologies, in consultation with the field authorities. The English, having given a lead in 1976, now rely on informal meetings and a series of circulars and other advisory documents to the field authorities. Where the Department itself cannot provide specialist facilities, or play a directly authoritative role, it can encourage the sharing of resources among regions or areas. In Scotland, the point was made that the establishment of a planning system can be an important means of clarifying the scope of the Department's authority and of modifying what can be perceived as inconsistencies of intervention. Accordingly, a key objective in the consultation between the Department and the Boards on the planning system has been the formulation of ground rules about spheres of control.

2.5 The relationships between the central departments and the lower level organisations in the NHS have changed substantially since reorganisation because of the difference in numbers involved. In Scotland, for example, the SHHD previously related to five regional hospital boards (and in a differing degree with local health authorities and 25 executive councils) but now works with 15 health boards. Previously, therefore, the central department would relate to a smaller number of chairmen, and with secretaries and senior administrative medical officers. It must now not only take up relationships with a larger number of authorities and a larger range of disciplines but do so in a context where members of executive groups who meet with them, play dual roles, as heads of professions in their authorities, and as members of management teams working through consensus.

2.6 The central departments face problems resulting from the changing political and administrative environment. Demands for delegation and devolution of powers from the centre have been strong and were promised as part of reorganisation. At the same time, however, health has become far more important politically and the health service, in common with other public services, is likely to be affected by acceding to the demands from particular groups. The introduction and running of planning systems, difficult

---

* See also the case study in Part III of this Report.

enough in themselves, have been affected by the changing economic environment. For the most part, therefore, departments may feel that they work by exhortation, rather than by prescription on overall plans. It is not easy for the centre to have a clear view as to how policies might develop and be made to stick. Yet uncertainty about role, and about the techniques required for forward planning, has not prevented some of the departments from attempting forward planning in consultation with the field authorities. The DHSS has a Planning Working Group which takes up thinking from the different levels of the health service. The Scottish Health Service Planning Council, with membership from the 15 boards, the Scottish universities and officers appointed by the Secretary of State, is trying to establish consensual methods of determining priorities. The problem is to make general judgements on health service futures emerge as authoritative and well backed statements upon which health authorities can act.

2.7 The uncertainties described in the previous paragraphs should not be over-generalised. Relationships between the centre and authorities within particular professional groups can be strong and seen, on both sides, to be supportive and to ensure that decisions are made which are compatible with understandings at all levels of the system. Where the point was raised in our discussions, however, the issue remained as to whether the Department was monitoring and co-ordinating the health service, or managing it. This uncertainty emerges differently in those countries where there are no regions. There the question is whether the central departments should have the managerial role of an English region as well as its central governmental functions.

Views Outside the Department

2.8 In discussing the role of the central departments, no strong feelings on their contribution or competence emerged from our field interviews outside the departments and the responses were patchy both as to the professional groups and the areas from which the responses were drawn. About two thirds of those participating made some kind of comment about the central departments. Of these, 12 stated they had no contact and no views at all .

2.9 Of those who directly answered the question, the majority (62) thought that the central departments were generally helpful in the advice they gave, in the content and style of their circulars and in the way in which they generally maintained their relationships with health authorities and workers within the health service. This approval which might seem to conflict with some of the particular complaints quoted below was somewhat general in nature, and was also voiced by some of the complainants.

2.10 The complaints volunteered by respondents were as follows: the central departments slowed down decision making unnecessarily (20) and this, perhaps, related to the criticisms of those (62) who felt that they indulged in too detailed control and, sometimes on no clear rational basis. One authority, for example, had waited nine months for guidance on the procedures to be adopted by nurses in verifying deaths and other similar examples were given. Decisions were too often mediated from central government administrator to health authority administrator rather than through the expert professional groups at both levels. There were some complaints that central administrators lacked direct knowledge of the National Health Service and that this is made worse by their habit of moving from one job to another after brief intervals. One respondent thought that the central departments were too much advised by academics and not by those with practical experience. Examples of inflexibility and non-responsiveness were given by 16 participants. A few complaints related to requests from central departments for detailed information which seemed unnecessary and time consuming. Decisions, often assumed to be politically motivated, were promulgated by the central government departments which cut into the ability of health authorities to use their budget according to their own overall plans. Instructions requiring more expenditure were given without the allocation of extra resources. For example, they were too easily yielding to trade union pressures in insisting that ambulances should be manned by two people instead of one, without giving budgetary enhancements to meet the extra costs. They interfered in incentive bonus schemes which were thought to be matters for management rather than government. They insisted on dust free pipes in one hospital at a cost of £100,000 which was thought to be an unnecessary waste of money.

2.11 Some complaints, however, concerned not over-control so much as lack of leadership. Some 16 complainants, mainly at senior levels, thought that the central department did not take an overall view, that they did not exercise expert leadership, that they acted as an arbiter, reflecting political pressures, that they had a poor sense of policy strategy and that "their own corporate planning might be in doubt." Groups of both regional and district officers thought the centre lacked unity and thus produced conflicting advice and instructions from different divisions.

Common Service Agencies
2.12 The team has not been able to make a detailed study of common service agencies which exist in Wales, Scotland and Northern Ireland, but has had some interviews with those responsible for them in Scotland and received a few responses on their working from those in the field authorities. Scotland and Northern Ireland have central agencies with a wide range of functions. In Northern Ireland the Central Services Agency has a strong role in the administration of general practitioner services, while in Scotland the emphasis is upon the central organisation of specialist services, not easily provided by individual health boards. The Scottish Common Services Agency comprises 16 departments responsible for services that include the design and commissioning of major building projects, supplies, ambulance services, blood transfusion, information, legal services, organisation and methods, health education, advice on laundry, catering and domestic services, and a communicable diseases unit, as well as dental estimates and prescription pricing. There is a Welsh Technical Services Organisation which is a separate health authority. It does not, however, cover ambulances and O and M.

2.13 The Scottish CSA is a statutory organisation established under Section 19 of the 1972 Act. This effectively brought together under one management body services hitherto provided by ad hoc agencies under the auspices of voluntary organisations, regional hospital boards and the Secretary of State. It emphasises its role as a service giver to both the SHHD and the health boards. The composition of its management committee (Chairman appointed by the Secretary of State from the service, seven health board and five Scottish Office members) reflects this dual role, and a concept of joint accountability to the Secretary of State and to the health boards. The management Committee provides resources and monitors performance; it is not concerned with the day to day running of the service, nor does it make policy. Its officers, who are not civil servants, act at the instigation of the health boards within the policy framework established by the Secretary of State and themselves. The larger divisions have their own directors, and some are decentralised into five local offices (previously the regional offices), thus enabling close working relationships to be established with at least the larger area health boards.

2.14 The dual relationship of the CSA with the SHHD and the health boards can be exemplified by reference to the building division. Health boards must establish their capital programme with the SHHD in consultation with the CSA division. Within this approval, boards submit briefs for individual projects to the division, stating user needs as agreed with the SHHD. They must satisfy the division that the statement of needs has been approved before it will act as a design and commissioning unit, and the division sets the standards with which projects must comply. SHHD approval of major capital schemes is given, taking account of the division's advice. Once a project is approved, the health boards set up and provide the chairmanship of project teams, while the CSA sets up the design team, at least for all projects costing over £100,000. User participation is thus brought into the system. At any point in the completion of the scheme, where there is unresolved disagreement between boards and the division, the matter is referred to the Department.

2.15 It seems clear that the relationship entails ambiguities. The health boards are the clients of the CSA, but the role of the CSA in applying standards and in giving advice to the SHHD gives them an authority beyond that of simple service-giving. And in the case of dispute between the CSA and the boards, it seems likely that the weight of influence will be on the side of the CSA. On the other hand, the CSA can, and on occasion does, act as advocate with the Department on behalf of health boards. And the CSA and its divisions are ultimately governed by a management committee with strong health board representation.

2.16 Only a few responses were received from the field, but these were, on the whole, favourable to the work of the common services agencies. Some of the bigger health authorities may feel that they should be able to carry through larger-scale projects according to their own user and design specifications. Occasional comment was made about the right of the CSA to appoint design staff. Some criticisms do confirm the apparent contradiction between the principle of boards' responsibility for the provision of health care in their areas and that of central standard setting or, indeed, of overall provision in some fields of work. There are conflicting arguments made as to whether ambulance services should be provided nationally or whether they should be more closely related to the pattern of service needed by individual authorities (although the contention of the CSA is that its organisation does allow for experimentation by individual authorities).

Summary

2.17 There seems to be general agreement that, despite the changed patterns of interaction since reorganisation, personal relationships between central government administration and professional advisers and their counterparts in the field are good. On both sides the uncertainty is about role and the requisite degree and boundaries of authority. The questioning in the central departments is reflected in the variability of criticisms in the field about degrees of control: for some control is too strong, and for others there is insufficient leadership from the centre. The ambiguities in the Common Services Agency's relationships constitute another element in this area of uncertainty.

Comment by the Research Team

2.18 The general arguments for common service agencies (or a central service agency, as it is known in Northern Ireland) are that there are many functions that need to be carried through coherently and on a sufficiently large scale over relatively small national systems such as can be found in Scotland and Northern Ireland. It might well not be appropriate for the central government department to act directly in a service giving relationship with the subordinate health authorities. The problem throughout is how common services can be provided without restricting the style of health care for which the health authorities are responsible. It is not possible to reach a simple judgement on the appropriateness of central services because of the wide range which they cover. Thus, there would hardly be dispute about the importance of a blood transfusion service to be made available to the Island Authorities with quite small populations. The economies of scale created by a unified supply system are also well known as long as "one off" purchases are possible (as they are) and a wide choice of supplies is available to the health authorities. There is an alternative means of providing common services, namely for health authorities to come together in consortium arrangements as occurs in other areas of public activity such as school building, where some Northern and Midlands local education authorities have worked together on common designs. Apparently, too, some such schemes were attempted between RHBs but without any great success. This would appear to entail an entirely different concept of a national health service, in which authority was shifted to the areas and in which the principles of integration, planning, prescription, co-ordination from the centre were under question. As it stands, in Scotland at least, the Common Services Agency would seem to constitute a crucial element in the relationship, uncertain as it is, between the Department and the Health Boards.

3. Structure: (ii) Levels of Authority

Context

3.1 The basic structure of the reorganised health services in England provides two statutory levels: Region, which undertakes major strategic planning for its geographical areas and monitors operations of its areas: and Area, which has responsibility for planning and operations. Areas are to be coterminous with local authorities, and may be divided into districts which are "natural" groupings for comprehensive health care provision. Both district and area teams are accountable to the AHA.

3.2 There is a major variation in structure between England and the three other UK countries. In Northern Ireland, Wales and Scotland, a line relationship exists between Area and District officers. There is no regional tier, although certain regional functions are performed by the Northern Ireland Department of Health and Social Services, the Welsh Office and the Scottish Home and Health Department.

Report

Region–Area Relationships in England

3.3 The need for the regional tier was strongly accepted. Fewer than 40 of all English health service interviewees thought that the regional tier should be removed either by areas relating directly to the DHSS, areas merging with the regions or the regions merging with the DHSS. Of these, 19 came from within one region, mainly from a single district area which had a teaching hospital. This may be attributed to the smallness of that particular region and to remembrance of the time when teaching hospitals had a direct line to the DHSS; these two reasons were stated by several interviewees themselves. Other respondents from the district level thought that the region was remote and that its impact on district functioning was not immediately evident. Still others, generally from areas, thought that area and region could merge, thus avoiding an overlap of policy making functions.

3.4 Regional functions were seen as allocation of resources, provision of regional specialist services, monitoring of national policies and standards, and strategic planning. The differentiation between regional and area functions made the relationship between these two tiers easier to accept and to operate. A few interviewees favoured the retention of the regional tier because it served as a buffer between the operational level and the DHSS. Region itself was seen as remote from the operational level, and this, too, was thought an advantage; it meant that the region was less threatening to districts than were the areas.

3.5 The working relationship between SDAs and their regions seemed to be slightly better than between regions and multi-district areas despite the strong reservation of one SDA about the need for the regional tier. In SDAs, the area tier was not a "middle man" between region and district and this may be a source of greater harmony and understanding.

3.6 The acceptance of the regional tier did not mean that problems did not exist. Several interviewees at the district said that the region was too remote from operations, and could therefore not understand their needs. Nine from area and region commented specifically on the duplication of work between these two tiers, while others implied that such duplication occurred at times. Six said that the region did not display a monitoring function either because they saw no evidence of monitoring or because the necessary data base was not yet developed. One area administrator said that monitoring was not possible because the regional officers were too involved in daily crises, which left no time for a well thought out monitoring scheme. A further six interviewees, from both area and districts, thought that the region interfered in the work of its lower tiers by overturning priorities for development agreed by area officers, or by involving itself in larger operational problems. Three at area tier would like to see more delegation from region to the area. It was pointed out by a regional interviewee, however, that areas did not always give adequate attention to priorities specified by DHSS policy. The RHA had to reconcile national guidelines with areas' own choices. Interviewees also thought that regional staff should be reduced; the numbers employed at that level could only be occupied as a source of interference in the work of lower tiers. In one region, in particular, the region itself was seen to be too small to have sufficient scope to function effectively; its smallness meant that it tended to get more involved in operational matters than was desirable. This raised the possibility of merging regions and giving them a greater span of control in resource terms. This would, however, have to be set against the problem of remoteness mentioned above. Lastly, some regional staff were seen to want to continue as an RHB, especially when the same regional officers held positions in the new structure similar to those that they had held in the old one.

Area-District Relationships in England

3.7 As one area administrator remarked, both area and district had the same master and so the relationship between them must be negotiated rather than imposed. Both had operational and planning functions and the opportunities for overlap of function and for conflict were considerable. The AHA, however, tended to relate to, and interact with, area officers; DMTs received little direct attention from their authority. The "separate but equal" philosophy was not seen to be realistic; AHA members needed to take an area-wide view which was supplied by the ATO, not the DMTs. The AHA chairman was based at the area headquarters, strengthening the link with the ATO. It was therefore not surprising to find a larger element of dissatisfaction and tension in the area-district relationship: a greater wish for control by the area officers and for autonomy by the district officers.

3.8 In multi-district areas, area officers felt that they had insufficient authority to ensure acceptance and compliance with area wide policies. Getting agreement on policy was a long process of negotiation which had usually to be conducted separately with each district team. Area officers also commented upon the inappropriateness of the separation of policy making and management; these were seen to be interactive processes which were made more difficult because they were carried out by separate teams. Both district and area staff agreed that there was duplication of work, through referral of issues from one team to another. District interviewees' complaints about area were that they were remote from operational activities, that they did not understand operational conditions, that they interfered with district decision making and that referrals between them and the districts caused delays. The area tier was also seen as a political device to pacify local authorities for the removal of health services from their control. However, there were some respondents at area and district who stressed the political or practical justification for each team and did not consider it realistic to consider modifications.

3.9 We interviewed in three districts which were part of multi-district areas. A more detailed analysis of views is as follows:

(a) one district, one of the largest in England, was part of a two-district area. The majority of district, and almost half of area level respondents, thought that the district, given its present boundaries, should be an area; it covered a large urban population with a clear identity of its own. Interviewees at area were more mixed in their views. Only two interviewees were in favour of three tiers, justifying this by reference to the importance of coterminosity. Others tended towards strengthening either the area or regional tiers, with the object of removing the other. These responses might have been influenced by the size of the region which has resulted in more of an overlap of functions between area and region than was found in other regions;

(b) the second district, in a three-district area, was a dense urban part of a larger urban unit. About half the district respondents thought that all three tiers were needed, and some wanted a line relationship between area and district. Their reason was the need for co-ordination of policy and operations among the three districts of the area. Other respondents thought that area could be removed as a way of simplifying the structure, and still others thought that there were too many levels without specifying a view on what would be an improvement. Only one interviewee thought an SDA would be best for the district. Of the 15 area respondents, almost half agreed with the need for three teams, again considering the need for a line relationship between teams. Others commented on the duplication of effort between area and district, or area and region. The difficulty of area working between district and region came out strongly here;

(c) in the third district, also in a three district area, there was general agreement that SDAs represented a better structure than the present one, but a variety of arrangements were considered. Some argued that the three district area could be divided into two SDAs; others thought that either region or area could be removed. A small number commented that with clarification of roles, the present structure could be made to work more efficiently. More than half the area staff interviewed were in favour of an SDA. Other possibilities mentioned at this level were a line relationship between area and district or the removal of either region or area team. No chief officer at area thought that the present structure should be retained.

3.10 The above paragraph shows the variety of opinions which exist, and the impact upon those opinions of geographic conditions such as the size of region, area or district. The interaction of service provision at district level within an area also affects opinions. The responses may also be examined in terms of the level at which staff work, but first a caution. The bare numerical responses to questions about the functions of and necessity for the different teams are, on their own, ambiguous. Not all respondents answered questions in the same way, so that some commented favourably on the creation of more SDAs, but did not specify how this should be done. A few felt unable to answer at all because they saw this as a political issue. Others, without mentioning SDAs, were in favour of removing a tier either above or below.

Still others opted for a line relationship which would reduce the discretion of the district. A further group said that there were too many levels without specifying which one could be removed. Some generalisations are nonetheless possible:

(a) only one fifth of interviewees at area and district, and one seventh at region, thought the structure either workable or necessary as it presently is; all others favoured some change, to streamline the number of vertical levels. Among these respondents, however, the majority would approve of a better distribution of work among the teams, and clearer role definitions. Some added the need for a line relationship between area and district, a view more prevalent among, but not exclusive to, area respondents;

(b) about one quarter of regional interviewees thought that the area should be the tier removed, as did just under one fifth of area respondents and one third of district respondents. Of these 15 regional replies, eight were within one region, reflecting perhaps that the old RHB had dealt with a larger number of HMCs than the present number of districts. The 10 area respondents included two chairmen of area advisory committees and one consultant member of an AHA, who, as practitioners, may be assumed to prefer decisions to be made at as low a level as possible; two others thought that the area tier as a whole could be removed, and the rest expressed views that either area or region could be removed or that the two tiers should merge, indicating that the concern was with duplication of function. In two districts, one quarter and one fifth favoured eliminating the area tier; in the third district, almost half the respondents preferred this view;

(c) one fifth of area and just under one fifth of district staff thought the regional tier could be removed; only one respondent at region favoured this. Of the area responses, half were phrased as either area or region, whilst only one district reply was in these terms. There was a very small number who thought that the region should merge with the DHSS;

(d) only six interviewees thought that the district could be removed, five of whom were staff in areas. Four of the six were in professions which saw the area as the best size for the provision of their services —dentistry, supplies and personnel. The other two respondents were concerned with the small size of one of the districts in their area;

(e) of the 31 practitioners interviewed at district, only one thought the structure should remain as at present. Most were more concerned with and aware of district infrastructure than with team levels. One third thought that the area tier should be removed; others mentioned that there were too many levels without specifying which they saw as redundant. Three, one of whom had previously worked in an SDA, specifically mentioned SDAs as preferable to multi-district systems;

(f) the most favoured structure was that of region and SDA as a more workable relationship. Almost half of region, two fifths of area and one fifth of district interviewees directly expressed a preference for SDAs, while a further two fifths at region, one half at area and seven tenths at district thought that one level could be removed which would in effect leave an SDA.

3.11 A general point made by respondents, whether they were personally involved in the situation or not, was that two district areas represented the least satisfactory system. It was thought that there was insufficient work at area level to occupy a full complement of staff, and that the discontent felt by district and area teams was thus greater than in MDAs. There were respondents who made this point at all levels. Likewise, the inappropriateness of the same structure for all types of situations was remarked upon. Some differentiated the needs of county and large urban areas; others those of teaching and non-teaching areas. But particularly in those regions which encompassed different geographical settings and demographic distributions, the need for flexibility of structure was recognised.

Line Management Relationships Between Tiers

3.12 In Scotland, Wales and Northern Ireland, there is a line relationship between officers at area and district. Our interviews showed that relationships between tiers were often seen to be even more strained and tense than in England and the complaints put more sharply. Personal relationships were said to be quite good, but structural relationships more difficult to operate. The kinds of difficulties experienced by district officers were similar to those of the English district: excessive duplication, constant interference by area officers, unclear terms of reference, insufficient delegation of authority, delays, insensitivity. Area officers were more likely to comment on the smallness of districts, the difficulty of splitting policy making and execution, and the struggle for some autonomy by districts preventing area officers from knowing what was happening. At both area and district, interviewees claimed that the size of districts and areas, and the creation of new administrative posts, meant that people "were not stretched" in their jobs. (Areas outside England are often the same size as English districts.) Insufficient work existed which encouraged a greater involvement in the work of lower tiers. More importantly, the line relationship between functional managers at area and district directly cut across the district teams' capacity to work consensually. Issues were more often seen as mono-disciplinary and the status of district teams' decisions was lower. These problems were most acutely felt in Wales and Northern Ireland.

3.13 There were some marked differences in views between area and district interviewees. While district respondents who specified a level were evenly divided between removing area or district, almost three quarters of area respondents were in favour of the district being removed. But there was a noticeable group at both area and district levels who were in favour of the present structure but with roles better defined. This view was more prevalent at area level than at district in Scotland and Northern Ireland but was more strongly expressed in both levels than in the other two countries. By contrast, only one interviewee in Wales at area level put forward this view; there were 10 respondents at district who thought the structure could be made to work. In both Scotland and Northern Ireland, there were interviewees who thought that the total structure was wrong for the country as a whole, and advocated changes in boundaries to make more viable areas and districts, both of which were thought to be too small.

3.14 NH Staff and members of CHCs or their equivalents in five districts were interviewed and their views are summarised as follows:

(a) 16 saw no need for an area tier; of these 10 were in Wales and 1 in Scotland;

(b) 15 saw no need for districts; of these 8 were in Scotland;

(c) 35 thought that there were too many levels without specifying which could be removed; of these 15 were in Northern Ireland;

(d) 6 thought that a new structure was needed, of whom 5 were in Northern Ireland. This related, as interviewees pointed out, to the fact that the whole country had previously been served by one hospital board; the present structure of four area boards and districts was seen to be over-elaborate;

(e) 27 thought the present structure adequate, although 10 of these said roles needed to be better defined. Only 4 respondents were in Northern Ireland;

(f) 35 respondents (half of whom were practitioners) did not reply to this question.

3.15 Of the 78 staff and members of authorities or boards interviewed at area level, 22 replied by commenting on the nature of relationships between area and district tiers, without either suggesting any change from the present status or agreeing with the justification for the present structure. The views of those who considered possible changes in the structure are summarised below:

(a) only one respondent at area level thought that the area tier should be removed;

(b) 33 respondents (6 in Scotland) favoured removing the district tier;

(c) a further 13 respondents thought that either district or area tier could be removed;

(d) a total of 12, divided between Northern Ireland and Scotland, favoured a wholly new structure, having fewer boards at area level and a smaller number of larger districts;

(e) 21 respondents thought that the present structure was justified in terms of policy making and operational levels and so no change was needed. Half the respondents added, however, that there had to be a clearer definition and distribution of roles to make the structure more efficient.

District Infrastructure

3.16 In all districts of the four parts of the UK, staff below chief officer mentioned that they had comparatively little contact with district officers, although there were exceptions. In general they were quite sympathetic to the difficulties experienced by district officers in decision making. But it was noticeable that area and region did not significantly touch staff in sectors. Their main concern was with the over-elaborate infra-structure of district organisation (a view shared by practitioners in SDAs as well). The impression given was that the reorganisation was discerned by sector staff and practitioners in terms of their own abilities to carry out their particular jobs. Unit and sector administrators were especially critical of the way in which decisions were pulled up from their levels to a higher one. Sectors and units were thought to have insufficient authority delegated, mainly due to increased functional management extending to district team levels (see below paragraphs 4.8 to 4.12). But the tenseness which permeated some relationships between district and area did not necessarily come through below.

Single District Areas

3.17 In SDAs, which exist in Wales and in English regions, there was a much higher degree of expressed satisfaction by staff. SDA staff commented, in comparison with colleagues in multi-district areas, that they were glad that they did not have to cope with those additional problems; they certainly thought their colleagues were far worse off than themselves in working relations. An area treasurer said "I decided I would never apply for a post in a multi-district area because it was obviously going to be fraught with difficulties".

3.18 Various reasons were given for favouring single district areas. Competition and rivalry between district management teams within an area and between area and district teams would be eliminated. The collective accountability of a sector management team was said to work well, and to soften the relationship which existed within a functional line. The corporate accountability of the team gave added weight to its individual members.

3.19 Those operating within them pointed out the disadvantages of SDAs as well as the advantages. Sector management took on a greater importance, and there was a need to clarify the proper degree of delegation to sectors. Practitioners and administrators within SDAs felt almost as strongly as their colleagues in multi-district areas that decisions were still too centralised and the district infra-structure too complex. The AMT was seen as (and felt itself to be) remote from the operational level. The area itself tended to be large, and some staff thought it difficult to identify realistically with it—loyalty and morale were important. Lastly, the members of the AMT often experienced conflict between management responsibilities and planning functions although these functions were said to be more interactive than in multi-district areas. This was particularly true of the ANO who had by far the largest staff to manage. The source of this conflict was seen to be an overload of functions for a particular role; chief officers were the final court of appeal as heads of departments but also had planning responsibilities which were distinct from management.

3.20 Of the 72 SDA respondents who expressed views about the number of levels, 45 thought that the SDA represented a better, more satisfactory, structure than MDAs. But even here there were respondents who thought that there were still too many levels. The largest number, 15, thought that the regional tier was unnecessary. Of these, 13 were in one SDA, showing again the impact of the size of a region on its working relationships. A further three thought that either region or area could be removed. Five thought that the area could be removed, leaving only sector or hospital and region; two of these respondents were junior doctors and three were from one CHC, reflecting perhaps a difficulty in dealing with a large and complex area. There was also the common concern with the infra-structure and its complexity.

Summary

3.21 This section is concerned with the relationships between the tiers in the NHS, in particular the ability to differentiate functions for each tier, and the necessity for each tier to exist. The relationship between region and area seems to be working reasonably well; there are more problems between areas and districts. The creation of more single district areas was strongly supported as a means of resolving some of these difficulties, but it was stressed that there should be no blanket solution to the NHS structure; structure should vary according to health service provision and with regard to geographic and demographic conditions. The line relationship between area and district officers in the non-English countries did not simplify working relationships between the two teams; its main impact was to lower the status and work of the district teams, leaving them less powerful than their English counterparts to manage district operations.

Comment by the Research Team

3.22 There are some general observations which may be made. One is that there are still staff hankering after the old relationship of HMC–RHB or Board of Governors—DHSS, which illustrates how difficult it is for staff rapidly to absorb new role relationships. For some, this is due to a new role resembling an old one in the same geographical setting, and relating to the same people as before. In this situation, it is natural to carry on as before, or to wish that one could do so. There needs to be more time and help and perhaps determination in learning new roles. But there are, too, structural problems which emerged clearly from the study.

3.23 There is obviously uncertainty of role and authority between district and area in multi-district areas, regardless of the quality of relationship between them. This demonstrates that the distribution of functions between area and district teams has not been sufficiently well analysed. There is too great a tendency for each level to mirror the structure and roles of the one above.

3.24 A third point is that the structure clearly shows the impact of a political decision (coterminosity) on working relationships (See Section 7). There are, of course, good reasons for encouraging liaison between the health and local authority services. But, in some areas, coterminosity created the need for multi-district areas whereas if health service operations alone had been considered this might not have been the result. While this is an important factor in England, it is even more strongly apparent in Scotland, Wales and Northern Ireland. Coterminosity has been asserted at the expense of creating non-viable management units. Only in Scotland were there officers at area level who felt that the present system could be made to work. In London, coterminosity has meant that areas work with more than one local authority for planning and joint financing purposes, whilst the districts work with individual local authorities. (See Section 7.)

3.25 The objective of integration places considerable weight on consensus management and corporate responsibility. These are difficult skills to exercise. Given the primary importance of integrative horizontal relationships within a level, the additional feature of complex vertical relationships between levels may need to be reconsidered. Line relationships between officers of the two tiers are in principle simple, but they are seen to cut across a corporate approach at the district level; most issues become mono-discipline rather than team issues. The collective accountability of a sector management team to an AMT may in fact serve as a better model.

3.26 In two regions it was pointed out that different structures were needed for metropolitan areas and for shires. We feel bound to draw attention to the view that local features should be respected by flexibility in structure.

4. Structure: (iii) Working Relationships

Context

4.1 The authors of reorganisation assumed that it was important to ensure the exercise of professional judgements about standards and to allow maximum local responsiveness to needs. These considerations would make hierarchical relationships in English regions inappropriate.* In their place, monitoring of performance by officials of one team of officers of the team below was seen as the mechanism by which a policy framework to ensure standardisation could be linked with local responsibilities. The agreement of objectives by officers at different levels should form the basis for monitoring and delegation. Functional management would give recognition of the expertise needed for the performance of particular tasks.

Report

Monitoring and Co-ordinating Relationships

4.2 Many administrators had exercised co-ordinative authority as group or RHB secretaries. But under reorganisation monitoring and co-ordinating functions were for the first time given a formal authority in the English regions, and between central departments and areas in Northern Ireland, Scotland and Wales. There were some interviewees at each level, for the most part professionals, who felt that these relationships worked well. When this was the case it was attributed to good personal relationships. Nowhere was it implied that the authority of a monitoring/co-ordinating relationship was easily accepted.

4.3 For most interviewees, monitoring and co-ordinating relationships presented difficulties. At all levels and among all groups, there were comments that monitoring was meaningless in the absence of accepted objectives or criteria against which performance could be measured. In this respect, it should be noted that of those mentioned above as having found monitoring acceptable, three were treasurers who could establish such clear objectives. Along with this was mentioned the lack of a sufficiently firm data base to allow monitoring.

4.4 The difficulty of getting compliance was seen as a drawback to monitoring relationships. This was a point noted in all multi-district areas by area and district staff, but especially by those who saw the area tier as the best

---

* The team has been able to find no explanation as to why this doctrine holds in England but not in the other parts of the UK.

base for their particular function: works, dentistry, pharmacy, personnel and planning staff often mentioned the desirability of a line relationship between area and district. However, this view was contradicted by three interviewees who thought that a stronger line relationship could not work at all because of the autonomy of the team being monitored. A weak form of authority, such as monitoring, was the most that was possible. Monitoring was also said to conflict with the reality of team management: if decisions were corporate a member of the team could not be held individually responsible for the way those decisions impacted on his work. It should be recollected that in single district areas, this difficulty was not found, because functional staff were not split between levels and teams below AMT were collectively accountable; there was little confusion over who made the final decision.

4.5 At least 15 respondents commented upon the cumbersome and complex nature of monitoring and how time consuming it was. Several thought it was too sophisticated for the NHS at this stage of development of management procedures. Monitoring placed a premium upon the establishment of good working relationships within which persuasion was possible; the authority of a monitoring relationship was not as clearly understood as that of other relationships.

4.6 Many of these comments were summarised by an administrator who pointed out that monitoring was more helpful to a health authority, regional or area, to keep its members informed of what was happening in lower teams than to the team officers, who had specific functions to carry out.

4.7 Co-ordinative relationships in themselves received fewer comments. They were seen as particularly time-consuming at the area level. The role of administrator was singled out as one presenting many difficulties especially in terms of co-ordination of the team of officers; the uncertainty about this was shared by administrators themselves and other team members (this will be discussed in Section 5).

Functional Management

4.8 Functional management was not new to the health service, being fairly well developed before reorganisation. The new structure, however, had considerably increased its importance and scope. It was commented on with approval or disapproval by more than half the staff below the DMT level. Naturally enough, functional managers themselves welcomed its development; for the career opportunities it created, for allowing specialised training to be developed and for the way in which expertise could be brought to bear on decisions. Problems associated with it occurred at the sector and unit level, where staff related to those below the senior functional manager level. In Scotland, Wales and Northern Ireland, where functional lines extended from district to area teams, functional management was said to conflict with the collective decision making of district teams.

4.9 As a group, nurses had many complaints about functional management. Ward sisters commonly (although not universally) felt that while remaining accountable for patient care, they had lost control of their ward, and could not get the services they needed, in particular domestic help and repairs. To get such services, there were many forms to complete and long delays, and although this kind of problem was experienced before reorganisation, it was felt to be more difficult now to get decisions at the unit or the sector level.

4.10 Unit and sector management suffered from similar feelings. Only one unit administrator said that functional management increased the challenge of his work. With the main functional managers working at the district level, the sector had to refer too many decisions, and the local co-ordinative role of the sector, and even more the unit administrator was diminished. A unit administrator remarked that, in the future, his post would be for more junior staff as it had comparatively little authority. Another commented that he was now able to contribute much less to the wellbeing of the patient, as so many decisions were taken at a higher level, and his job was mainly passing messages. Consultants, too, were strong in their criticisms of the inability to get decisions taken at a low level and of lack of clarity about who at local level was responsible for different functions. The infra-structure at the district level was clearly seen to be overloaded and confusing. An issue closely related to this was the extensive network of consultation now necessary and the additional burden this places on those who want an immediate decision. It was said by a few interviewees that the elaborated structure partly resulted from concessions to staff anxieties about the loss of jobs.

4.11 These problems were found as much in single district areas as in multi-district areas, and in non-English districts as well. Long functional lines cut across territorial groups be they district or sector teams; no area/district or single district area had yet found a way of sufficiently delegating authority or of co-ordinating needs of different teams so that decisions on local needs might be made both quickly and at the right level.

4.12 Below the DMT or AMT, then, horizontal integration was seen to be lacking. The boundaries of roles of different functional managers were said to be unclear, and there were misunderstandings about the extent of authority of functional managers, and about how much ought to be delegated to lower levels. Functional managers were in a service-giving relationship to other staff, yet it was not clear that the meaning of this was understood. Personnel, in particular, came in for much criticism, and indeed several personnel officers themselves recognised that their expertise was not clearly understood or readily accepted by those used to handling their own staff. The increasingly complex work on industrial relations, for example, and conditions of service were thought to be matters needing expert treatment and this was not fully appreciated.

Summary

4.13 In this section two types of relationships, monitoring/co-ordinating and functional management, are examined. Both of these impinge considerably on the ability of staff to participate in decision making, and to exercise the degree of authority assigned to their roles (which may conflict with the degree of authority they feel they ought to have). Monitoring/co-ordinating relationships were not thought to have sufficient authority attached to them to enable the setting of standards; and this criticism was particularly prevalent among second line area officers and chief area officers in multi-district areas. The problems of functional management were not new, but had been further complicated by reorganisation, especially at unit and sector level, because of the splitting of functions between levels or, in single district areas, longer functional lines.

Comment by the Research Team

4.14 Reorganisation confirmed in the NHS, at least in England, types of relationship which are more sophisticated and complex than those which were universal before. In part the difficulty may be technical—lack of objectives which are measurable, lack of information; it may also be structural, as far as misunderstandings of authority attached to a role are concerned, and conflict between vertical and horizontal relationships. In Section 3, it was noted how loyalties have developed to a team rather than to a professional group; the attempts to establish even weak forms of authority such as monitoring and co-ordinative relationships may be seen as threatening the corporate identity of a team and its authority over its own staff. The inherent difficulty of monitoring must be related to the extent to which a planning system is in operation, which, in theory at least, should provide agreement about policy and operational activity.

4.15 Comments from district staff show that they feel that it is difficult to get simple things done, and that authority has left the hospital level. This is felt most strongly by practitioners in the different health professions, many of whom refer back to the time when the hospital secretary, matron and medical superintendent (whose role survived in Scotland until reorganisation) were able to meet requests and sort things out on the spot. It was then perfectly clear to those who needed services that both the board of management or the HMC and the officers directly working with it were charged with the running of the hospital and its management. It is no longer felt to be clear where hospital decisions have to be taken. It may be by community medicine specialists working in the hospital, or the sector administrator, or the district officer or area officer. In part, the difficulties may arise from the need to adjust to a new system the top of which may not be visible to all practitioners. There were difficulties of this kind before reorganisation. But in the view of many interviewed, they have increased considerably since 1973 and 1974. This point is further elaborated in Section 13 on the impact of structure on decision making.

4.16 Functional management difficulties are basically those of ensuring sufficient delegation to an operational level, although they also reflect problems in defining the role of the administrator in the NHS. The extent of delegation possible depends partly upon how tightly funds must be controlled, but there was a general awareness in all areas and districts, English and non-English, of the need for stronger sector and unit management so that operational decision making could be decentralised.

5. Structure: (iv) Individual Roles

Context

5.1 During the field survey, some general comments were made about the content of various roles. The difficulties which officers in a particular function experienced in all or almost all areas were said to be due to ambiguities in the structure or in the loose definition of the role itself.

40

Personnel

5.2 As a specialist function new to the NHS, the personnel role was not always understood and often seen to conflict with the responsibilities of line managers. Several personnel officers at area and region thought that they ought to be members of the team of officers, because so many decisions had personnel implications; the three Regional Personnel Officers interviewed all felt that they were often brought into discussions too late to exercise any influence. Team members, however, did not accept this view, stating that personnel should be in a service giving relationship with the team, and not part of it. Issues which both line managers and personnel officers thought to be their concern were study leave, locum appointments, duty rotas and the firing of unsatisfactory staff. Line managers resented the interference (as they saw it) of personnel officers in these matters.

5.3 The placement of the nurses in personnel carried a dual responsibility to the personnel officer and to the nursing officer which was ambiguous in organisational terms and occasionally created uncertainty for the nurse. Most of the nurses specialising in personnel work thought that they could be integrated into the personnel department, and this seemed in general to be welcome to personnel officers since it would give them a more comprehensive department. Nurses within districts were not always pleased with the nursing personnel role, seeing it as a function detracting from their role as manager. Only one divisional nursing officer expressed the view that the area nurse personnel should be solely responsible for nursing personnel work, with no involvement from the personnel officer. Another nursing officer thought that the personnel nurse should be concerned only with wider issues of personnel work, such as safety legislation, equal opportunities legislation and the like, leaving the daily personnel function to nurse managers.

5.4 The personnel function was further complicated by the lack of skilled personnel officers, particularly in nursing personnel and in district personnel posts. This hampered the acceptance of the function, as it did not operate satisfactorily.

Area Based Services

5.5 As mentioned in Sections 3 and 4 some services saw themselves as needing to be area based in their planning and development activities in order to meet the criteria of efficiency and equity. In multi-district areas, the budgets for some of these services had been delegated to the district level, and area officers thought it difficult to develop an area wide policy. In *dentistry, pharmacy, works* and *supplies,* the splitting of functions between teams hampered the giving of leadership to these services. In single district areas, similar problems might also occur, although not so frequently, or so severely. There, for example, the sector management team might give one set of instructions to a works officer, and the area works officer another. Confusions might be sorted out, but they created additional stress on staff and delay.

Nursing Structure

5.6 Almost without exception, nurse practitioners said that the nursing management hierarchy was too long and incomprehensible, and Salmon sometimes aroused much stronger comments than did reorganisation. The need for the grades of both Nursing Officer and Senior Nursing Officer was questioned. Nurse practitioners thought that decisions were taken too far from the patient, but equally, a divisional nursing officer claimed that there were too many levels between her and the patient. Nurse managers were seen to be remote from the working situation and unable to understand the immediate needs of ward sisters. Another frequent comment was that the increase in nursing administration had stripped the working level of experienced staff. But it should be noted that several nurse managers disputed that nurse administrators had multiplied considerably, either post-Salmon or post-reorganisation. In one region, it was said that there had been a slight decrease in the numbers of nurse administrators since reorganisation.

5.7 The levels of the nursing structure were said to be unrelated to other services, particularly administration. Unit administrators reported difficulty with the number of levels or nurse managers which nurses seemed unwilling to have bypassed. Several nurses were unhappy with the need to move into management in order to advance in their careers; they identified a need for a career structure which encouraged nurses with greater experience and expertise to remain in clinical practice. These comments received support from consultants and other clinicians.

5.8 In SDAs, the dual role of the ANO as head of the nursing service and as AMT member, was said to be especially difficult. The ANO of one SDA estimated that 35 per cent of her time was spent on non-nursing administrative duties, but she was managerially accountable for 40 per cent of the staff employed in the area. Both operational nurse managers (divisional nursing officers) and area nurses were effectively second line officers to the ANO and this created considerable monitoring and co-ordinating demands on the time of the ANO. Area nurses might be drawn into a managerial relationship with divisional nursing officers, because of the demands on the ANO's time. It was said that the gap between an ANO and a divisional nursing officer was too great for effective management.

Administration
5.9 Mention has already been made of some of the difficulties and confusions experienced by administrators who felt they had lost the stronger authority possessed before reorganisation. They no longer felt able to initiate actions, and in general, many felt a good deal of frustration when actions were not taken which they considered they could have handled themselves. Former group secretaries who said that they could get decisions out of their HMCs, or make decisions in consultation with a chief nursing officer and chairman of the medical committee, now found themselves as district administrators who felt that they had to refer too much to both the DMT and ATO. Former hospital secretaries who had seen themselves as responsible for the running of a hospital and its services now felt too subordinate to a long functional line of management. Services hitherto subordinate to administrators such as catering or engineering now fell more strongly under functional management. Administrators' sense of relative impotence, which found expression at all levels, was in some cases exacerbated by their knowledge that others saw them as too powerful. Some felt themselves accused of trying to act as chief executives when, in fact, they believed that even the most consensual form of management required some co-ordinative drive which they had been trained to provide. The position of the administrator as co-ordinator

was particularly sensitive; many team members recognised the need for some leadership to be exercised within a team, yet were reluctant to sanction what they considered to be a return to "primus inter pares". Others saw the position of the administrator as deriving too much power from being the focal point for receiving and distributing information; in Northern Ireland he was also the accounting officer.*

5.10 The burden upon senior administrators, in terms of both amount of work and weight of responsibility, was brought to our attention not only by administrators themselves but by others too. Their co-ordinative work included that of their own second line staff as well as the servicing of committees and, unofficially, the team of officers. But additionally they had to be accountable for the work of subordinates to whom they had inevitably, particularly in times of intense policy making activity, to give a large measure of independence

5.11 At the area level, two area administrators mentioned the uncertainty of the boundary between the roles of the area administrator and the area medical officer, particularly regarding responsibility for medical administration and co-ordination. Both these officers were seen as generalists on the team and the division of responsibility is unclear. This view was mirrored by a district community physician, who expressed uncertainty as to responsibility for planning between himself and the district administrator. (See paragraph 5.13 below). In SDAs, the clinical members of the AMT were also much involved in medical co-ordination.

Community Medicine
5.12 The roles of area/regional medical officer and district community physician were thought by their role holders to contain what could easily be two full time posts: medical administration and specialists in community medicine. Although no precise information was given, the impression was that medical administration was extremely time consuming and the detailed work involved required frequent attendance at meetings. The administrative work load for other SCMs was equally great, entailing liaison and medical advice to local authorities, acting as head of specific services and co-ordinating services provided by different authorities or different parts of one authority for a specific client group. One SCM estimated that 60 per cent of the job was pure administration.

5.13 Besides administration, the planning function of community medicine implied an increased level of research and data refinement which could lead to evaluation of services and modification of priorities among services. This aspect of community medicine was largely overlooked because few community physicians were able to avoid the demands of medical administration, including a great deal of work with hospitals, which took up the community physician's allocation of time. Despite these problems, specialists in community medicine found that the new structure had enhanced their role and

---

* The interpretation of this role is not clear. The chief administrative officer is responsible to the Board for the ways in which its capital and revenue monies are expended. But other chief officers are budget holders and responsible to the board for the control and management of their resources.

provided greater opportunities for their work than had existed, for example, under local authorities. One interviewee commented, however, that while community medicine required its own expertise, it need not be the only source of recruitment for medical administration.

Summary

5.14 The content of this section illustrates in more specific circumstances the problems of functional management experienced at the operational level and between levels. The lack of clear boundaries between particular roles was said by respondents to be a source of individual stress and organisational tension insofar as decisions were delayed or referred unnecessarily.

Comment by the Research Team

5.15 The points mentioned above show the difficulties experienced by staff in attempting to carry out their roles. Many of the dissatisfactions relate to insufficient authority to carry out functions. They also derive from decisions taken during or just after reorganisation. Officers were appointed because the role was mentioned in the Grey Book,* and because of pressure from staff, before the need for such roles was established. Each tier thought it necessary to have a full complement of staff, and some said that the maximum numbers of appointments had been encouraged "from above", possibly because of trade union pressure. In at least one area, it was thought that the size of the area staff would be insufficient to cope with all functions, and these were delegated to districts, although officers at area level would now prefer to undertake them themselves. The administration is seen to be cumbersome and overmanned in some functions, and the ability to initiate limited. In this situation it is hard for individuals to feel responsible for work. This will be discussed further in the section on decision making.

6. Consensus Management

Context

6.1 Consensus management teams are the main manifestation of the importance attached to co-ordination among different professions. It is generally held that decision making cannot be undertaken by a chief executive of a single authority because of the integrative complexity of health care provision. Management and officer teams are consensus bodies in that the agreement of each member is needed for a team decision. Further, the team is collectively responsible to its authority for the carrying out of its policies.

Report

6.2 There were two principal advantages of consensus management. One was that it gave a wider dimension to decision making, bringing in different points of view, allowing these different views to confront each other, and portraying the impact of one set of factors upon others. Several members who participated in team meetings mentioned how much broader their own

---

* Or in the equivalent documents for Northern Ireland, Scotland and Wales.

understanding of the health service was through such group membership, and treasurers in particular appreciated the new opportunity team membership presented to them to gain such an overview. Secondly, it might bring with it a stronger commitment to decisions and result in better implementation. There were no specific examples given of this, but it is worth noting that interviewees mentioned this as a potential gain.

6.3 Support for consensus management was wide-ranging, and only a small minority of respondents thought that it could never be successful. In one regional and one area team, there was nearly complete agreement that it worked well, a product of the degree of commitment by team officers to it. In other teams views were more mixed, and endorsement of it was generally stronger among team members than among second line officers. Most respondents, while believing in team management, indicated that it created problems.

Composition of the Team
6.4 The composition of the teams of officers met with general approval. In Northern Ireland, finance officers, who are second line officers, wanted to be members of the Executive Teams, while other officers stated that having both finance and most general information in the hands of the administrator made that role too powerful. In England, Wales and Scotland there were occasional pleas for various second line officers (supplies and personnel) to be team members. Some chief officers, of dentistry, pharmacy and works, while having the right to attend team meetings and to participate in discussions affecting their services, still felt excluded and thought that full team membership would be appropriate. But these were not consistent demands and would seem to relate more to a lack of involvement with a particular team than to a structural deficiency. There were two interviewees in England (a GP and a DCP) who thought that, at district level, the social services, although not part of the health services, should have team membership. In Northern Ireland, where health and social services were integrated, there was a strong minority feeling that having social services represented made team functioning more difficult. Four consultants thought that the teams were heavily biased against clinicians; six nurses thought that there were too many medical members of the team. But it is fair to say that there were no consistently strong demands for altering the team composition.

6.5 Indeed, there was a strong recognition that the teams needed to be kept small to make them manageable. In one area, and one of its districts only, additional team members attend on a regular basis and some, although not all, felt that extended membership might hinder the team in developing a corporate spirit and reaching consensus.

The Problem of Team Leadership
6.6 Whilst there was some support for the idea of a chief executive, it was usually recognised at the same time that such a management form would be unacceptable to professional groups. The different groups of staff wanted to have a say in the management of health services and at the same time recognised the need for groups other than their own to have a voice. The health service required the co-ordination of many different professional groups and therefore needed their consent and involvement in decision

making and planning. No one person could speak for all and it was interesting to note that only one team member definitely recorded in favour of there being a chief executive. Those members and staff who favoured a chief executive thought that it would be more efficient in taking decisions and allowing strong decisions to be made. The question of a chief executive was often linked in discussion to that of team leadership.

6.7 A major worry which interviewees expressed about consensus management was the degree to which teams would be susceptible to domination by a particular personality. All team members were formally equal but not in professional status, and a dominating personality was thought to be bound to emerge, which, it was assumed, would have an adverse impact on the quality of decisions. This comment was usually framed in the abstract and, except in two cases, no evidence was presented to show that this in fact happened. It was a fear expressed more frequently by non-members than by members of teams.

6.8 The fear of personality domination was linked, however, to the need for some form of leadership of the team. There was a marked reluctance to consider the administrator member of the team as the obvious co-ordinator, although this was formally part of his role. This conflicted with the idea of a team of equals and was seen as perhaps too close to the previous role of the secretary to an HMC or RHB. At the same time, there was considerable awareness of how much teams needed leadership to function efficiently. Some teams elected a chairman on a rotating basis, varying from one month to a year. This solution at least acknowledged the need for leadership, although it lacked continuity. Generally administrators tended to think that they ought to be acting as a co-ordinator, but were aware of the sometimes quite open hostility to this. The leadership issue remains one of unresolved dissatisfaction and ambiguity.

Other Problems

6.9 Another source of uncertainty faced by teams was the distinction between an individual's sphere of management within his own professional group and team members' responsibilities; team members wore "two hats". For many years, this problem was one of which they were well aware and felt they were gradually sorting out. It was said by team members and non-members to be a source of delayed decisions and inappropriate decision making. It was of concern in SDAs because the AMT was the only cross-over point and issues could take a very long time to reach it. Its impact was to fill agendas with minor items, to hold back staff further down the line from being able to get on with their work, to centralise decision making and to make team meetings exceedingly long. Some professional officers who were not team members expressed annoyance that decisions which they felt competent to make were referred to teams. They felt that their expertise was being denied and their opportunities for decision making inhibited, with no benefit to the final decision.

6.10 In addition, there were other associated "pathologies". Individuals were seen to use the team to protect themselves from difficult decisions within their own sphere of competence. People tended to display an interest in problems relating to their own sphere, perhaps hesitating to question others on their work, or being too eager to let others decide; a "patch" system of interests developed and a corporate sense was missing. A reason given for these comments was that the general quality of administration was seen to be poor, and some felt there was a need for better training for nurse and medical administrators.

Conflict Within Teams

6.11 All teams found that not to reach consensus was difficult to handle; immediately after reorganisation, this was often seen as a failure. Some interviewees commented that issues were dropped if no agreement could be reached. In some teams the absence of consensus was reported to the health authority as a majority recommendation with dissent noted, or with full options and objections displayed. Chairmen of authorities might also be called in to bring about agreement. At all levels, some respondents expressed concern that team decision making fudged genuine divergence of opinion, and that important as consensus was, it might at times be equally important not to consense. Feelings about conflict within a team were ambivalent. The occasional absence of consensus might demonstrate the real commitment team members have to those decisions reached by consensus, but too much conflict might also show a lack of commitment. There is clearly some pressure on team members to reach consensus but it was not possible to understand whether the pressure is harmful apart from a specific decision. (See Case study No. 2 for further discussion of this point.)

The Speed of Decision Making

6.12 For many of the above reasons, team meetings and decisions took a considerable amount of time. From the sector level in single and multi-district areas, there were several issues mentioned as having been centralised, for example, study leave, unpaid leave, and staff replacement posts. These were usually decided by either the DMT or AMT but staff below that level saw no reason why authority should not be delegated.

6.13 But speed at which decisions were made was not the sole criterion. Some interviewees felt that it was necessary to take longer, that one got better decisions sometimes, or at least more considered decisions. The need for policy decisions to be taken quickly was thus queried; it was in decisions on operational matters that speed became important. The speed of decision making was also linked with functional management issues. It is difficult therefore to separate out the impact of consensus management on this particular issue.

Quality of Decision Making

6.14 There were mixed views about the quality of decisions, but there was no consistent pattern to these views except those which were obviously attached to a particular team. The general fear was that consensus meant compromise, that a weak decision was more highly valued than no decision. "Peace at any price" was the phrase used by a GP member of a DMT, but in general it was second line officers who made this point more frequently than team members.

6.15 The quality of decisions was said to be adversely affected by the reluctance of a team to seek advice from other specialists. This view was expressed by second line officers and chief officers who were not members of a team. In some places, it was said that the team operated as a "closed shop". Not only did other chief officers feel cut off from decision making, but they claimed that the consequences of decisions were not fully considered because of the absence of their advice; decisions had to be made twice, or difficulties occurred which could have been avoided.

Northern Ireland, Scotland and Wales

6.16 In four of the five non-English districts, it was apparent that the line relationship between officers at district and area made the functioning of a district in two of the three countries almost meaningless. District team meetings "exchanged information", were "a talking shop", "dealt with trivia". Here decisions were seen to be more monodisciplinary than team matters and team decisions were said to be reviewed by the area. In Scotland, team members felt they had more scope for decision making and the team had a purposeful role to play. (See also paragraphs 3.12 and 3.25.)

Views of Authority Members

6.17 From the viewpoint of the chairmen and members of area and regional health authorities consensus management was seen to be functioning well. One AHA chairman would have preferred a chief executive and several chairmen were in fact said to function as if they were the chief executive. The principal concern of health authority members was that consensus management might be filtering too much from team meetings, so that conflict was hidden or good ideas lost before they reached the authority. For further discussion of this point, see Section 10 on Authorities.

Summary

6.18 The use of multidisciplinary groups in the health service was generally agreed to be the most acceptable form of decision making. Most team members thought that consensus management was working better than did their second line officers. Nurses and treasurers or finance officers were found to be more pleased with team working than administrators and medical officers, perhaps inevitably, in that their membership of teams has given them a formal recognition that they did not possess before. There was widespread support for the present composition of the teams as being suitable, although some second line officers thought that they too should be members. The main concerns over consensus management were the degree to which individual personalities could dominate, the attributed delay in decision making, the difficulty in distinguishing team responsibilities from monodisciplinary management, the possibility for weak compromises rather than hard decisions, and the burden which team membership places on the time of the chief officers.

Comment by the Research Team

6.19 Consensus management is a key feature of the reorganised health service and many team members feel that they are improving their ability to work together. It is not surprising that difficulties have been experienced as it is within teams (and in their recommendations to authorities) that many of the conflicts of values found within the health service come for resolution.

6.20 Many of the comments about consensus management did not attack the principle but the operation of it. Thus, consensus management is not incompatible with a strong co-ordinative role effected by the lay administrator or, indeed, by a member of the team chosen by his colleagues for his personal qualities. Another element of team behaviour is the importance of delegating some team functions to individual members. Not all need be involved in everything, even when confirmation or support by the whole team is necessary. Nor does consensus necessarily mean unanimity.

6.21 Consensus management has several arguments underlying it. It may make for less efficient but more acceptable decision making because different groups will know that their point of view has been heard. It is true, of course, that accommodations then have to be made if a controversial decision is to be acceptable to the whole team. Those who want clear and strong decisions must find compromise unacceptable. The advantages of acceptability and compromise conflict with other criteria such as the speed and rationality of decisions. The research team have not found it possible to relate impact of team functioning to the quality of decisions. This is, in part, because consensus brings many conflicting criteria into play: coherence of working within a team to keep the whole system functioning well; the safeguarding of professional standards and interests which are important to the different working groups within the service; loyalty to the health authority so that clear and unambiguous recommendations are made to them.

6.22 Clinical involvement in consensus decision making is discussed separately in Section 9.

7. Relations Between Health and Local Authorities

Context

7.1 We have discussed earlier the attempts to integrate the hitherto separate health services. The new health authorities were also required to relate their work to that of the local authorities. The changes were to be of four kinds. The areas administered by the health authorities were to be geographically *coterminous* with those of local authorities, as far as was possible. *Local authority members* were to be appointed to RHAs, AHAs and CHCs (see also Section 10). The English and Welsh health and local authorities were to establish *joint consultative committees* to develop collaboration and joint planning, Scotland still has no formal machinery for collaboration and planning, although some authorities have established joint liaison committees and a recent SHHD Working Party has recommended systematic provision of this kind. Latterly, arrangements have developed for the *joint financing* of appropriate projects and services. And, in the particular case of Northern Ireland, the health and social services were to be administered by a single authority separate from those of either the local authorities or the boards set up by central government for such services as education and libraries.

7.2 In advancing these themes, reorganisation took up long-standing policies. Throughout all areas of welfare and social services, waste, potential conflict and clients falling into the gaps between services have been thought to result from different services working with the same clients but going their own ways. The same theme is celebrated in the assertion of corporate management within local authorities, and the attempt to create joint social planning within central government.

Report

Are Relations with Local Authorities Better?

7.3 About a third of the respondents spoke directly to this issue. A slight majority thought relationships with local authority services to be no better, or worse, than before reorganisation. The negative returns, however, included those who were able to say that they had kept the relationships established over many years in their previous roles as, for example, health visitors or community nurses. Those who thought relationships had improved were primarily the medical administrators, nurses and paramedical workers (but all by slender majorities only) whilst administrators and medical clinicians predominated among those who thought that they were no better or worse. Once again, however, it is difficult to see whether the problems are those of principle or of practical working relationships. The responses tended to cluster in particular areas. Thus, there were approving references to the relationships between the authorities for education in one area, and for collaboration in the allocation of housing in another. Elsewhere, the splitting of child health from the social services was thought to be disadvantageous (but see the sections on Northern Ireland below) whilst at the same time joint work for handicapped children had developed since reorganisation. Relationships were seen in a few detailed cases to be good at field level but not good at administrative level. Occasional references to problems such as the sharing of confidential material were also made.

Coterminosity

7.4 A surprisingly large number of respondents, and in all disciplines, positively expressed the view that the principle of coterminosity was irrelevant, or worse, to the running of the health service and its relationship with the cognate local authority services. One respondent described the principle as "tommyrot". But a close analysis of one of the regions studied shows that attitudes varied significantly according to level and location. The great majority supporting coterminosity worked in the community or were local authority members of health authorities or community health council members. Hospital staff saw little need for it. Those furthest away from the operation of the community health services, as in the regional levels, supported it least. Some said there were far more important considerations that should determine the boundaries of health authorities and their districts, even if coterminosity could bring some advantages. In some cases, coterminosity was thought to have produced areas not appropriate to patterns of health care needs because the catchments for local authority and health services were not the same. There might also be a mismatch of levels within those areas where the district team appropriately related to the local authority but was not itself a health authority. Some, however, felt that coterminosity might later enable health and social services to be integrated—a prospect viewed differently by different respondents. Another viewpoint was that the fact that it was seen as irrelevant reflected the failure to achieve an integrated health service and to reduce the dominance of hospital interests and needs.

Joint Working

7.5 There were not many responses on the JCC mechanisms or on joint financing. The 42 responses slightly tilted towards saying that the arrangements were not working well and that they were "a waste of time", or that they "frittered away time". The meetings of members in the joint consultative committees and of the most senior officers on both sides in the various planning teams were not thought to be particularly relevant to the creation of better operational procedures. Joint financing could hardly get off the ground when, as a few respondents put it, there were insufficient resources for new developments. Joint care planning teams and joint working needed more fundamental structural change, in the view of some of their critics. It should be noted, however, that some planned co-operative schemes are already off the ground between health and local authorities, if not universally. We take up the issue of joint financing or funding in the Appendix to this section which is based on interviews in three local authorities and their related AHA.

Northern Ireland: Integration of Health and Social Services

Context

7.6 In Northern Ireland, the social services are part of the area health and social services boards. The Director of Social Services is a member of the Area Executive Team and District Social Services Officers are members of District Executive Teams. We were told that social workers approached integration with some trepidation. Although they thought that they had been inadequately provided for by many local authorities and disparities in social services between areas within the province were marked, they felt that there might be dangers in being swamped by the powerful health service interests. Moreover, the Northern Ireland social services had not enjoyed the growth of funds that had occurred in England and Wales after the Seebohm Report was implemented. For these reasons, the Northern Ireland Department of Health and Social Services made particular efforts to protect the social services by earmarking funds, so as to ensure their growth at a time when the total funds reaching the health and social services boards were to grow at a far less favourable rate. This was part of the more general policy of advancing community care services, including community health services.

7.7 Of the 73 interviewed in Northern Ireland, 54 responded on the question of relations between health and the social services. They came from all levels and disciplines but, inevitably, there were small numbers only in each working level and group interviewed. In particular, whilst social workers at district level were interviewed, no basic grade field worker was included in the lists prepared for us. It should also be emphasised that what follows here is based on one Northern Ireland area only, and at a particular point in time whilst relations are still developing.

7.8 Of the 54 who responded, 34 pointed to some degree of benefit from the integration of health and social services although many of these also made criticisms of the results. The improvements mentioned included the opportunity for social services to have access to stronger organisational and resource systems. They were not only now part of a larger body with many specialist resources, but also one in which professional rather than local

51

authority member judgements predominated. When social services joined health they brought with them a big backlog of work to be done, for example, in terms of the provision of aids in private houses; and the health and social services board had been able to cope with these problems effectively. At the professional level, standards of practice had improved, in the words of one social service administrator "beyond all expectations". The senior and directing staff were of a high calibre. There were improvements mentioned specifically in work on non-accidental injury, on relationships in the health services with GPs and nurses, and on work for the elderly. Joint work on the At Risk Register was going ahead well.

7.9 Where there was geographical proximity between the different working groups, relationships had improved. A reduction in the overlap of visiting between health visitors and social workers had occurred. Although some explicitly looked back to the old hospital almoner system, other hospital nurses referred to the way in which social workers worked well with them. They were "on the bleep" and worked together with them about patients. Records could be shared.

7.10 On the level of detailed joint working, it is notable that the warmest testimonials to the benefits of integration came from six out of the eight hospital and community nurses interviewed. Nurses in the wards found it easier to get adaptations made to the homes of patients before they were released from hospital. But in other respects, as well, relations seem to have improved. There was, for example, good collaboration in the dispensing of drugs in old people's homes between social workers and pharmacists. The feeling of development in the wards and in the community was shared, as well, by nurse administrators at both area and district levels, although they perceived some of the difficulties more strongly than their operational colleagues. The general opinion among senior nurses was, however, that in spite of difficulties, integration was worthwhile.

7.11 There was satisfaction in the social services that their growth had been protected. They were, however, sensitive to the comparisons naturally made by their medical colleagues. Social services might have enjoyed a similar rate of growth had they remained separate. But the fact that a unitary authority had to dispense monies differentially undoubtedly caused discontent on the health side,* which, in the words of one administrator, "made nonsense of corporate management".

7.12 Although 17 respondents explicitly said that integration worked badly, this figure should not be compared with the 34 respondents who thought that there had been some advantages in integration because many of the latter had reservations. Area staff (including some of the most senior social service administrators) had doubts about the good working of integration. Medical clinicians within the hospitals and in the community were all but united in speaking of the difficulties resulting from it.

7.13 Some of the accounts are, indeed, important not because they can be at all generalised but because they reveal some of the apprehension about

---

* In 1977/78 £139,000 were earmarked for social services and £51,000 for community health services out of a total of £35m on the area's current account.

social work, such as the picture of social work assistants who "do three months of sociology" and then come back to make judgements they are not qualified to make. A source of anxiety was the belief that social workers were taking on tasks on the borderline of health care, at a higher cost than that associated with the health service and without the expertise that some of their medical colleagues felt they needed. "They cannot deal with the most serious cases and are costly in dealing with the less serious ones". They could not be trusted, another version went, to manage patient needs. They were not to be trusted with confidential records. Another comment, which conflicted with the testimony to improved relationships on cases of non-accidental injury, was that social workers, perhaps acting out of feelings of inferior status, were over-assertive. (Social workers might retort, however, that doctors, more than most, find it difficult to get used to being answered back.) They treated doctors merely as a technical resource rather than as colleagues and required them to give evidence of a medical condition but did not ask them to join in the decision on the disposal of cases. Social workers were thought to be reluctant to give way to medical leadership when the medical issue predominated. Again whilst doctors have to act at once, social workers reflected on the wider circumstances of the client before taking action. One clinician felt that social workers would deal with one out of five cases who needed social worker intervention and left the other four to the clinicians to help.

7.14 Senior social work administrators were well aware of some of these differences. One of them described them in terms of the health service being used to patients taking on a willingly dependent role whilst social services were concerned with independence of clients. A lot of time was therefore spent in explaining to each other different professional attitudes. Other differences were those of, perhaps, the more explicit political ideology. More than once in our survey, social workers were associated with "socialist" attitudes. More fundamentally, again, however, one senior administrator referred to the break up of concepts of illness. Whilst social workers used funds to help children and old people, the health services must help people who work and contribute to the economy and society to keep on their feet. Thus the waiting lists of 30 to 40 year olds for medical treatment compared unfavourably with the spending of money on "holidays for children who get on badly with their parents".

7.15 This line up of attitudes will not surprise observers of the two groups of services. The difficulties of working together could have been predicted and one interviewee pointed out that the argument for integration was not as well made in the Green Paper as had been the integration of the health services. The case of the elderly was quoted, but that was the easiest case to argue. The argument really stemmed from the administrative and political point that with the reorganisation of local government in Northern Ireland there were still 26* relatively small local authorities. These carried somewhat narrow functions and had no responsibilities for or connection with

---

* Previously there had been 8 major county, city and borough councils and more than 70 local authorities. The major authorities had administered a wide range of services. But they disappeared when 26 district councils came into being and the personal social services no longer had a viable county council base.

either education or housing which were under a separate system. That being so, it would have been anomalous to put the newly integrated social services into relatively puny local authorities. The granting of protected monies for social services meant that what would have been a difficult integration anyway was further exacerbated. It is noticeable that unfavourable comparisons between social service expansion and the holding back of developments in health expenditure are not a cause for comment in the other three countries.

7.16 Moreover, more than one interviewer spoke of the way in which the services were already being integrated prior to 1973. Health care and social service workers were already collaborating on geriatrics in many parts of Northern Ireland. One former MOH had already succeeded in involving social workers in a growing relationship so that the welfare authority had begun to work in health centres.

Comment by the Research Team

Northern Ireland
7.17 In putting together the Northern Ireland health and social services, it was too lightly assumed that medical staff in the acute health sectors would willingly accept the viewpoints of a far less well developed social work service. The feeling of disjunction was accentuated by differential allocation of funds within the system that was supposed to become corporate and integrated. Moreover, there might be fundamental differences of opinion about the alleviation of human problems which organisational amalgamation in itself cannot bridge. The differences in philosophy, working styles and roles of officers made integration *at the systems level* difficult. *At the working level* the sharing of specialist resources and working together between social workers and nurses becomes possible. The problems arise, however, with the higher status groups in the health service who, seeing their own resources at a standstill and their expertise challenged, feel that integration is a "shotgun marriage". However, it is difficult for the team to be sure as to whether some of the problems might result from the particular circumstances of a small country faced by exceptionally severe political problems.

General Comment
7.18 A general issue is exemplified by the experience of Northern Ireland. Where work is highly technical and specialist, or is based on particular philosophies, as is true of the whole range of health and welfare services, working together may not be easily secured by the simple application of solutions such as co-terminosity or organisational integration. Joint consultative committees and joint financing are obvious ways of ensuring collaboration between separate authorities but two preconditions seem necessary. In the first place the sanctions for *not* working together need to be more obvious. There is no authoritative point in the total system which can insist on working together. But if the arguments are to go beyond rhetoric, detailed agreements on quite technical processes need to be secured. Such agreements take time and specialist input. Secondly, planning has proved difficult to get off the ground in the health service (see Section 12). It assumes internal coherence of objectives, processes and working

relationships. Until both the technology and style of forward planning are secure within the health service it will be difficult for effective joint planning between authorities to take place. Coterminosity for its own sake does not seem to be a good policy. Yet in spite of objections to rigid application of the principle, it should also be noted that heavy burdens of communication would result if there were no correspondence between health and local authority boundaries.

Appendix

A Study of Joint Financing in One AHA

7.19 A specific way in which health and local authority services are encouraged to work together is through the mechanism of joint financing, in which the NHS contributes up to 100 per cent of the cost of a local authority service meeting social care needs of health service clients. It is seen by both health and social services officers as one of the more imaginative ideas associated with central government, and one whose aim of transferring funds from hospitals to community services is well supported by those involved. In the AHA in which joint financing was studied in detail, the funds allocated for such projects amounted to nearly £500,000 for the current financial year. This represents approximately 0·7% of the AHA budget.

7.20 Joint funding has been in operation for two years only. The account which follows is based on interviews with seven health and local authority officers. It illustrates some of the problems experienced by an AHA, its districts and related local authorities, in attempting to establish a dialogue enabling both health and local authority services, social services in particular, to benefit from this scheme. It illustrates the types of obstacles which may stand in the way of good liaison even when, as was clear from respondents, the intention and desire to make it work well are present. Often it is assumed that individuals block good working relationships; perhaps insufficient attention is paid to different organisational objectives, structures and styles.

Who Benefits?

7.21 On first sight to those in the NHS, it seems that joint financing of projects has been an open gift to local authorities; they are enabled to increase services offered to their communities at a considerably reduced cost to rate-payers. Evidence cited by NHS officers to support this view is that almost all schemes so far submitted to the Joint Consultative Committee (JCC) have originated from the local authority side, and almost all have been approved by the AHA. "The relevance of (joint financed schemes to) health service needs was never questioned by the area, and the health service never asked whether it was getting value for money" commented a senior area officer, while a local authority officer said that local authorities were in the driving seat because the AHA had to spend the money on local authorities or not spend it at all.

7.22 But the gains from joint financing do not always appear so "pure" to local authorities. To begin with, a limited time period exists for the operation of joint financing, and there is concern that local authorities may acquire costly responsibilities at the end, for which no additional revenue grants from central government, either directly or through the NHS, may be made. For a political body, sensitive to the interest of its rate-payers, this cannot be a minor consideration, and so joint financing is viewed with some suspicion.

7.23 Likewise, it may be noted that although joint funds may be spent on community health facilities or services, this does not seem to be readily accepted by the health service because of long term revenue implications. For certain long-stay groups such as the elderly, a move to the community may increase demand for such services, which may be extremely difficult to meet on the cessation of joint funding in a field where current demand already so far outstrips supply.

7.24 A further reservation is the extent to which the interests of health and local authority services diverge. Moving patients from hospital to community may benefit the health service in that it releases beds for other patients or other uses. Moving patients to community facilities increases responsibilities of social services—domiciliary care, social support, building and maintenance of hostels or other accommodation. It does not relieve local authorities of any existing responsibilities, nor necessarily tackle any current and urgent problems. In areas where social deprivation is fairly high, taking people from a situation in which they are adequately, even if not ideally, cared for may not be the highest priority. So priorities of the two service authorities may be very different. (See paragraph 7.34.)

Impact of Health Service Structure

7.25 In the area studied, co-terminosity between health and local authority services occurs at health district level, with one district serving two local authorities. When joint funding began, each local authority had its own JCC, which for this area meant four separate JCCs. The local authority members of the AHA thought this arrangement cumbersome and repetitive for the health service, and after a year, the four committees were combined into one JCC for the AHA and all local authorities together.

7.26 An obvious advantage from the AHA viewpoint is that a unified JCC would make it easier to put forward health service priorities to all local authorities at once, and to be able to compare schemes put forward, choosing those of greatest benefit to the health service. However, officers of two of the local authorities consulted think that this type of JCC organisation is a disadvantage. First, each local authority will not have the same needs as the others, and area health service priorities may not be able to operate with sufficient flexibility or sensitivity to meet these differing needs. If AHA priorities are adhered to too strictly, then some local authorities may find it difficult to participate in joint funding projects. Next, projects need to be worked out between the local authority and health district; the JCC based at area level takes attention and perhaps responsibility away from the district tier. It also means that JCPT or JCC meetings are large gatherings and much of the meeting may be of little interest to those from three of the four local authorities present.

7.27 Moreover, with both health district and area involved in discussions, local authorities must reach agreement with two levels before final approval is given for a project. Again, this is a complicating but not overwhelming difficulty, and its real impact may be psychological rather than in outcome. It creates the potential for agreement to be reached at one level, with the knowledge that it can be overridden by another, or for both health service levels to leave the real work to the other, so that little may be accomplished. The impression is that local authorities are left in some doubt as to where or by whom decisions and agreements are made or, at best, there is a duplication of effort.

7.28 In addition, the AHA relates to its RHA for particular functions, but the RHA, covering part of a metropolitan and a county area as well, cuts across geographical boundaries within which local authorities are used to working. The urban area is served by four RHAs, and so on the health side there is no single strategic body to which local authorities may relate.

Impact of Local Authority Structure
7.29 The differences in authority structure of the NHS and local authorities are well known and certainly well documented as a potential source of difficulty. Although both services have officers and members, these carry different roles and function differently. However, both local authority and NHS officers involved in joint funding think that the health service does not take this sufficiently into account.

7.30 Local authority officers tend to refer to a local authority as "democratic" and to the NHS as "autocratic". Thus local authority officers will refer to elected members before committing the local authority, whereas NHS officers feel freer to speak on behalf of the AHA and have a more open and individual role in decision making. Moreover, local authority councillors will often consult with the local political party for guidance and agreement on issues, and this results in delays in decision making at meetings, to allow for such consultation.

7.31 There are also different sections of a local authority involved in joint financing; there are service departments such as social services, education or housing, and also the finance department. The complexity of financial aspects of joint financing was said to be underestimated initially by local authorities and the health service, and it is only recently that local authority finance officers were brought into direct participation. The inclusion of several service departments and the finance department, however, contributes to the size of the JCPT and the number of advisers at JCC meetings.

7.32 It may also be noted that local authorities are grouped differently for different kinds of programmes. Of the four local authorities brought together within the AHA, three are linked to other local authorities outside the AHA for various urban development programmes. Yet, in some way, planning of both health and local authority services must be brought together.

Objectives of Joint Financing
7.33 The overall objective of joint financing is seen as keeping patients within the community or returning patients to the community more rapidly. But there are differing views of how joint financing is to achieve this:

(a) helping local authorities to fund services or facilities which are already in their plans;

(b) helping local authorities to provide services which they would like to develop but which are not in present plans;

(c) getting the most economic use of funds available.

7.34 The distinction between objectives (a) and (b) is an important one but perhaps more in concept than in outcome. If joint funding is used for a provision that a local authority is already undertaking, then health service funds may be used to finance, say, social services without any additional benefit to the NHS. If joint funding is used only for additional provision, then local authorities may incur recurrent expenditure which they will have to meet after the joint funding programme ends. Moreover, it may mean that a local authority will have to give higher priority to a service or facility in order to participate in joint funding than would otherwise have been the case (see paragraph 7.23).

7.35 Objective (c) poses a further distinction among objectives. Finance officers from health and local authorities tend to see joint funding being most economically used to fund capital projects, because it would enable local authorities to limit interest costs and thus lower the total cost of capital developments. But officers of service giving departments, particularly from the local authority, do not always agree with this. Their concern is more to support people within their own homes by providing services directly, by fostering self-help groups or by other voluntary efforts. So financial considerations may need to be examined in relation to practitioner concepts. Guidance from the DHSS has been ambiguous; while priority has been given to revenue schemes over the past few years, circulars on joint financing stress capital projects.

Time Spans

7.36 Local authority officers have expresed doubts about the usefulness of the joint funding programme, given its limited period of operation. While, for example, wards, units or even hospitals may undergo change of use or closure in a comparatively short period of time, it may take much longer to build up resources and services within the community. Staff must be recruited, and possibly trained, and administrative backup support services provided. An extension of services in one direction may necessitate structural changes within an organisation. Bringing about such changes requires considerable organisational effort, which may have to be undertaken by staff fully occupied with existing responsibilities.

7.37 The pace at which such changes can be absorbed within an organisation undergoing expansion may be slower than thought possible or desirable by those outside the organisation. The feeling expressed by local authority officers was that while an impact may be made on community services for, say, the elderly, over a ten year period, rapid change over a five year period may be impossible because of the demands placed on its departments and the fairly radical reorientation of effort and staff this would require. Thus, different expectations may be held by health service and local authority officers as to what can be accomplished over the present period of the joint financing programme.

The Mechanics of Joint Financing

7.38 We have already mentioned some of the problems of finding the most convenient and effective level at which to establish JCPTs and JCCs (see paragraphs 7.26 and 7.27). Area health service officers are currently concerned to institute systematic procedures for joint funding, for both financial transactions and planning arrangements. The establishment of such procedures has been hampered by staff changes among those in the NHS most concerned with the JCC, so that only one of the three principal officers involved has worked with the JCC since the beginning of the joint funding programme. The establishment of set working procedures would enable the approval of JCC recommendations by the AHA to be made at the same time as the AHA considers its own operational plans. Thus health and joint planning could be linked together.

7.39 Local authorities, too, appreciate the difficulties which have emerged due to the absence of procedures. There has been confusion on both sides as to what should happen after proposals have been agreed by the decision making bodies of the authorities involved. But local authority officers stressed that establishing proper procedures would resolve only some of the difficulties. From this viewpoint, the joint funding programme could be run more smoothly if there were a better understanding of the needs of each authority. This would mean developing closer working relationships with the health districts so that in each case joint concepts of needs and corporate objectives could be evolved. Their feeling is that the concern with procedures held by health service officers overshadows the need for joint financing to take place within a framework of joint planning: without such a context, joint funding may seem to be simply a mechanistic activity, a series of one-off exercises.

Concluding Comments

7.40 The material given above is only a "snapshot" of a situation still evolving, but this example of a particular activity linking health and local authority services does show how the reorganised structure can affect the facility with which different authorities may work together. A common programme for both authorities may provide unequal and dissimilar incentives for its operation. No provision was ever better intentioned, but joint funding demonstrates the difficulty of creating inter-organisational working when the contributing organisations have different objectives, political environments and modes of working to reconcile.

8. Advisory Committees

Context

8.1 Professional advisory committees are a means by which practitioners within the health service may participate in the policy making processes. Professional participation has different functions; management needs to receive up to date information about professional needs and developments; professional workers need to commit themselves to agreed proposals for change. Professional advisory committees, established at the area and regional authority levels, are to be consulted before major planning and allocation decisions are made.

Views on Advisory Committees

8.2 Although advisory committees seemed to be more fully operational in England than in other parts of the UK, the principle of advisory committees was, on the whole, accepted by both authority members and NHS staff. However, the impact of such committees had so far been idiosyncratic and highly dependent on the attitudes and expectations of individuals. Quite opposing views were given of the impact of an advisory committee in the same authority by chief officers, committee and authority members, and it was difficult to get an overall view of their working. With a few exceptions relating to the medical advisory committees, the general feeling was one of quite meagre impact and of additional burdens on the consultative process.

8.3 Practitioners seemed to be no more pleased with the advisory structure than officers; a general comment was that involvement often came too late and at too short notice to substantially influence developed attitudes. It was difficult to judge the extent to which staff felt themselves to have a real role in policy making through advisory committees. Nurses did cite some examples of agreements reached on policy matters, although these seemed to relate more to an ANO's management responsibilities than to policy making of authority. Consultants and general practitioners were individualistic in their views on the success of advisory committees, although for them, advisory committees were closely related to their involvement with management teams. On the whole, advisory committees did not seem to have found ways of engaging the active interest of staff.

8.4 A point common to most advisory committees was the ambiguous role of the chief officer who was usually responsible for the administration of the advisory committee concerned. Advice by a committee might appear at times supportive and at other times threatening. An officer might present both his own and a committee's advice to an authority or underplay differences of opinion. Cases of conflicting views at times seemed awkward for an authority and the officer to handle. This difficulty would occur less in the medical than in the other advisory committees.

Dental, Pharmaceutical and Paramedical Advisory Committees

8.5 The views concerning dental, pharmaceutical and paramedical advisory committees were similar. Their impact, as seen by the chief officers of these services, had been minimal, and many felt dissatisfaction with the way in which they worked. Chief officers felt they were at least as competent, if not more so, at giving advice to authorities and saw little need for this function to be carried out by those whose views may be particularistic. This might relate to the difficulty of getting a balanced composition of a committee; combining independent contractors or retail pharmacists with hospital workers did not necessarily make it easy to develop composite views. There was little evidence that advice proferred was actually taken.

8.6 On the other hand, there was a strong feeling that the committees did bring together different elements of the profession, and helped to generate a better understanding of differences in views and problems, even if the benefits from this lay in the future. Another gain, as seen by members of these professions, was the increased status given to their groups by the existence of the advisory committee and the potential this gave for getting ancillary services represented in strategic plans. Not surprisingly, chairmen of these committees tended to be more satisfied with them than other members or chief officers.

Nursing Advisory Committees

8.7 A total of 80 nurse practitioners and nurse managers were interviewed with regard to their views on the nursing advisory system.* Although the overall impression was critical, 20 nurses, all but three managers, considered the advisory committees as fulfilling important functions. The most frequent comments here were that the committees were "working well", that they "gave good advice", that their "advice was taken by the AHA" and that they were beginning to improve. Six nurses mentioned the importance of these committees for the development of nurses, so that they learn how to participate in policy making. Others thought that the advisory committees brought together nurses from different practice settings and this was valuable for the development of better understanding. The chairman of a regional nursing and midwifery advisory committee mentioned the boost which having an advisory committee gave to the morale of the nurses. Some nurses felt strongly that if medical advisory committees continued, then it was important that the nursing ones did as well.

8.8 The impact of the advisory committees on nurses may be shown from the response of nurse practitioners (ward sisters, health visitors, community nurses). Here, of the 17 practitioners interviewed, only two thought that there was a definite role for the advisory committees. Eleven others made no response to the questions about the advisory committees, three thought that there was no impact and one thought that it was a body for nurse managers. If the intention was to provide a forum for nurses to bring problems from the service level to the advisory committees, it must be of concern that so few nurse practitioners were familiar with the advisory committee system.

8.9 The majority of comments made by nurses about the advisory system tended to be critical, and their responses focused on two issues. First, that the advisory system could be in conflict with the hierarchial structure of the nursing service, and that because of the hierarchy, there was no need for a separate channel of advice. About one fifth of the nurses interviewed commented on these points, drawing attention to duplication of advice by officers and committees, and pointing to the apprehensiveness and unwillingness of some chief nursing officers towards interacting with the committees. The second main criticism was of the inexperience of nurses in committee work. Some specific points made were the dependence of a committee on the area or regional nursing officer for leadership, parochial attitudes and lack of real contribution from committee members. Few nursing advisory committees generated their own ideas, but tended to react to requests for advice. Nurses also commented on the lack of feedback to the committee from the authority, and from the committee to non-members.

---

* This excludes nurses from Northern Ireland whose advisory committee operates at the DHSS (NI).

Medical Advisory Committees

8.10 The medical advisory system is more complex than the others, encompassing separate committees for GPs (LMCs) and hospital consultants (Hospital Medical Staff Committee, Hospital Medical Executive Committee) as well as joint District Medical Committees (DMC), Area Medical Advisory Committees (AMAC) and Regional Medical Advisory Committees (RMAC). At the regional level, there are often specialist sub-committees.

8.11 There was no one who thought that the medical advisory committees were unimportant or that all of them were unnecessary. One senior administrator commented that adequate machinery for professional debate was essential, because the medical profession should be giving the lead in development of health services. Clinicians were more ambivalent in their responses, expressing resentment against committees and the time they took but not saying that there was no need for medical advice.

8.12 In general terms, there was more satisfaction expressed with RMACs. One RMO remarked that public relations with the medical profession had improved and that the "best brains" were drawn into the advisory system, while another cited the ability of the RMAC to speak authoritatively for the region's consultants. Chairmen of the RMACs thought their advice was taken seriously by the RHA and RTO, and one administrator mentioned that the RTO "had learned to its cost" to ensure consultation with the RMAC. The functions of the RMAC were described by a chairman as reconciling competing interests, putting a brake on the "wild" ideas of the RHA, reconciling teaching and service interests, and giving professional advice on broad planning issues.

8.13 The problem of an over-elaborate system was remarked upon. RMAC chairmen mentioned the amount of consultants' time the total system needed to operate well; one called it a cumbersome way of bringing together general practitioners and hospital consultants. One region was advised by 47 committees. A senior administrator said the system was reasonable only if it were used selectively. An RHA chairman thought the system untidy and complex although helpful to the authority.

8.14 As more doctors would be involved in DMCs and AMACs, it was at these levels that the majority of complaints about the number of committees were made. In one single district area the fact that the AMAC worked well was attributed to the absence of a DMC to draw attention away from the AMAC; the AMAC was thus the focal point of integrated professional advice. One interviewee pointed out that it was important to have medical advisory committees as near to the operational levels as possible, an argument against large single district areas, but not against all single district areas. By contrast, in multi-district areas there were complaints from doctors and administrators about the overlapping functions between the DMC and AMAC. Besides these two committees, the advisory system in general seems to have revived interest in Hospital Medical Staff Committees, so that in many places, consultants may be involved in four advisory committees considering the same issue: HMSC, Cogwheel, DMC and AMAC. For areas which have several small hospitals, the system could become oppressive and a medical administrator commented that in his area, consultants felt "imprisoned" by their own committees. From the consultants' viewpoint, such a structure meant many committee meetings, duplication of discussion and the possibility of decisions being overridden at different levels. One consultant summarised his view by saying that the system worked well within a level, but poorly between levels.

8.15 The composition of the AMAC was, in some cases, said to contribute towards poor functioning. In multi-district areas, if the AMAC brought together district representatives, it incorporated district rivalries of sizes or of teaching versus non-teaching needs. If it reflected medical specialities, it might ignore important district needs and fail to engage the interest of clinicians. Some interviewees thought that general practitioners and consultants had so little in common that there was no point in a joint body. The problems of general practitioners were homogeneous, but those of hospital consultants varied; the danger was that the AMAC became dominated by hospital concerns and, in one area, the general practitioners had withdrawn (one said "been ousted") from the AMAC. In another area the AMAC has ceased to meet, because of the lack of interest by its members.

8.16 If consultants were ambivalent in their feelings about the medical advisory system, Area Health Authority members were likewise. In only one authority was there clear and unambiguous support for the quality of advice coming from the AMAC; all other authorities, through members and chairmen, expressed a need for medical advice while being discontented with the advice they were now getting. In two authorities, the AMAC was seen as insufficiently detached from its own interests. In another authority, members saw it as legitimate for the AMAC to protect its interests, but its advice did not in their view help the authority, and in fact added to the difficulty of decision making. Another authority was less critical of the advice received, but noted that the AMAC tended to react to requests for advice rather than to put forward its own ideas. An authority chairman commented that the low level of contribution made by the AMAC reflected the low morale of the medical profession in general. Some members of AMACs complained about the tight time limits within which advice on complex issues was demanded.

8.17 Comments about District Medical Committees tended to be of the same nature: complaints about duplication with other advisory committees, and the disparate interests of general practitioners and hospital consultants were the two main comments. In one authority, two active DMCs were thought to be responsible for the lack of interest in the AMAC. Several consultants mentioned the overlap between the Hospital Medical Staff Committee or "Cogwheel" and the DMC, and the impression given was that if there were a choice between the two, most consultants would prefer to attend their "Cogwheel" which related directly to their own institutions.

8.18 There were few comments on the Local Medical Committees (LMCs), except to express satisfaction on their functioning. General practitioners considered that advice offered by the LMC was well received by the FPC, that its meetings were well attended and that it was very supportive of the GP representative on the DMT. Favourable comments were also made by the administrators of Family Practitioner Services about the Family Practitioner Committee. These committees were virtually unchanged by reorganisation. It should be noted, however, that the LMC and FPC are established at the area level, and thus in multi district areas the interest in participation by general practitioners may be diverted away from districts.

Regional Scientific Committee

8.19 One of the problems experienced by the advisory committee system was to find a common focal point which enabled an authority to get the advice it needed and practitioners to feel that their advice was taken. An instance of an advisory committee which was said to achieve this was given by a Regional Scientific Advisory Committee. In this committee, requests for equipment were made to peers, representing different scientific disciplines, who are aware that granting funds for equipment for one discipline might well mean that their own may not get its requests accepted. Both the chairman of the committee and its officer agreed that leaving the allocation to the committee gave the debate a framework of reality within which to work. The authority rarely rejected its advice.

General Views of Authority Members

8.20 At both area and region, the medical advisory committee tended to receive the most attention; comparatively few comments were made about other advisory systems. A general point was that it was difficult for an authority to deal with different advice coming from different committees. The chairman of a regional authority commented that advisory committees might contribute less to the authority when its strategic plan had been agreed; advisory committees might thus focus more on purely professional matters than on advising on policy.

The Views of the Unions

8.21 Interviews were conducted systematically in one area with branch officials of four major unions and in another area a chairman of a confederation of local health service unions was interviewed and other members seen informally. Several respondents mentioned the unions' ultimate aim of integrating the NHS with local authorities. Most considered that there were too many levels for swift decision making and that the formality of procedures was obstructive. In both areas, union officials spoke of a tendency to ignore or by-pass districts because decisions were obtained at area. "Conflict is inherent in the present arrangements of extensive bureaucracy, and delegation of management powers is needed." Grievance procedures were felt to be too protracted or non-existent.

8.22 The Joint Staff Consultative Committees were criticised by four of the five respondents as being negative, limited in scope (since they cannot negotiate pay), and concerned with trivia. The management was said to shelter from the unions behind the JSCCs which alienates staff from management. Two officials complained of a lingering resistance to unions which impeded their work, especially in the nursing hierarchy, although an RCN representative thought that attitudes had improved. This covert hostility was, they thought, unfortunate since branch officers were well informed and could help management. There was scepticism about the consultation procedures: unions' comments were ignored or they were consulted over what were really faits accomplis. Three officials said that managers were less trained in procedure than union officials: there was a need for skilled management at district rather than area level since that is where pressures and industrial disputes arise.

8.23 A major point, agreed by all union officials interviewed, was that the "bureaucratic" multi-tier structure hindered management-staff relations. The unions' current practice of negotiating with area directly when possible must be seen in the light of their expressed desire to deal with competent management at the operational level. The trade unionists interviewed felt that the good of the NHS was one of their main concerns, as well as the well-being of their members, and they wanted more institutionalised modes of co-operation with management on all matters. (For a different view of the trade union role see Section 14 of this report.)

Summary

8.24 Despite the general importance attached to advisory committees, there are few examples of good practice. Pharmaceutical, dental and para-medical advisory committees are thought to be more important in bringing together practitioners in different settings and in advising the chief officer than in advising authorities. The Nursing and Midwifery Advisory Committees, both at area and region, tend to be seen as competing with advice coming from the nursing management structure. In addition, nurses themselves commented strongly on their inexperience of committee work. Medical advisory committees are thought to be more significant to authorities than other advisory committees. Difficulties experienced here were the duplication of advice from different levels, the amount of time needed to participate in and to consult with them, and the difficulty of finding common ground between hospital consultants and general practitioners. In almost no case was the impression given that advisory committees were acting as a source of independent professional advice to authorities, although a variety of relationships existed between an advisory committee and the relevant professional administrative officer.

Comment by the Research Team

8.25 The sharpest comments made by advice-givers and advice-receivers were that there are too many advisory committees. The need for so many is not accepted by the professionals involved, a view expressed most strongly by doctors. Some AHAs and RHAs suffer from advice overload; this is seen to slow down decisions considerably and devalue advice-giving in general. It may therefore be worth re-evaluating the necessity for the present advisory system with a view to streamlining it.

8.26 The number of committees in the medical advisory system relates partly to the reluctance of consultants to allow their views to be represented by colleagues, so that specialist sub-committees or panels are set up. But it would seem to relate as well to a basic ambiguity in the advisory system—for whose benefit is it to operate? The advisory committee constitutes a forum within which professionals may agree change, exchange views and assess developments. But it is also an advice giving body to an authority. These functions are not always compatible, and to be effective, may call for different types of members. For the first medical "politicians" (referred to as such by several respondents) may be needed for negotiation about developments and defence of specialisms. For the second, medical experts may be more appropriate than representatives. The danger lies in not recognising the distinction between these functions: experts may not be representative and representatives may not give good advice. Comments by AHA or AHB members seem to indicate that they do not always get adequate advice from advisory committees.

8.27 A further reason for clarifying the purposes of committees is that rejection of what is intended as advice is discouraging and tends to denigrate the value of a committee. Those doctors who felt their advice had been ignored expressed considerable anger at a system which seemed to override the views of a pivotal professional group. The lack of feedback from an AHA may be a contributory factor, for it allows the worst interpretation to be made. It was pointed out, however, that when advice is rejected it is not necessarily ignored.

8.28 Another aspect needing clarification is the relation between the chief officer and the professional advisory committee. If "creative tension" or differing advice is intended as part of the system, it should be recognised as such so that potential conflict of opinion may be understood and legitimated rather than becoming a source of anxiety. This may be difficult when the committee is serviced by the chief officer.

9. Involvement of Clinicians in Management

Context

9.1 In England and Wales, the District Medical Committee (or Area Medical Advisory Committee in single district areas) elects two representatives to the DMT or AMT. "As full members of the DMT, the DMC representatives will take part in all its discussions and decisions. As team members, they are parties to the consensus decisions of the team and share in its collective duties and joint responsibilities. But unlike other members of the DMT, they take their places not as heads of hierarchically organised professions but as elected representatives of equals. They must enjoy the confidence of their colleagues, so that they can speak for clinicians not as mere delegates, unable to commit their peers without reference back, but as representatives using the discretion vested in them as a basis for action." (Grey Book, paragraph 4.10).

9.2 In Northern Ireland, the Chairman of the AMC is a member of the AET and the Chairman of DMAC a member of the DET. In Scotland the DMC representatives are not full members of the DEG; arrangements for the involvement of clinicians at this level vary between health boards, and may entail the attendance at DEG meetings of representatives of other groups, such as dentists or pharmacists, as well as doctors. The pre-organisation working party on the integration of medical work in Scotland took the view that the position of all chairmen of medical advisory committees vis-à-vis the administrative structure would be "strengthened by their independence from it and by their dependence on the confidence of their colleagues". (SHHD Review of Medical Advisory Structure.)

9.3 The Field Interview Survey covered eight DMTs (or their equivalents) and two AMTs. In all five English teams, there was considerable expression of the importance and benefit of having clinician members of the teams, by both clinicians and other team members. The contribution of clinical members lay in bringing "shop floor knowledge" to team matters. "They bring in realism to decisions; it would be unacceptable not to have them", "We contribute sanity and realities to team discussions", "We check flights of fancy". These comments illustrate the feelings of clinicians and chief officers that the clinical members did make a real contribution and the necessity felt for medical involvement. It is interesting that more favourable comments about clinical representatives were more often made by members than by non-members, perhaps indicating a change of attitudes through personal involvement. Similar comments were made by members of sector management teams about clinical involvement at that level.

9.4 It was noticeable that the same degree of interest in clinical team members and their contributions was not found in Scotland, Wales and Northern Ireland. Comparatively few responses were made to questions about clinical involvement. The clinicians shared similar problems of representing colleagues with English counterparts, but as the importance of team decisions was lessened by the line relationship with area officers, this limited the value of clinical members and their ability to influence decisions.

Models of Participation

9.5 Clinicians presented different models of participation* as team members. On two management teams, both the general practitioners and consultants were clearly representatives not delegates. Both GPs said that they made up their own minds: "it is more important to manage local affairs than to represent local medical opinion, although this must be kept in mind". One consultant said that in the last analysis, he was not a representative. "We have to do the best we can in a management situation." Another said that "if the views of consultants are in conflict with his committee (DMC) then he has to act as an individual".

9.6 In another management team, the opposite view was argued. In this area, the Area Medical Advisory Committee had passed a vote of "no confidence" in its representative for conforming with a decision with which consultants strongly disagreed. The consultant representative then resigned, and the new representative was very conscious of the limitations of acceptability which the medical staff might place on the management team decisions. A consultant member of the team said: "Inevitably there will be painful episodes when the consultant has to use his own judgement, but the overall sanction must be the views of his colleagues. Clinical members are to some extent representatives of their colleagues, not just one sixth of a consensus decision. There are times when medical members of the AMT have to demand that the AHA should make the final decision".

9.7 Other clinical team members functioned as liaison officers, explaining medical views to the management team, and management decisions to medi-

---

* See the case study reported in Part III.

cal colleagues. One consultant said that decisions would be worse without clinicians, even if they have no special contribution to make. A GP spoke of his role as a watchdog, making certain nothing adverse was done to GPs. Another GP mentioned the "persuasion" content of his role, speaking to his colleagues before decisions were made to try and affect the views of doctors.

Problems of Involvement

9.8 A fear shared by many of the clinical team members was of being seen by colleagues as the "administrator's man", a kind of administrative officer. This concern is especially strong now that in some areas services are having to be contained within strict financial limitations. This goes against both past traditions in the service (for many years services were allowed to expand provided a good case could be made for extra resources; those in areas affected by RAWP are feeling its impact now) and the ideals of consultants who aim to provide the best treatment available for patients regardless of cost. The tension between management and clinical aims was apparent and some consultants mentioned this as a reason for the reluctance of clinicians to become involved in management teams: the very nature of the decisions needed would be going against clinical interests. It may well be unfortunate that clinicians were encouraged to become more involved in management at a time of cutbacks.

9.9 In almost all areas, it was thought that there were good opportunities for clinicians to become involved in management; the main difficulty was interesting them into taking advantage of such opportunities. It was frequently mentioned by GPs and FPS administrators that the time burden was considerable. (One GP estimated that he spent one day, and another two days, a week on management matters) and the financial returns did not really meet the extra costs. GPs must find their own cover for their practices during the times they served on committees or teams. Three FPS administrators specifically mentioned the lack of competition for GP places on teams due to the time and work commitments it entailed. Even consultant representatives thought that an extra burden was placed on colleagues because they could undertake less clinical work. One consultant team member said that he kept outpatient sessions at four different hospitals, just to keep in touch with colleagues. Another consultant mentioned the lack of secretarial support given to team members which he thought would lead to an absence of continuity in team clinician working, if only because the filing and finding of papers took time to get right.

9.10 It was apparent in Northern Ireland, Scotland and Wales that the interviewees saw fewer opportunities for clinicians to be involved, and this related to the overall feeling that medical views were largely ignored. Decisions were taken at a level remote from actual practice and doctors had no voice in them. In one country, it was said quite strongly by almost all consultants and GPs that the relationship between doctors and administrators was one of confrontation, or "of aggro" as a senior registrar put it. In these countries, as well, the medical advisory systems were thought to be less satisfactory and the doctors were seen to be particularly demoralised by the new structure. The problem in the reorganised structure of obtaining a medical focal point at hospital level, exacerbated by the relative lack of authority of the unit or sector administrator, seemed in Scotland to have created some nostalgia for the role of the medical superintendent. The intention that medical divisional structure should, through the chairmen of divisions or the development of a role of "Chairman of Chairmen", provide the means of establishing a medical presence in the institutional management had not been realised. The problems of representation and of engaging clinical interest in management reasserted themselves at this level. However, there was an awareness of the problem and evidence of endeavours to use the divisional structure for its solution on the part of some health boards.

9.11 There was divergence of opinion over how much general practitioners were involved in management. There were some respondents who thought that GPs were more involved with the health services than before. An area administrator mentioned that the GPs had gained a voice in hospital matters while consultants had not gained a say in general practice; an FPS administrator thought that GPs had done well out of reorganisation in terms of opportunities for consultation. But the majority of comments on this topic were that GPs were basically not more integrated or involved in health service work than before. The evidence cited for this was the direct link between the FPS administration and the DHSS (or Welsh Office, DHSS, Northern Ireland or SHHD), the different method of payment for GPs, the ambiguity of accountability felt by FPS administrators to the area administrator or the FPS, the open-ended nature of GP expenditure, and the focus of GP representatives on area (through LMC) rather than district. There is no evidence from the interviews that the integration of FPS services in Scotland and Northern Ireland had made any substantial difference to the involvement of GPs in general health service management.

9.12 A few respondents were certain that it was a waste of time for clinicians to be involved in management; they lacked the necessary training and it ought to be left to professional administrators. There were many others who thought that clinicians did not want to be involved in management. Specific comments were the adherence to independent status, lack of trust in political authorities, lack of understanding of team or committee work and refusal to be represented by colleagues. Clinicians were said to have no appreciation of management needs or financial constraints, nor were they used to justifying their actions to other professionals, a point that led one non-medical respondent to press for medical audit. Some mentioned a need for a change in medical education to include knowledge of the NHS and how it operated; one or two others would add knowledge of medical administration to training courses.

9.13 There were also respondents who thought that doctors should combine independence with involvement in management. GPs naturally adhered to this view, but so did consultants, some FPC administrators and other administrative officers. The argument was that while a medical input to decision making was needed, the patient ultimately benefited from the independence of administration to ensure that patients' needs were being considered. Many doctors saw their role in management as defending the needs of patients against the administrative and financial considerations of administrators.

Summary

9.13 As in Section 8 on Advisory Committees, the views expressed here illustrate the difficulties of establishing a new work pattern in the NHS. While it is true that, prior to reorganisation, the Cogwheel system provided medical input to hospital management, the new system of team membership for practising clinicians installs them as decision makers at the operational level. The effectiveness with which this works relates in part to the effectiveness of the representative machinery by which clinicians achieve consensus views, but equally to the willingness of clinicians to take part in management. In the English districts, despite some difficulties, one can see the beginning of an effective interaction. Much less importance was attached to clinical involvement in the other three countries. As with advisory committees, the main difficulties lay in learning new roles and in the time commitment which clinicians need to make for participation.

Comment by the Research Team

9.14 The somewhat bland assertions of the reorganisation documents that clinicians will take part in team discussions and be full partners in consensus management understate the considerable novelty and difficulties of this role. Despite the critical comments made about the involvement of clinicians in management, both by clinicians and others, it is important to note that where a management team sees itself to have a real role in decision making, the clinicians do succeed in carving out a role for themselves and contributing to the management process. It seems to us significant that we can point to such examples of this happening. The appreciation of clinical membership by other team members shows that the experience of making decisions together can generate understanding and sympathy for the difficulties of each other's roles. Consultants and GPs have gained a greater awareness of the constraints of management situations, and chief officers have come to appreciate the important and difficult role carried out by clinicians. This must surely be a hopeful sign.

9.15 It should be of some concern that in some areas medical staff feel cut off from management involvement. A regional administrator said that in his view the raison d'être of reorganisation was to give the clinicians a voice in management. A split between management and clinicians is almost inevitable where clinicians themselves do not see this as the case. And then the incentive is for clinicians to withdraw from involvement, to be defensive, to act "irresponsibly" (in the eyes of other officers). It seems to us that, in parts of the UK other than England, the structure hinders the participation of clinicians as team members, and is unable to engage their interest at either district or area levels. In Scotland, the DMCs feel that they have no function or power because, in their view, the DEGs have none, and the DMCs have inadequate access to AEGs and AHBs.* The same factor may operate elsewhere.

9.16 What has received very little recognition from non-clinicians is how unrewarding and thankless the role of clinical team member may be. The

---

* Source: SHHD Review of Medical Advisory Structure, 1977 (unpublished).

70

clinician runs the risk of pushing his colleagues too fast while going too slow for other team members, of being seen as the "administrator's man" and as someone who must constantly refer back to colleagues before taking decisions. Any uncertainties or ambiguities in the role definition may be exacerbated by the attitudes of colleagues and officers. The role may be limited by the willingness of colleagues to accept representation, while at the same time be stretched by the demands of management.

9.17 Although medical clinicians are now being challenged by the development of more comprehensive planning processes there is no controversy about their key role in effecting changes within the health service. They are different from other staff groups because they are not within a management hierarchy. This accentuates the problem of ensuring that they are involved in management. Yet they cannot be allowed to remain separate from decision making beyond their own individual clinical boundaries. At a time of limited funds, the tension between professional ideals and accountable management becomes sharper because it is less easy to meet individual demands, but the relationship of doctors to management structure, in their individual roles as practitioners, as representatives of other doctors and as members of management teams, is still far too unclear. Individual clinical needs and overall management policies will always be in tension but conflicts need to be expressed in such a way that resolutions can be found. This throws heavy burdens on to the role of the clinical team member which is only now developing but which is never likely to be easy.

10. Authorities and Member Involvement

Context

10.1 The functions of authorities have changed as has their pattern of membership since reorganisation. Previously, the health services were governed by regional hospital boards and hospital management committees, local health authorities and executive committees. They have now come together into *unitary* regional and area *health authorities* in England and area health authorities in Scotland, Wales and Northern Ireland.* What is now a district, subordinate in varying degrees to area, often has the geographical boundaries of a former hospital group governed by its own hospital management committee. This has enabled health administration to become more *"professionalised"*; for teams of officers (known variously as the District Management Team, or the District Executive Team or District Executive Group) now operate instead of the HMCs or their local authority equivalent. It has also meant, however, that many members of the health service who previously had direct access to the governing body find that they must refer to a team of officers and are at what they feel to be several removes from the governing body. This is, perhaps, most keenly felt by consultants, by former group secretaries, chief or principal nursing officers, working formerly at group level, or by their equivalents who have transferred from local authorities. A further important change is that a *third* of both

---

* The Northern Irish area boards also take in the functions of administering social services previously performed by local authorities.

regional and area health authority *members* are *nominated by local authorities*, except in Scotland and Northern Ireland where the proportions are somewhat different because there are nominees from voluntary bodies. Other members are appointed so as to include representation from the main professional groups within the service and such other relevant interests as the universities. Yet a further important change is that the consumer interests are explicitly separated from management by the creation of the community health councils. (See Section 11.)

Report

10.2 In general terms, there were no differences between the opinions of regional and area staff about the way in which health authorities were working or about the way in which members at the two levels were working.

Staff Views of Members' Role

10.3 Opinion was evenly divided among those staff who thought that the authority had developed a clear role and those who thought that they were uncertain of their role. There was a slight tendency for administrators of all levels to feel that members were uncertain in their role and this relates to some characteristics of member behaviour which will be discussed later. The components of the members' task were seen to be as follows:

  (a) the monitoring of the activities of the Regional and Area Teams of Officers and District Management Teams who should be accountable to members. This was variously expressed as a watchdog or monitoring or a policeman role and was advocated both by members and staff;

  (b) final responsibility for planning (though this was sometimes thought to be too complex for members);

  (c) responsibility for specific major issues such as decisions on whether to close hospitals;

  (d) acting as a catalyst of public opinion and then arbitrating between the professionals in the service and public demand. They should apply commonsense criteria to complex problems. They should be able to balance the lay counterview against that of the professional.

10.4 In one area both members and staff felt that members should and do have the function of *management* as well as monitoring the managers and determining the larger policy issues. This might have tied up with the fact that the area had a particularly strong chairman. One chairman, elsewhere, however, expressed the authority's role as "to get a team and to plan and co-ordinate policy" which suggests more of a policy making than a managerial role.

Members' Views of Their Role and Functioning

10.5 Members were mainly interviewed in groups and breakdowns between regional and area opinions cannot be specified because of the overall numbers involved. Moreover, opinions about their role and functioning clustered strongly according to the authority to which they belonged. The majority of members interviewed, however, felt that they had a clear role or that it was developing satisfactorily although strong dissatisfactions were expressed in some authorities. They saw that the authority had a clear role but were divided on whether they, as members, could make an impact and were in good enough contact with the service. "The authority has been told to have second thoughts even on consensus decisions", a member said of one area where many members of staff thought that the authority's role was effectively that of rubber stamping. One chairman conceded that early on there was little option but to take officer advice and that it would take five years before members came to grips with the service. Another thought that the very existence of the authority was enough to ensure that officers went into the issues properly. But the overall impression of member feeling was that they found it difficult because of lack of time as much as of knowledge to come to grips with so complex a system. This was not because of defects in member quality which varied enough to ensure that at least some of them were able people. Members appeared to be and felt remote from the management process. Only the chairman was well enough placed to make an impact on the decision making of officers.

10.6 It was perhaps inconsistent, if natural, that members found that they had insufficient time to come to grips with so complex a system but at the same time felt that the consensus mode of decision making employed by management teams meant that members were being offered sets of proposals that were already worked through, thus leaving little room for member initiative (see also Section 10.12). Some members thought the solution was to insist that argued options should be put to them. Members certainly expressed some unease that they were so little involved in policy making. They could be no more than referees who became redundant when there was agreement among officers. But here it should be noted that in some respects, and in some authorities only, staff felt that members did not tackle the larger policy issues but concerned themselves more than they should with details (see paragraph 10.14 below). Some members also felt that they were inundated with a large amount of advice from the statutory advisory bodies whom they were compelled to consult and that their own role was somewhat questioned by the existence of CHCs who, too, were supposed to represent the community interest (see also Section 11).

Quality of Members
10.7 Some of the criticisms of the members' exercise of role related more to their representative status and to their behaviour than to quality or their perceived or actual functions.

10.8 The great majority of respondents of all disciplines and levels thought that members were, on the whole, of good quality. (But see Section 10.10 below, on local authority members). The contrast between this general evaluation and the criticism of the way in which they function was perhaps, a result of some of the uncertainty of role already referred to. Where they were criticised, and similar criticisms came from many quarters even if none of them were backed by a large number of respondents, a wide range of issues was mentioned. They were criticised for failing to act in a corporate way in the sense that they might promote particular viewpoints. "Parochialism" was a quality often imputed to some members. Other examples of particularist viewpoints were criticised. In one area university members were felt to be too powerful. In another, members were felt to lack specialised knowledge of matters in which they took a particular interest, such as building. Some members were felt to be unresponsive and unsympathetic to staff problems, in contrast to the good relationships now imputed by some to the previous HMC and RHB members. Some were not felt to be confident enough to exercise their role and were the "staging post" between an area team of officers and the region. Some chairmen were thought to be reducing the role of officers by establishing a direct relationship not only with the Secretary of State but also with his officers.

10.9 Some NHS employees felt that other forms of experiences should be more systematically brought in. Industrial and business experience was greatly appreciated and in some authorities more of it was thought to be necessary.

10.10 There were various criticisms relating to the political nature of members' behaviour. Two structural issues emerged. First, there were differences in relationship between health authority members and their officials and local authority members and their officials which might account for some of the criticisms of local authority members of health authorities. Secondly, local authority members appointed to health authorities were in a dual role, the two components of which might not easily be reconciled and might lead to fragmentation of the corporate responsibility of the health authority. These difficulties meant that members were felt to be beating some local authority drum rather than taking on the role as members who should be committed to the health authority. Few, indeed, spoke in favour of the local authority base from which some of the members had sprung. In one authority, criticism was related to the suspicion that local authority members would favour a local authority take over of the health service. On a more general issue, there was some feeling that appointments to health authorities were made by the Secretary of State for political reasons.

10.11 A somewhat contrary point of view concerned the lack of political base and legitimacy made by two members of staff as being a factor likely to make members insecure in the decisions they took. Yet other complaints were concerned not so much with local authority origin but with behaviour based on a desire to make political impact rather than to consider the case being discussed on its merits. Political activity such as a reference by one member to "consultants lining their pockets" was disliked. Other evidence of political interference included a failure to agree to a closure, which would have yielded enormous benefits in terms of saved resources, because of health council pressure, and a decision to reduce loans on cars if they were not of British origin. Some thought that there should be more representatives of NHS employees. Yet, in some areas, the difficulties faced by members reflected the serious tenor of local politics. One chairman of an authority was said to have lost his seat in a local authority because of a tough policy on hospital closures.

10.12 In general, however, in spite of these criticisms, most staff respondents thought that at least a key minority of members asserted themselves responsibly and well. Officers were, however, ambivalent about the extent to which they wanted members to be strong. One referred to "a built in tendency to rubber stamp". But if they did more than rubber stamp this would imply that officers' advice was inadequate. Officers, it was said, should be able to outline the right policies. But this point was not followed through to its conclusion: no interviewee said that health authorities were unnecessary.

Perceived Impact

10.13 If in spite of the many reservations stated above, members were felt to be generally competent, and their role to be either certain or developing, their impact on the service was felt to be slim. The great majority of respondents at all levels either felt that the impact was weak or recorded no comment at all about members. The nearer that one got to the operational level, the more frequently did respondents find it difficult to record any impression at all of the way in which members worked. Some were disappointed by their lack of contact with employers. The thinning out of contact is not surprising. But it is interesting to note that many felt that members were good people with a job to do, but all the same had little impact. This feeling corresponds with members' own belief that they had no real opportunity to get a grip of the system.

Officer–Member Relations

10.14 Those within the service were generally discontented with relationships with members. One objection was to the way in which members took up detailed issues and made what were considered ill advised decisions. In one area the decision to set up an administrative unit concerned with particularly sensitive issues of management was considered costly and unnecessary and taken directly against the advice of officers. In one case, a chairman involved himself personally in detailed problems of industrial relations and "got things wrong". But in another area the Chairman was almost affectionately regarded as yet another member of the area team and was able to deal with the unions on delicate matters in a way impossible to officers. Some members fiddled about with details such as the manufacture of sterilised water in hospitals, and without much technical knowledge. An AHA approved the award of study leave even when regulations laying down conditions for it had already been made. One authority approved individual car loans to officers. In another authority there was uncertainty about the decision to seek the advice of second line officers rather than that of the chief officers. Chief officers did not object to this as long as their advice was usually that taken. Otherwise they could hardly sustain authority over the system they were required to manage. Working within the teams meant, in some views, that decisions were not made enough by officers but were unnecessarily forced up to the authority, and this touched on the feeling among some that there should be a chief executive. Consensus management could also mean a limited role for authority members (see paragraph 10.6) particularly where teams took the view that to have to take a matter to the authority constituted a failure in the consensual mechanism.

10.15 So far, examples of over-obtrusive member action have been given. Examples to the contrary were also given. Both members and officers related ways in which members did not fully develop their policy making role. They received, probably encouraged, and then endorsed, recommendations instead of making firm courses of action themselves. In some areas, RAWP gave members options among which to choose for the first time. In at least two of the authorities visited, members felt that they had never been given policies to decide but had a vague fiduciary role which was not an adequate way of securing public control over the work of a highly professional and technical service.

Complexity of Issues

10.16 A few officers challenged the whole principle of lay membership. The more difficult issues were also technically complex. For some respondents complexity meant "professional matters" such as those which doctors, dentists, paramedicals or nurses might feel they ought to decide. Others were more concerned about the sophistication, variety and detail of the data to be grasped in planning and maintaining an extremely complicated service, reliant upon such a range of expertise.

Access of Staff to Members

10.17 Particular problems could be identified in the non-English areas where the district did not have direct access to the area authority. There were certainly stated feelings in the Scottish and Welsh districts that those who were responsible for operational decision making were excluded from contact, either functional or social, with the policy makers. In England, too, however, some staff felt that they had lost contact with members. As is often the case, those in contact with politicians and governing bodies might find it a time consuming experience. But those with no contact felt that the "real" decision makers were removed from reality.

Members' Powers

10.18 Members' views were not far different from those of officers as discussed above. Local authority members felt that they provided a democratic base which the health service would otherwise lack. Few were fully satisfied with the control that they had over the service. Some were then asked why they did not make changes in structure or procedure if they found them unsatisfactory. Their reply was often that they felt constrained by the rulings laid down by the centre or in legislation.

Summary

10.19 The role of members and their relationships with officers displayed common features throughout the study. The choice of members was felt to be sufficiently good to ensure that authorities should be able to function adequately. There was, however, considerable criticism of the way in which local authority members did not sufficiently change role and take up the committed stance appropriate to health authority membership. The strengthening of the "professional" and the associated emphasis on the consensus mode of working in the service might mean a corresponding reduction in the leadership role that could be played by authority members. The variation in roles and relationships was, however, more the result of local political traditions than of the structural relationships laid down by legislation and the guidance documents associated with reorganisation. Where members' grasp of overall policies is uncertain, because of lack of time available to them, or lack of systematic offering of options, a strong interest in detailed management issues becomes evident.

Comment by the Research Team

10.20 It is not possible to be clear if the lack of impact of members derives from the structural changes which have located membership participation at a level higher thân that of the former HMCs. Alternatively, it could be the result of the behaviour of members, possibly accounted for by the fact that they must perform complex tasks on a voluntary, part time, basis. Their difficulties are also compounded, perhaps, by their responsibility, at area level, for relating to more than one team of officers. It should be noted, however, as in the case study on members' inquiries (in Part III), that members can have impact to the point where they are felt to be entering the managerial role.

11. Community Health Councils

Context

11.1 Community Health Councils and their Scottish and Northern Ireland equivalents* (Local Health Councils and District Committees) were newly introduced with the reorganised health service. They are an institutionalised method of representing the interests of the public in the health service (and of the social services in Northen Ireland). They enable representatives of the public to get to know establishments run by the health authorities, to consider matters relating to the health services' operation, planning and development, and to give advice to the area authorities. The development is of considerable interest because it deliberately separates community representation and review from executive authority which is the business of the health authorities. CHCs are not formally concerned with conditions of employment or of working conditions for employees. They have access to the area authorities although their geographical coverage is most often coterminous with those of health districts.

Report

Principles Underlying CHCs

11.2 The great majority of those interviewed, at all levels of the service and from all disciplines, accepted the principle of having CHCs although the majority also thought that the CHCs were not as yet working well in practice. The arguments of principle in favour of the CHCs were that they would be able to link community feelings and needs with health planning, that they would enable community health services to involve the consumers, and that they would disseminate information to patients and potential clients. It was felt by many who criticised that there was a need for a separate system of critique which could act as a "watchdog", "keep people on their toes", "act as a ginger group", "establish a creative tension between the health service and those whom it served". There would be benefits to the health service itself because CHCs would stop introspective attitudes from developing. It was, therefore, a responsibility on the health service to work with the CHCs. An administrator put it that "if they don't work, it's our fault rather than theirs" and that it was the best way of reconciling health service operation

---

* For ease of reference "CHC" will be used to cover all three usages.

with public wants because "you can't answer criticisms once they appear in the press". It is better to anticipate them.

11.3 Far smaller numbers, again from all levels and disciplines within the service, felt that the CHC concept was wrong, first on grounds of legitimacy. The area boards were felt to be as representative as the CHCs. A few felt that power without executive responsibility meant the irresponsible use of power. Others thought it virtually impossible to define the community interest, to identify "anonymous public opinion" or to ask the right questions on behalf of the whole community. CHC relationships with community and client problems were sometimes unfavourably compared with those of the former hospital management committees or house committees or local authority members concerned with health.

11.4 A few respondents saw CHCs as a further elaboration of consultative machinery. CHCs were "another stumbling block" and "another way of hitting officers". They were another body to consult and "an unavoidable encumbrance". If they picked up complaints the Davies Committee assumption that remedies should be first sought from the organisation complained about would be ignored. They would lead to "defensive medicine" as experienced in the USA. A few respondents felt that CHCs exercised lay pressure on professionals whose exercise of judgement was critically important to good health service work. CHCs were evidence of the public obsession with the NHS. They were also seen as another financial burden at a time of economic stress.

11.5 Two respondents thought that they were seen as "bound to fail". They would find it difficult to become effective as against the system but if they became better informed, they would then become part of the sytsem.

Judgements on the Way in Which CHCs are Operating
11.6 It was noticeable that the working of a particular CHC often produced similar responses among clusters of role holders on whom they had impact, irrespective of discipline. If any variation in pattern among groups at all can be discerned, it was that those who spoke well of CHC work were particularly dependent on public co-operation and response, such as those concerned with community medicine and health education. They thought the CHCs to be operating better than did those who delivered acute services. But, it should be emphasised that opinions could vary strongly as between districts, areas and regions. Some, not only those at district and operational level but also at region thought that they worked well and usefully, whereas in some districts and areas criticism of them was widespread and sustained.

Favourable Judgements: NHS Views
11.7 A minority from members of all disciplines and levels felt that CHCs were helpful, that they communicated well with consumers, that they raised important issues and monitored well. They raised complaints in the areas where it was not easy for clients to do so and could be good sources of information. In one of the larger authorities, a senior officer felt that there were only "two odd-balls out of a quite large number". More than one respondent mentioned that CHCs could express the views of those within the service about improvements that needed to be made though not all

thought it proper for those inside the health service to raise issues through their contacts with CHCs.

11.8 Examples of action taken by CHCs were noted. They spoke on behalf of small communities who genuinely needed to retain the smaller hospitals due for closure. In some areas they helped educate the public on the need for preventive medicine. Good booklets on the health services were provided. A poster competition for health education was held by one CHC. Pressure might be put for the provision of local clinics, about waiting lists, or even on a case of a faulty roof on a health service building which no one else had noticed. CHCs had caused Parliamentary Questions to be put down which might result in more capital resources to flow towards an authority. A CHC would take up a particular issue, by monitoring, perhaps, work in the services for the mentally handicapped which might otherwise not get the priority that some felt it deserved. A few officers felt that their CHCs had a greater impact on the service and its improvement than did the area health authority. Because they could raise issues they might become "a focal point of discontent", and thus help to defuse unhelpful hostility towards a service that was doing its best.

Favourable Judgements: CHC Views
11.9 The CHCs themselves, whilst not, for the most part, disguising unease and uncertainties about their roles and their development, also pointed to some of their successes. They ensured that transport was arranged for a health centre. They were able to look at parts of the health service, and particularly the geriatric, mental and physical health care systems, and the balance of community care as against hospital care. Some had surveyed patients at local health centres. Critiques might be backed, but only in one case were, by work with academics competent in the field of health services and the assessment of impact on clients. Some saw themselves as having an informative and educative role with the public on health matters. They reviewed public documents and commented on them. Doctors and other practitioners were beginning to ask the CHC to take up problems of individuals. Local authority members of the CHC lobbied for the health service within their local authorities. They felt that they gave unbiased consideration to area policy in a way not possible within the area boards which were strongly influenced by their officers. Employees in some (but not all) districts in multi-district areas almost saw the CHC as the district authority. One CHC could speak in glowing terms of its relationship with district and area and the work it had been able to develop. From our accounts, there seemed to be few middle positions: either the CHCs worked well and successfully, or were distinctively frustrated and disliked in what they tried to do.

Criticisms by those in the Service
11.10 Criticisms of their working from within the health service were often strong, although the majority interviewed thought that health councils were of potential benefit.

11.11 The first complaint was that they *did not act as if they represented the people and the consumers*. Because it was difficult to formulate a general community interest, members indulged in personal views rather than representing the whole public interest. Some officers remarked, indeed, that they would much prefer "real" pressure groups because at least it was then possible to identify the standpoint from which criticisms were made. They could not represent the full range of priorities in a community because, for example, they were hardly likely to speak up for teaching hospitals or for priorities on behalf of the whole region. One set of health councils was criticised as being "too middle class" and too approving of everything they saw. The implication was that they passed on the small problems of their own friends rather than looked out for some of the difficulties in, say, outpatients' reception areas. Others maintained that they could be influenced by dissatisfied NHS staff.

11.12 In more than one area they were accused of *seeking political advantage* or playing political games. There were too many councillors fighting battles which they had lost elsewhere. Local authority members often came in for mention as stirring up trouble for purposes of publicity, which the press were eager to encourage. (But a CHC officer pointed out that political activity and connections were necessary to achieve action. The councils were right to represent districts without too much heed to the region or area, a point made as well by NHS officials.) There were a few comments about the poor attendance and rapid turnover of members.

11.13 Because CHCs could not take account of the whole range of issues facing a health authority covering a wider area, they tended, it was felt, to *deal with niggling parochial issues.* The one most often stated was that they were invariably against hospital closures* and would, if they had their way, allow sub-standard emergency units to be kept open in deference to local anxieties and wishes. Against this, however, it is noteworthy that the CHC in one area experienced a protest march against it because it supported a hospital closure. Other issues mentioned were demands for an emergency dental service which assumed that independent contractors and money could be found for it. CHC opposition to fluoridation was held by professional officers in some areas to support a medically inadvisable policy to which they had been led by poor advice from biased groups. They might advance "fashionable views on mental illness" which took no account of what can be provided. Pressure from a CHC led to the decoration of a ward that did not need it, while other priorities went unattended.

11.14 Against these criticisms of ill advised purposes, employees and members of health authorities maintained that *some were not attending to issues which required pressure.* Where clinicians did not provide a good waiting list procedure they had not acted. They never visited the waiting area of an outpatient department to see how the services actually worked. They seemed to need to drum up business and thus asked staff which complaints they should pursue and then got a distorted picture from individual members of staff. Or they indulged in "doctor bashing". One CHC insisted that family practitioners should be asked to display leaflets in their surgeries advising patients how to complain about their GPs. Because they had no real sense of priorities "they attracted support only from the moaners" and were "a complete waste of time". They were "bad value" as a complaints procedure.

---

* See the case study on hospital closures in Part III.

11.15 These *complaints of irresponsible and overcritical behaviour* came from virtually all levels of the health service and all disciplinary groups except that the regional authorities were perhaps more detached from community health councils and felt less the impact of their behaviour, either good or bad, and, with a few of the districts and areas, identified some CHCs as positively helpful. More than one administrator implied that the CHCs regard the service as guilty until proved innocent. An irresponsible attack by a health council almost caused a much needed administrative building to be lost from a building programme. Advertisements in the local press asking for complaints were not a constructive way of working. They almost always failed to bring out the good points about the health service. They saw the consumer as necessarily opposed to the management system and portrayed health service officers as villains.

11.16 These allegations of niggling parochialism, and distorted priorities, link with a more substantive issue. Quite a few respondents thought that they were *not technically competent* to monitor the health service. This relates to the councils' own complaints about the lack of information upon which they might act, and their need for more staff and technical resources.

11.17 There were complaints that CHC behaviour *abused openness of procedure* in ways demoralising to staff. Statements would be made without full investigation which were immediately taken up by the press. Indeed, at hardly any point did anybody on any side have anything good to say about the role of the press in reporting on health service matters.

11.18 A further complaint was that there were *too many health councils impinging on health authorities*. One district administrator, unusually however, had no less than three councils with whom to relate. One region had 17 health councils in it. It would mean "17 different interpretations". Taken with the massive statutory consultative machinery this meant a formidable and often inconsistent set of inputs to decision making. One area had 30 groups, including the health councils, to consult. Another area enumerated five health councils each of which took a different view. The results could be delay and high cost. One respondent thought that health councils could delay decisions by 6 to 12 months on changing the use of resources. One district official had three complaints put to him by the CHC on the day of interview. Another official reckoned that about a half of one administrator's time was taken up in dealing with CHC matters.

11.19 Dissatisfaction was often inconsistent. CHCs were held to have a nuisance role. Staff might feel under "inspectorial surveillance". They might complain of "disruptive" visits. They might object to outsiders influencing professional judgements. They might feel that they are "expected to jump". They might object to the Council acting as an inspectorate and as a complaints system. But others, if only a few, maintained that they were easily manipulated by officers and may not always create a sufficiently independent critique of the system.

Complaints About Working: The CHC View
11.20 The complaints about the way in which the system was working were numerous, came from all quarters, including the CHCs themselves, and make

it plain that a review of both principles and working of CHCs is necessary. Some felt that *their task was too large* ("To give us the whole health service to keep an eye on is too much"). The former hospital management committees (whose areas many of the CHCs now often cover) had their work cut out to grasp what was going on in the hospitals without as well having to concern themselves with general practitioner and community services and, in Northern Ireland, the social services as well. They felt that they did not have the resources they needed to make a full study of the service and one CHC wanted a full time research officer.

11.21 In all, many CHCs felt that the *role was still developing*. Some felt that the public did not realise that the CHC existed and a national campaign to increase awareness would help. One group of CHCs (the Northern Ireland district committees) felt they benefited from having a national association.

11.22 Many members felt that the *NHS staff did not co-operate with the CHC*. Officers had not received adequate guidance on how to treat CHCs. CHCs tried to contribute constructive criticism but were often given incomplete information and half answers. The attitude met from some administrators might be that *they* were giving a public service and knew what people wanted. Not all CHCs were given access to board meetings. Some resented the fact that area authorities, required by law to consult a very large number of consultative bodies, maintained that there was no need for the health councils because the advisory bodies gave them the advice of paid professionals, as if the consumer viewpoint was less important. It had become an "us and them" relationship. Some of the CHCs said that it was virtually impossible to develop a general interest in health matters. So it was necessary instead to focus interest on opposition to, say, hospital closures, or on developments that it felt the health authorities were not sufficiently undertaking.

11.23 Other problems concerned *formal status*. In Northern Ireland, the Secretaries to the Council were the district administrators who were employees of the health service. Advertisements for CHC staff appointments had to be put, in one area, under the health authority's name. Officials rather than members observed that this must lead to a conflict of role.

Summary

11.24 Almost all respondents approved of the principle of having community health councils separate from the health authorities. In some areas, they had established themselves as bodies thought to be useful by those who were affected by them. But the majority of those interviewed thought that they were not functioning successfully. Moreover, even those who approved of them in principle might also add that there were other developments, such as the advisory committee system, which were also good in principle, but which created overloading on an already over-elaborate system. Yet in reciting these varied and persistent complaints, it is important to note that many respondents appreciated that the health councils were recent inventions, that their creation was an attempt to differentiate management from representation and that the health councils might have to relate to a health service which itself was uncertain of its own systems and structure ("they are useless because they relate to a useless system" as one interviewee put it).

Comment by the Research Team

11.25 The research team felt that the principle of community health councils was being advanced at a time difficult for the health service. Members and officers uncertain of their role would find it the more difficult to work out with the CHCs what their role should be. It is noticeable, in this respect, that some members of the health service are unclear on how community health councils should operate. They tend to confuse their right to offer a critique with what they conceive of as their duty to be helpful to the health authorities. Thus it is not compatible to act as spokesman for the community and also to provide a public relations function for the health service, as some members and officers have suggested. Others object to them having an "advocacy role" which is, however, completely consistent with their formal terms of reference. Similarly, however, members of CHCs may not always understand that they lose their own status as legitimate critics if they attempt to get too close to management.

11.26 The research team were concerned to notice how poorly the resources and role of the CHCs were defined. They can hardly do their job properly if they do not have secretarial resources enabling them to relate effectively to the authorities and to their potential clients. They need access to the full flow of relevant information. Yet they need independence of health authorities and thus should be able to advertise for and appoint their own secretariat as is the case in many areas. They also need technical resources enabling them to assess the impact of health services on clients and patients which are not tasks easily undertaken on an amateur basis. These changes would, however, increase costs and exacerbate the shortage of competent staff already felt by some to exist in the NHS.

11.27 A few of the interviews confirmed the research team's analysis of what is now lacking. Because health councils are uncertain of their role, resources and access to information, they might be defensive, over critical and combative. There is no clear process through which they are entitled and required to act. For example, it must be harmful if complaints are raised in an open meeting in front of the press and officers are expected to give answers off the cuff which then become the basis of a press report. Due process demands that the health councils take up a matter systematically with the health authority. When they have assembled the facts, they then might draft a report to which, in natural justice, those reported upon should have access and a right of response. Both the report and the reply could then become public if it were felt to be useful. As it is, members feel they are being hastily criticised. This may increase the institutionalisation of the CHCs and some spontaneity will be lost as a result, a point made to us by one CHC secretary responding to our request for comments.

12. Planning

Context

12.1 In England, Wales and Northern Ireland, the central departments have required authorities to produce strategic plans* and have produced

---

* The Northern Irish Boards were also required to produce social service plans.

NHS planning guides. (In Scotland the position is different and is dealt with in paragraphs 12.4 to 12.17 below.) Proposals for the next ten years ahead were requested and these were to relate the region and area's own circumstances to national levels of provision. Within the guidelines developed from strategic plans, district, area and regions were required to produce operational plans covering three year periods in which the first year contains firm proposals and the next two years provisional indications.

12.2 Through these measures, the NHS imposed on itself tasks of great complexity which demanded sophisticated techniques for identifying health needs and wants, for matching them to existing resources and resources likely to be available in the future. *Forward looking rationality* was thus one demand placed on the system. The *impact of planning* on such important long range issues as the balance between hospital and community services became key issues. Another was the ability of planning systems to be relevant to *current operations.* In so doing, however, sensitivity to the needs and feelings of those who worked within the NHS involved the need to ensure adequate *participation* in the planning process. There are also criteria of *planning costs,* particularly in terms of administrative manpower to be taken into account.

Report

Has it Got off the Ground?

12.3 Most respondents in most, but not all, areas and districts did not feel that planning had got off the ground or had a meaningful impact on operations.* A large number of respondents (96) in fact made no comment at all about the planning system. The general impression is conveyed by a statement in a report on the management functions of a region and its areas: "planning in the reorganised NHS is still far from completely developed. There has not been sufficient time for authorities to operate the full planning cycle and procedures laid down by the DHSS and the benefits that should accrue from working within a more integrated service are still far from apparent". (January 1977). Administrators, particularly at the regional and area parts of the system, formed a minority group in their tendency to believe that it was already working.

12.4 Some areas had made a start with a few health care planning systems but had not developed comprehensive strategic planning which might replace some historic commitments in favour of perceived future needs.

12.5 The stage of development reached is well summarised by a senior officer in an authority where matters were relatively well advanced. The following extract from our interview note touches on many points to be dealt with in more detail later in this section: —

"When implemented the planning system will develop corporate planning which will be of particular help to the health service. At the moment plans coming to the (authority) are not very realistic; they require breaking down into costed items and strategies, with priorities indicated. There is no sequential thinking or development of alternative strategies. This is partly because the professionals do not give enough

---

* But see the case study of one region, area and district, in Part III.

attention to finance, the changing economic climate has not been grasped and staff are still acting as if the health service can continue growing. It also partly reflects the calibre of financial staff at (different) levels. They can handle day to day events but cannot supply high level strategic thinking. Innovation is stifled and is likely to remain so until 'new blood' works its way to the senior positions." (But) "The health care planning teams, often with poor research facilities, are felt to have achieved a lot in understanding the position and needs of various client groups".

12.6 Yet, as one chairman of an authority put it, planning might already "release uncertainty". Many other respondents from all disciplines said that it would at least start the discussion on where the service should go. Another regional senior officer believed that the planning cycle was working, because the regional team of officers decided that it would have to work. They had to encounter the fact that people did not like making choices among options all of which seemed to be of high priority, and that staff were not used to being specific in requests and costing of requests. The earliest stages were terrifyingly difficult but once the logic and grammar of planning began to be understood, the task became easier over time and more beneficial.

Different Perceptions of Planning
12.7 The official statements implied long range and synoptic thinking. Thus, the Guide to the New Structure for Health and Personal Social Services for Northern Ireland (November 1972) referred to programmes of care as being perhaps the most radical new approach in the proposed structure. There, the areas were to consider comprehensively a range of different services each catering for the needs of an identified group of patients or clients through programmes of care. Yardsticks would be established, and a more rational development of services related to clear objectives could then get into effect. Similar statements are found elsewhere. One Regional Strategic Plan (December 1976) roundly declared that it had been prepared for the decade ending 1986/7 and stated the objectives against which operational plans prepared during that period will be measured. It was based on area strategic plans and comments from a number of interested bodies. It was affected by initial consultations with formal advisory machinery and area chairmen. It was concerned with such major issues as the use and distribution of hospital beds, and the relationship between them and community services. In another region, strategic planning was thought to be concerned with frameworks of guidance on factors such as population, indicators of the level of services provision, availability of resources, broad priorities between different care groups, broad directions for growth and contractions in service and criteria for resource allocation to area authorities. The product of strategic planning was an overall framework to which all operational planning related. Operational planning, however, was concerned with defining and executing specific developments in health services.

12.8 These statements did not always correspond to conceptions of planning as perceived in the field. Some indicated in their answers that they mistook strategic for operational planning. In such cases respondents referred to anything from the creation of large scale building projects to the forward ordering of equipment of vehicles as if they were planning in the sense being used in the documents. The most common mistake was to confuse planning of capital projects with the whole planning operation, and this confusion existed right across the disciplinary groups although it was less obvious at the higher levels of the system. But very many of those who understood the distinction believed that planning was not fully comprehensive and covered too short a time span, although others thought that long term planning must be unrealistic when resources are uncertain. There were quite strong responses in this respect among area staff (but less so among regional), most strongly from administrators but also from many other groups as well. Such comments as "planning has meant the more objective allocation of resources", and that planning did mean that the needs of the period of five to ten years were being discussed, have to be balanced against the feeling that broad policies and objectives had been inadequately considered before resource decisions were put into the planning framework.

12.9 There were a few references to an inadequate analysis of needs, to a failure to move away from the historic commitments implied by existing distribution of resources, and to the failure to explore new objectives or evaluate the fulfilment of existing ones. Whilst there was some enthusiasm for planning from among members of health care planning teams in different authorities, some nurses thought that they were medically dominated. A contrary view of the whole process came from an authority member who felt that planning was too global, as were budgets, inasmuch as there was no delegation of either to the working units. But this criticism tied up with other criticisms about an authority stating budgets for districts half way through the financial year in which money was to be spent. Other complaints about the lack of conceptual range concerned the failure of the service to provide adequate training for planning. But this point was thought by one respondent to be an excuse for inaction and a projection of respondents' lack of interest in implementing a planning system.

Quality of Analysis
12.10 A minority of respondents referred to the level of data required. In the words of one senior official, "planning is like computers. If you put (muck) in, you get (muck) out". But all who did mention it felt that data were lacking, even when sophisticated computer systems were available, and that the analytic capability required was generally absent. This complaint relates to the general criteria for a good planning system stated in paragraph 12.2.

Role of Central Departments
12.11 The few respondents who referred to the usefulness of DHSS guidance found the material helpful but not always in line with their particular needs. There was some complaint about the way in which data required for a central department were not the same as those required for regional or area strategic planning. It is not, in fact, clear that the central departments adequately consulted* the regions and areas before formulating their requests. "Some difficulties have been experienced in following (the requirements of the NHS Planning Guide) which, though meeting national needs, do not fully

---

* This point of view is, however, modified by the case study on a planning system (Part III).

meet regional needs. Discussions will therefore be necessary in due course with the DHSS to modify the format for the future so as to accord more closely with the needs of the service". The DHSS guidance* was felt to be clear in its priorities but too complex for present manpower. It was often followed too slavishly. Guidelines were not clear on resources. A more general complaint was that departmental decisions on planning were slow and that they interfered in details.

Level of Participation

12.12 The majority of those who mentioned participation in planning felt that it was inadequate. There was, however, a particular clustering among the staff of those districts who felt that area was not delegating them sufficient authority. There was more satisfaction, in fact, with membership of health care planning teams, by those who were in them, than with the way in which the main structural relationships worked. Some thought, however, that the planning system brought those in the field into a nice balance with management. But some did not feel that their participation was truly effective because administrators did not relate district planning to the strategic plan of the authority. Others again, thought the levels of participation too high; "horrific" was one word used and another commented, in the planning context, that it led to delays and that attendance at meetings had become a virility symbol. This touches, however, on another point made which was that planning should not be regarded as something which can be undertaken by groups of 20 to 30 people meeting together (as has been reported to the team) but by small teams of technically competent people who can analyse data and place it into a comprehensive statement. The onus on them was, of course, to consult everybody affected by the plan. It did not involve first line participation for all concerned.

Relevance to Operations

12.13 The majority of those who replied on this question, and at all levels, felt that, so far at least, planning was not relevant to operations although in a few of the more advanced areas, it was felt to be beginning to bite. "Institutionalised planning merely means more paper work, more red tape and more jobs for the boys", (thus a clinician). Others thought that it was dangerous because, paradoxically it was both Utopian and restrictive.

Costs of Planning

12.14 Some respondents, from all levels and disciplines, but not very large in number, spoke of the time and staff involved in the planning system. It meant duplication of work between the health care planning teams, sector teams, patient resource groups and the different disciplines. Some spoke of it as confusing and complicated. Some comments, indeed, referred to the same objections as those held against participation. There was one case, it was claimed, of "several meetings of 40 people to discuss a 30 bed wing", but note here the limited operational sense of planning.

Planning in Scotland

12.15 There is, as yet, no formal planning system operating in Scotland, and although the SHHD was felt to be moving towards the establishment of

---

* The NHS Planning System, DHSS, June 1976.

one now, doubts persist in the Department about its value and feasibility. The framework exists. The Department has a Policy Group, supported by a small Planning Unit established in 1974. There is also machinery for consensual determination of national priorities in the Scottish Health Service Planning Council (on which each health board is represented), working through national programme planning groups, and in the national advisory committee structure. The Planning Unit potentially has a key role, in that it services each of these bodies.

12.16 Not surprisingly, views on planning did not come through strongly at area and district level in Scotland, although there were positive comments from some respondents on area programme planning. What follows is largely derived from interviews with members of the Department. The delay in establishing a planning system has to some extent been deliberate. There was concern about complexity and over-elaboration, and a feeling on the part of some that formal planning was less needed for monitoring and co-ordinating purposes in a country of this size. At the same time, there have been severe problems of resources. The Planning Unit has six staff and lacks key kinds of expertise, such as health economics and operational research. Statistical data are provided by the Information Services Department in the CSA whose resources are available to the 15 health boards. The resource problem has been compounded by the enforced diffusion of the Unit's activities. The demands on its time of its functions of service and support to the Health Service Planning Council, the programme planning groups and the seven national advisory committees have made it impossible to give any priority to its functions of co-ordination of Departmental planning and the formulation of authoritative strategic statements for the Policy Group.

12.17 There has been planning activity, but as yet it has not been co-ordinated or fully consultative and there is some uncertainty about its impact. The finance department produced SHARE, the Policy Group "The Way Ahead", and the doctors and nurses have worked on manpower planning.

12.18 In some respects, then, the Scottish approach to planning may be said to have been tentative. (It will be remembered in this context that there is no formal machinery for joint planning between health and local authorities either). However, the framework established was highly ambitious. It brought up to national level the challenge of reconciling the need for participation and consultation with the demand for the application of sophisticated technology to long term strategic planning.

Northern Ireland

12.19 The DHSS (NI) has programme planning teams which study the needs of specific client groups. These are mirrored at the area board level by programme planning groups of officers. Difficulties were being experienced, however, in bringing the whole planning system together, as well as in securing good working relationships between the different disciplines in the working groups.

Comment by the Research Team

12.20 The evidence is overwhelming that the planning system is not fully off the ground. But from the point of view of policy development, the more important issue is whether the range of concepts of planning is generally understood throughout the service. The confusions between planning in its strategic and large scale operational sense and broader general decision making are to be noted. Multi-disciplinary management may help create the favourable environment for planning, but it is not the same thing. The central departments put out clear theoretical guidance on the way in which planning could relate long term purposes and objectives to patterns of health need and resource frameworks. Application of the guidelines showed how theory needs to be related to the practical problems experienced by the health authorities. Moreover, theoretical constructs need to be tested and changed as experience within the system grows. Finally, rational planning conflicts with political pressures both from within and from outside the NHS.*

13. The Impact of Structure on Decision Making

Context

13.1 The guidance from the central departments stated that the objective in reorganising the national health service is to enable health care to be improved. The Grey Book on the English reorganisation went on to say that "management plays only a subsidiary part, but the way in which the Service is organised and the processes used in directing resources can help or hinder the people who play the primary part". The basic principles were maximum delegation and decentralisation within a framework of national, regional and area policies.

Report

13.2 To ask interviewees about decision making is to ask about the dynamics of the structure; how the various features of the structure, described in isolation in the other sections of this report, operate together. Comments are grouped under four main headings, but there is considerable overlap among these sections.

The System is Top-Heavy and Over-Managed

13.3 In Northern Ireland and Scotland, this criticism, voiced equally by district and area staff, reflected the difficulties of a two tier structure in small geographical and demographic areas. In England and Wales, respondents, while concerned with the number of tiers within a region, were particularly vexed by the administrative structure within a tier. There was a general feeling that administrative staff had increased greatly, although this was challenged by some who pointed out that any increase was directly related to additional consultative functions, and a greater awareness of administration since so many more people were involved in decision making than before.

13.4 Comments were frequently made about the Salmon structure for nurses, with nurses as critical as others. An area health education officer said that for a health visitor to contact her she had to go through her nursing officer, senior nursing officer and divisional nursing officer who then contacted the health education officer. An area nursing officer said that

---

* See case study on planning in Part III.

89

application for a six month training course went to divisional nursing officer, district nursing officer, area nurse (personnel), DMT and AMT, taking a total of four months. A ward sister mentioned that "ten people now do what matron did before". Many nurse practitioners commented on the duplication and lack of differentiation between nursing officer and senior nursing officer posts; there was considerable doubt as to whether both were necessary (See Section 5).

13.5 Another evidence of over-management was the multiplication of channels of communication. A district occupational therapist reported receiving the same memo from three different people. Circulation lists for quite trivial documents sometimes occupied more than two sides of closely typed memoranda sheets. Any one role holder might find that he or she must choose between several points of reference. A consultant, for example, might refer to the chairman of his medical advisory committee, or the clinical member of the district management team, or the district medical officer (where they exist) or the administrator at unit, sector, district or area level, or the regional medical officer. No doubt, lines of communication established themselves by usage but many of those interviewed remained unsure as to where they might legitimately apply for action to be taken. In hospitals the separate lines of nursing and administration did not mesh well together; things got "lost" going up different functional channels, and often different messages came down.

It is Hard to Locate Responsibility for Decision Making

13.6 This comment was again most prevalent among the non-English countries, particularly district staff, but was put forward in English regions as well. Functional management with long lines of communication meant that decisions were taken at a high crossover point away from the level which had the problem. Uncertainty of authority in a role led to unwillingness to make decisions and thus matters were referred upwards. It encouraged cautiousness, lack of trust and territorial attitudes, according to a physician superintendent. The increased number of people who were now involved in hospital decisions, although located outside the hospital, was commented upon by a nursing officer: sector administrator, district medical officer, district finance officer, district catering manager, area records officer and general administrator for building. The uncertainty of who could make decisions led, according to a consultant, to the "rule book syndrome". A unit administrator mentioned that buck-passing had become the national sport of the NHS. An area paramedical officer thought that separate funding of hospital and community services produced a need for inter-linkage between the two services which confused decisions and communications.

13.7 Generally, the involvement of so many different people and groups in decision making had resulted in an inability to make decisions. The points at which this was felt most strongly were the hospital (a senior registrar said that there was no focal point for decision making within the hospital and this view was shared by a number of nurse managers) and sector administration, as described in a previous section. Some of the points made above, duplicate channels of communication, referrals between tiers and incompatibility of nursing and administrative structures, were also relevant here.

Decision Making is Too Centralised

13.8 It follows from the two previous sub-sections that there was a strong feeling that decisions were made, and perhaps could only be made, at too high a level. As before, centralisation was an umbrella term for various features. Uncertainty of role boundaries between teams of officers necessitated frequent referrals. Consensus management and the Salmon structure were thought to be features which pulled up decisions. It was often said that managers in the NHS managed at "too low a level" so that chief officers dealt with matters seen by themselves and others as trivial. A sector administrator likened his role to the middle part of an egg timer. There were other comments that sectors were subject to endless controls from above, that policy made at area and district dealt in too much detail, leaving too little freedom and manoeuvrability at the sector and hospital levels. It was mentioned by several interviewees that regardless of whether decisions needed to be made centrally, overturning decisions or agreements reached lower down was destructive in that it undid considerable work put in to reaching agreement, and created bad feeling among staff involved.

13.9 To many practitioners, the management structure was seen to be remote. Decisions were made somewhere "up there" by people who were usually unknown. In interviews it was noticed that practitioners were unfamiliar with the structure, composition of teams or names of officers. But the feeling of remoteness was not confined to practitioner level; several chief officers at area and district also mentioned their own feelings of remoteness from the patient level. Extended lines of communication were seen to be disadvantageous to both extremes. (See Section 14.)

13.10 Centralisation of decision making was said to occur due to by-passing of levels. This was particularly noted in two of the non-English areas but also occasionally mentioned elsewhere. Consultants especially had informal lines of contact which cut across the formal structure. The District Medical Committee was by-passed on occasion by consultants going directly to the Area Medical Advisory Committee, so that the ATO made the decision rather than the DMT. The consultants' view was that the sector and district teams had insufficient authority to make decisions, so one might as well go "straight to the top". Such by-passing caused considerable confusion and resentment below, as other staff could be unaware that issues were simultaneously being considered elsewhere in the structure and often had their own decisions pre-empted. From a source outside the Field Interview Survey, the team was made aware that serious consideration was being given in Scotland to establishing management responsibility at unit level, through strengthening the role of the unit administrator, finding means of incorporating the medical profession into management at institutional level, and taking a new look at the implications of the nursing structure for the delegation of responsibility to nurses in hospital.

13.11 Another point mentioned by interviewees in all regions was the quality of management which in itself necessitated a greater degree of centralisation. The inexperience of administrators and nurse managers was seen as a source of decisions being referred to higher tiers, and for managers to pull up decisions. The post of sector administrator was mentioned several times as being undergraded and poorly paid, thus attracting inexperienced staff. (See paragraph 4.10.) The loss of senior managers in 1974 was pointed out by many as the source of some current difficulties; people were inexperienced in "making the system work" (a physician superintendent).

Consultation Has "Gone Mad"

13.12 Consultation was seen as necessary; it was expected by different groups, and could potentially add to the wisdom and acceptability of decisions. But there were many criticisms of the consultative processes now existing. Consultation was blanket, rather than selective, so that there was consultation of groups, marginal to a given issue, which extended the time taken. It was difficult to judge the best time to start consultation; too early might mean positions hardened before all options were known. Consultation "reduces the enthusiasm of staff to take initiatives and make decisions" (a catering manager), "democracy has led to bureaucracy" because of consultation (a sector administrator); "it encourages play safe attitudes" (a general practitioner), "abdication of responsibility" (a district personnel officer), and "inaction by the length of time it takes, so that things get dropped" (a medical university representative).

13.13 Managers felt that they had lost control of their own departments and that their decision making scope was severely limited by consultation. On capital works projects, an area treasurer claimed that there was scarcely time in the financial year to fit in the consultative processes. It was also noted that these may be so long that the problem has changed before consultation has been completed. The consultative process was made more cumbersome by the number of committees involved; committees were said to have "proliferated" since reorganisation. The machinery for handling these groups was not yet well developed; there was a lack of synchronisation among them, so that much time got lost through referral and delays between meetings. A chief administrative medical officer claimed that "neutrality and inertia have been created through the balance of power groups" which had the power to obstruct.

13.14 Various examples were given to illustrate these difficulties. We have already alluded to the case where approximately 40 bodies were involved in the consultation associated with the occupation of a new hospital wing, and the discussions had been underway for almost three years as it involved acceptance of a change of the use of beds. In another case it took three years for a catering manager to get a new rota accepted. An area nursing officer claimed that it took three to four months to get a decision from the Area Nursing Policy Group, because of consultation with ANO, SNOs via divisional nursing officers, Area Nursing and Midwifery Advisory Committee and possibly the JCC and Area Staff Consultative Committee. An administrator said that over 1,000 copies of the area plan had to be sent out for comments, although very little came back.

13.15 Some consultation was seen as "window dressing"; there was only one viable option yet consultation still had to be taken. The chairman of an AHA spoke of the "fallacy of the consultative process where the facts may point to a particular solution before the exercise begins. It is necessary to consult both politically and for purposes of morale, but the whole decision making process is thereby lengthened". Other practitioners and managers thought that consultation was often meaningless because too little time was allowed for it to be seriously conducted. The lack of feedback from consultation contributed to it being regarded with cynicism.

Budgetary Control

13.16 Two aspects of budgetary control were seen to hinder decision making. One was the late notification of budgets. Sector administrators tended to stress this factor as a reason for their own inability to plan and make decisions within their sphere, but works officers were also sensitive to this issue. An area works officer commented that the late allocation of funds meant that one considered not the most needed projects, but rather those which could be completed within the financial year. The second was the necessity to adhere strictly to budgets which had resulted in decisions being taken centrally so that an overall view could be retained.

Impact on Patient Services

13.17 It is not easy to relate these characteristics to the actual delivery of services to patients. Especially in community services, nurses and doctors seemed to have little contact with the administrative structure, and did not feel hindered in carrying out their functions through lack of decision making. The units within which they worked were small and independent, and decisons about work were almost wholly taken by staff based within the unit.

13.18 Practitioners and managers within hospital settings expressed mixed views. A superintendent radiographer said that he "was not messed about by elaborate administration because his department was essential to acute services". A senior house officer said that clinicians had hardly perceived the effects of reorganisation, and this was supported by comments of other consultants. But on the whole, those working in hospitals felt varying degrees of frustration in the way they could perform their work. Some of the specific comments made may appear minor: weeks to get a coat hook on the wall; three days to get a light bulb changed; delays in getting electrical points wired up. The difficulties of co-ordinating support services by nurse managers and administrators mentioned above related more directly to the patient, and because of these difficulties, there was a feeling that services to the patient had become worse—less efficient, more bureaucratic and more costly. A district physiotherapist suggested that practitioners tended to absorb the frustrations themselves, thus minimising the effect on patients. The opinion that patient services had suffered is hard to document, and we can only report that in hospitals many staff held such a view.

Views of Regional Officers

13.19 While area and district respondents were able to cite multiple sources of problems in decision making, the comments at regional level tended to cluster around two issues: consultation and the number of levels which are involved in decision making. This is perhaps understandable insofar as the region is the final arbiter within the NHS. Focusing on policy issues, its decisions are highly political and it is subject to representation by a wider range of groups. Several respondents pointed out the frequency with which groups go on arguing after a decision has been made, mistaking consultation for agreement. Region was dependent on other tiers to supply information and to accept its decisions, and it could observe difficulties of decision making in these tiers. Respondents at region were thus more likely than others to comment on the complexity of the total decision making system and the importance of the will to make decisions.

Some Positive Comments

13.20 While there is little doubt that most people in the NHS feel decision making has become more difficult, there were comments which were less pessimistic. Some respondents questioned whether decision making had been that much better before reorganisation. A number of chief officers thought that their new positions enabled them to make better decisions, even if this did take time. In general, the right of consultation was welcomed as a good feature although its excesses may have been deplored. Consultation contributed to the validity of decisions, and to an understanding of the potential impact of decisions. The openness of decision making was also thought right. Several interviewees recognised the impact of financial restraints on decision making and thought the structure was being wrongly blamed for all problems.

Summary

13.21 In this section respondents express their feelings about the decision making process. Many of the perceptions about different aspects of the structure, reported in the previous sections and that which follows, are related to what is considered here. Examples are quoted but these should be seen as illustrative only; there has been no attempt systematically to follow through particular decisions. The majority of opinions expressed concerned the length of time needed to take decisions; and comparatively little was said about the quality of decisions. The principal problems were seen to be the number of levels through which decisions have to pass and the number of people who become involved, uncertainty as to where decisions were made, centralisation of decision making and the consultative process. Members as well as staff were highly critical of the decision making process.

Comment by the Research Team

13.22 From the interviewees' replies, we can identify different types of decisions, and relate some problems to those. At the regional level, for example, it is not so much delay which the structure imposes on decision making as a rather complicated process of consultation. Policy making and strategic planning may not need to be done quickly and acceptability may be a more important criterion. However, the consultative process at all levels was seen to be over-elaborate, and it is likely that decision making would benefit from its streamlining.

13.23 At the operational level, the problem mentioned most frequently by practitioners and first line managers was that of getting quick decisions on service giving functions, and this raised questions about functional management structures and delegation of authority.

13.24 In between these two levels, there is a range of decisions which may begin at the operational level but have policy implications, or alternatively, arise from policy issues but impact on operations, and it is here that the greatest difficulty of identifying decision making roles seems to exist, and that external factors may impinge on decision making structures. The issue of relationships between teams was again raised, and problems of decision making can be seen as an aspect of the separation of policy making and management mentioned in Section 3. It may also be possible that management decisions, because of the lack of clarity of roles, get caught up in policy making procedures and are mishandled in this sense. The principal external factors which impinge are the importance attached to participation, so that everyone gets consulted regardless of their centrality to an issue, and financial constraints which have led to a need for greater control over expenditure.

13.25 It is not possible to say whether in fact decision making does take longer now than before reorganisation, but it is true that staff strongly think it does, and this colours their perceptions and feelings about the structure. Without structural modifications, the decision making process may improve when planning has become a more established and certain activity, and as staff gain in familiarity and skill in working the system. Some of the problems discussed above are related to the structure, but others are inherent in the health service.

14. Morale

14.1 Towards the end of the interviews we asked about the state of morale in the health service. The question was not precisely formulated and it is evident from the responses that morale is equated with a general state of content or discontent which might relate more to general feelings about the NHS than to feelings of satisfaction with their jobs or working context. Many comments made in response to other questions had already touched on questions of morale and, partly for this reason, perhaps, 122 interviews contained no record of response on this question. 124 specifically said they thought morale was low and a smaller number (70) thought it was reasonably good or even high. Among these, however, 10 respondents said that morale was high at their own working level but low in the rest of the service. Low morale was assumed, often by others, on the part of hospital doctors who were more likely than community or administrative doctors to point to declining attitudes towards work and service for patients and some of whom were particularly damning on specific developments such as overtime payments for junior doctors, the bureaucratisation of nursing and the over-elaboration of administrative structures. A few volunteered the information that their own personal morale was either low or high, but in no significant numbers.

14.2 It is important to note, however, that where low morale existed, it is explained not only by problems arising from reorganisation but by other factors as well which, taken together, elicited a larger number of responses. Economic circumstances, the status change of clinicians and managerial groups, and the growth of trade union power and working attitudes, rather than reorganisation, were seen as significant factors in declining morale.

14.3 The reasons given for low morale varied according to the areas where the question was asked. For example, in some areas, senior officers at the district level were particularly upset at the failure of the area to clarify roles and to delegate sufficient authority and discretion to them. But apart from this particular point, there was no clear indication as to level or professional group in relation to sets of dissatisfactions.

Structures, Attitudes and Resources

14.4 The largest group of stated dissatisfactions (63 respondents) complained of *over-elaborate organisation* with too many levels creating a system that was both big and remote. Associated complaints from far smaller groups were the *reduction of role certainty* and authority. Many junior administrators felt that functional management had reduced their role and *status*. However, others criticised the creation of *too many administrators* with too much power over other specialisations. Some administrators maintained that management was the target of *unfair criticisms* and that this was demoralising. Next to complaints about the over-elaborate organisation, however, sizeable numbers (43) spoke of the *changing attitude towards work*. They spoke of frequent absenteeism. They objected to uncaring attitudes which were not hitherto a characteristic of the service. Many of the 43 specifically said that the growth of *trade union power* had caused trouble where none need exist. One administrator said that every three or four weeks he finds himself in an industrial dispute. Of similar intensity were complaints about resources. 41 complained about *poor resources* and shortages of staff and another far smaller group about the *over work* resulting from staff shortages. Very few said that *salaries* were poor. Indeed, some said that salaries were now fairly high for most people. Only a few complained of poor working conditions. 17 respondents, and not all of these were doctors, said that the *declining relativities* were a source of unhappiness and a further 21, not all of them doctors again, referred to the doctors' loss of status as a contribution to low morale.

14.5 It is worth noting, however, that a small group went out of their way to say that resources were not short but they were, if anything, misused. Again, it should be stressed that there are groupings of opinions according to the area where the question is asked. It is likely that the research teams were not conducting their enquiries in the worst off areas. Certainly some respondents pointed out that standards were high and resources and facilities good.

Reorganisation

14.6 Other complaints were related to reorganisation and, in part, to other changes in *social attitudes* which were contemporaneous with the restructuring. The changing relativities and loss of status for some has already been referred to. A few referred to the popular *distrust of the NHS* which was often built up by the media. 17 respondents talked about the *uncertainties* that reorganisation had brought and there was some apprehension that there might be yet further changes to absorb. A similar number talked about the difficulty of adjusting to the new structure and the exceedingly unfeeling way in which reorganisation had been undertaken. "Staff feel battered by reorganisation" and this battering included the removal from established posts, the requirement to go through elaborate recruitment procedures and to resettle into a new and strange organisation.

Comment by the Research Team

14.7 Both the questions and answers on morale have to be taken in conjunction with answers on other issues. They reflect, however, many of the feelings about the general results of reorganisation and the working of the service. For the most part, work for patients goes on regardless of the changes in the structure and the social and economic climate in the context of which it takes place. But when the question is asked, discontent with the system is evident.

PART III
The Case Studies

Introduction

1. Whilst conducting the pilot and field interview surveys the team sought help in identifying subjects for closer study. It was not possible to cover the whole range of interest contained in our terms of reference and, as has already been indicated, the choice of studies was determined in part by what was most easily accessible within the timetable of the research.

2. In the event, however, the four studies served to illuminate an important and interestingly wide range of themes. *The study of a planning system within a metropolitan region* reveals many facets of both structure and of decision making process. It shows how the best attempts to plan providently and rationally, to establish meaningful objectives, and to specify the ways of achieving them, encounter almost, but not quite, insurmountable obstacles. First, there are multiple concepts of what the health services should be (objectives), as perceived by the national, regional, area, district and practitioner levels. These concepts need not conflict with each other but may imply different scales, intensities and contents of what is felt to be needed which may be difficult to reconcile. Then there are the difficulties of running a system which, in principle, should invite participation from many groups and thus lead to what many consider the overloading of an already overloaded system. Thirdly, there are the problems created by the fact that health planning is expected to be a *technical* process but even so becomes *political*. So "planning statements come to represent the balance found between different concepts of rationality". The study shows something of the actual problems faced by the NHS. These include historical assets sited in the "wrong" places and the longstanding practices embodied in professionally sanctioned procedures whilst demography, changing health care practice and social values may require a rapid reallocation of resources.

3. From the study of macro-planning, the reader is invited to turn to three particular instances which all, however, demonstrate a common theme: that health care services are the subject of public and professional concerns which cannot be decided by any simple, comprehensive and non-conflictual decision making system. The problem of producing acceptable plans is highlighted by the fact that authorities vary in their style from those with a bias towards control by management to those who are controlled by politicians. *The study of the allocation of responsibilities in bio-medical engineering*, which is concerned with the competing claims for control by the Works and Physics Departments goes directly into a primary issue in the health service—of how clinical members of management teams can reconcile their management and representative roles. It demonstrates, too, how the wide range of disciplines at work in medical care contribute towards complexity in decision making. "The incorporation of clinicians in management, the requirement of consensus decision making, the roles of the authority members, of the DHSS, and of the region and . . . the impact of structural changes upon power are all brought under scrutiny." The capacity of the structure to promote good decision making is thus examined. The policy conclusion reached is that ambiguity in the reorganised structure needs to be clarified without, however, attempting too drastically to destroy the tension between conflicting but equally legitimate aims and principles. Again, we hope the reader will gain

101

an impression of the vastly complex and difficult human issues with which the NHS has to cope.

4. The study of two *examples of hospital closures,* in describing the process of closure, brings out the interaction of judgements which are brought to decision making through consultative procedures. It shows how different meanings are attached to the currently vogue words of "consultation", "negotiation" and "participation". It illustrates how consultation is perceived and practised. It evaluates the *costs* of consultation in terms of delay but also the *benefits* in terms of the development of relationships with those with whom health authorities must work. It reinforces, in more detail, many of the issues brought out in the study of planning.

5. Our fourth case study appears, on the face of it, to be concerned with a somewhat exotic aspect of decision making in the NHS. But *the use of members' committees of inquiry,* in an authority area where member commitment and involvement in management as well as in policy making are marked, again demonstrates aspects of policy and decision making well beyond the confines of the procedures directly studied. These fourteen inquiries into organisational "errors" were not only a monitoring process but also a "critical investigation of decisions taken at the operational level". The use of such committees, at least in the cases under study, was a management device strengthening the authority's control over the service. The issues identified included "a perennial problem in the NHS, namely, the separation of the lay members from the clinical organisation, and their problems in understanding and controlling the service as a whole". The anomalous position of the layman in a highly professional service and the conflict between lay control and multi-disciplinarity are also brought out. The equally difficult role of professional administrators is exemplified. It is they who seemed to have been "most often criticised by the committees, and most exactingly questioned by the members". So, too, are the relations between area and district in an authority where the hierarchical line relationship is strongly emphasised.

6. Each of these studies is, we hope, worth reading for its own sake. Between them they touch on many of the overarching issues illuminated by the field interview survey. We emphasise that they can be no more than glimpses of a complex and varied reality. They are in no sense a sample which can be taken to reliably demonstrate how the NHS works in all of its aspects and in all of its field authorities. Between them, however, they constitute a powerful plea to the Royal Commission and any others who might read them to accept that those working within the NHS incur extraordinary complex and arduous personal and organisational burdens. We have done no more in these studies than to lift the corner of the curtain on a scene of vexing difficulty. Our gratitude to those who allowed us to do so is great.

CASE STUDY NO 1

Planning System in a Region

by Nancy Korman and Maurice Kogan

I Introduction

1. This case study was undertaken in one English region and one of its areas and districts. A study of the planning process seemed appropriate because it demonstrates how the complex policy making system for health gets to work on determining its future service patterns in terms of finance, manpower, physical resources and time. It thus reveals many facets of both structure and of a decision making process.

Factors Affecting Planning

2. The study of planning in the health service also illustrates the way in which multiple considerations, all of which are legitimate, have to be reconciled before policies can be created and put into effect. Some of the considerations are exogenous to the health service. For example, as we will see in the region to be studied, the changing population numbers are a dominant factor in much of the macro planning. The fluctuations in the economy at large, and in the resources made available to the NHS in particular, also help to determine the resource boundaries within which planning takes place. There are then factors intrinsic to the planning of the health service. There are changes in medical technology ranging from the extremely expensive and technically sophisticated devices for screening, such as the scanner, to radical changes in pharmacology which may contribute towards changes in patterns of service requirements. Then there are changes in concepts of health care such as the generally accepted policy in favour of a reduction in institutional caring, towards caring in the community. There are the changing concepts of how to provide hospital services. Quite recently notions of what constitutes the best size of the district general hospital have become more varied. The concept of the nucleus will enable either old or new units to be linked together either to ensure flexibility of provision in the face of changing demands, or for reasons of economy, depending on one's point of view. A large proportion of the stock of hospital buildings is in need of repair or replacement or transfer to sites where they can meet the needs of newly formed populations.

3. Other potentially conflicting concepts concern the politics and the processes of decision making and all are present in the planning system we have studied. The current philosophy of planning assumes that it will be comprehensive and rational inasmuch as it will attempt to enumerate the whole range of needs and relate them to the whole range of resources that might be manipulated by health authorities. It also assumes, however, that planning will be participatory so that many groups with a legitimate concern in decision making will have a voice in it: community health councils, local authorities, consultative committees, staff associations, MPs and others who are not directly accountable for creating the executive policies. These participatory contributions then have to be related to the increased professionalisation of the health service as represented by the extension of functional management as well as by the more traditional clinical freedom of individual clinicians. And there are also strains of an optimistic assumption that all of these contributions can, and should be, brought together in order to achieve consensus about the future. In practice, however, some partici-

105

pants would say that there are no right answers, but only the most acceptable, to be found.

The Areas Studied

4. The study is based on one region and one of its areas and districts. We studied a number of current documents from the DHSS, regional, area and district levels and also interviewed 25 people directly concerned with planning at the different levels. The list of documents consulted can be found in the Appendix to this Report. The study was sent in draft to those who had participated in it and this report takes note of their comments.

II Characteristics of the Authorities Studied

5. Several marked characteristics of general demography and of health service provision dominate the thinking of the regional and area authorities about planning. In overall terms, the regions may be divided into three types of areas. One is in Inner London, an area of declining population with a notable imbalance between types of hospital beds and population needs, where some hospital facilities are out of date. The second is in Outer London, having a more stable population and a better balance between bed provision and bed need, and a more mixed hospital fabric. The third area is in a county identified for future population growth and having a deficiency of acute beds estimated to become worse as need grows.

(i) Regional Characteristics

6. The distribution of population and its forecasted movement present the region with the identified need of shifting resources from areas of decreasing population to those of increasing population. This identified need is made even more dramatic by comparison with national norms of bed provision, which indicate considerable over-provision of acute beds within the region as a whole, and within the Inner London areas specifically. To reach a more favourable comparison with national norms, the region has estimated that it will have gone a long way to achieving a reduction by some 4,000 beds by 1986/87.

7. The needed redistribution of beds identified on a geographical basis has also been examined on a basis of bed use. The regional excess of beds lies in acute services, while for more chronic and long-term illnesses there is a shortage in comparison with national norms. Within the framework of gross decrease in number of beds, the region has indicated a shift in bed use to increase geriatric and decrease mental illness beds, and to work towards provision for mental handicap patients within their own areas to conform more with national norms and current standards of good practice.

8. The region, in producing these assumptions, seeks to place reliance on community service support to influence the ability of area and districts to meet the norms they propose, which are themselves, however, somewhat more generous than the national bed norms created by the DHSS. It remarks, however, as to the relatively small degree to which primary care and community services are under the control of regions and areas, because general practitioners are independent contractors, and virtually all other services,

other than provision for day centres, home nurses and chiropodists, are in the hands of the local authorities.

9. Redistribution according to the national Resource Allocation Working Party (RAWP) will cause resources to be redirected so that facilities will be more in line with national norms and this implies the region will face the possibility of a decrease in its share of health service funding over the next decade: at present its funding is 17 per cent above the mean of all RHAs.

10. The region contains, in whole or part, eight postgraduate institutions and four undergraduate teaching hospitals. The region produces a sixth of newly trained doctors and a tenth of newly trained dentists for the country.

(ii) *Area Characteristics*

11. The area studied is a three-district area containing two teaching districts and one non-teaching district. Of the six areas in the region, this area has declined most in population. Its present population is less than half that of 1901, and the projections are that it will continue to decline. The area's demography has dictated a major characteristic of its strategic plan, namely, that no less than 18 hospitals have been proposed for closure or a change of use in the decade ending 1986/87. Others have already closed. The second dominant characteristic is that the "burden of sickness, handicap and social deprivation . . . is demonstrably heavy". Despite the fall in population in recent years the absolute number of elderly have increased. The health of the population generally compares unfavourably with the national averages and this includes a high infant mortality rate, a higher rate of sickness benefit claims a higher rate of admissions to hospital, a "300 per cent higher incidence of tuberculosis and a 9.2 per cent higher death rate" than the average for the rest of the country. Mental and physical handicap in the area is higher than the average as well. The social and environmental conditions of the area are poor, as measured by all of the standard indicators. It is also an area of high immigration.

12. At the same time, the distribution of both acute and non-acute services is patchy. The area now contains a total of 18 units providing acute services, which it hopes to reduce to 6 by the end of the decade 1986/87. Two large teaching hospitals are listed alongside one middle-sized district general hospital and several very small units. Besides the two teaching hospitals there are also a dental institute and three nurse training schools. The provision for chronic, geriatric and other long-stay categories is adequate in terms of numbers, but not located in the right place. For example, most long-stay mental handicap patients are in hospitals outside the AHA; the same is true for a proportion of geriatric beds used by the area. There is an excess of maternity beds and a lack of day care facilities for mentally ill, elderly and mentally handicapped groups. Besides its own population, the AHA also provides service for a "commuter" population from areas surrounding London. The area also contains a number of regional and sub-regional specialities.

13. In the area of most serious primary care need, general practitioners are thought to be too few in number and this is one of the disputed justifications used in the area against the closure of hospitals which have taken the burdens

normally carried by general practitioners. In practice 14.8 per cent of the general medical practitioners in the area in 1974 had list sizes exceeding 3,000 compared with the national average of 15.9 per cent. But other indicators, such as the numbers of GPs who work single handed, who are aged over 60 years, who graduated outside the UK, who have higher qualifications in general practice, or who are resident at the surgery were substantially less satisfactory than the national averages.

(iii) *District Characteristics*

14. The district studied is the non-teaching district of the three, and this has strongly determined both its physical provision, as inherited from the past, and its current revenue incomes. The district's population is 50,000 larger than the next largest district in the area yet its income from the area is approximately £10 million as compared with £28 million and £31 million for the two teaching districts. Parts of the district, however, brought with them an inheritance of good community services for child health and for the health visitor service in general. At the time of reorganisation (1974), the district contained 11 acute hospitals; by 1986 it is proposed that there will be four. But the first nucleus hospital in England is to be opened within the district.

15. The regional and area characteristics may be summarised as a demand for reallocation and rationalisation of resources among and within areas. In addition, services within the community require development on a more comprehensive and equitable basis. These changes will have to take place within a regional allocation which at best will increase only slightly and at worse remain the same as the present level. Moreover, these reallocative processes have to be carried through in a particularly complex political environment. One area is a mixture of old county and new town. Another area has a strong tradition of working class and particularly manual occupations and the political characteristics that go with them. Yet another is socially mobile and, in it, new and articulate pressure groups vie with the more traditional political groups. In this respect, a regional health authority is unlike a local authority where there is at least an identifiably dominant party representing if not a single style then at least a consensus of styles and approaches towards policy problems.

III The Planning System: Stated Objectives

DHSS Concepts

16. The DHSS had worked for some time to produce planning guidelines. The earlier documents put a great deal of emphasis on the districts' role. The first document for consultation appeared in 1975. Then, in June 1976, the DHSS published "The NHS Planning System" which served as a guide to English health authorities in creating and running their planning systems. The manual was issued as a working document to guide planning in the NHS so that both strategic and operational plans could be devised. The proposals for the district and area plans and the planning timetable had been tested in specific locations over two years and had been the subject of widespread consultation. But the Department's proposals on strategic planning and the regional strategic plan were meant to be subject to scrutiny and adjustment as time went on. In the words of one interviewee, the DHSS documentation

was "the only thing we had to go on, it was an important first guide to action", although the region has since developed the DHSS system. The DHSS is now considering ways of making the strategic planning system easier to operate.

17. The manual defined planning as "deciding how the future pattern of activities should differ from the present, identifying the changes necessary to accomplish this, and specifying how these changes should be brought about". The DHSS referred to different but related activities: policy analysis and policy making; strategic or long-term planning; operational planning and programming; budgeting and project planning. In practice, however, the immediate activities followed through in the region under study have been those of strategic and operational planning and most of the regional, area and district documents refer to those two phases directly. The region's strategic plan indicated the need for further study of general topics such as interaction of community and hospital care, improvements in productivity in acute care, patient benefits from care and several others. These begin to activate the need for policy analysis and relate regional to national concerns.

Planning Criteria Set Out by the DHSS

18. The DHSS stated criteria which would have the broad aim of improving the performance of the whole health service. Two were not so much criteria as basic considerations: *relevance to health needs and supply* are, perhaps, obvious elements within the planning framework. Other criteria are more exhortatory: *realism* so that planners should be on their guard against unrealistic resource assumptions, *consultation* with the community and *involvement* of members, the professions and other health service personnel, *compatibility* so that plans are related to others within the same area or region or relevant local authority, and to the longer term strategy, and *flexibility* to offset the danger of unduly rigid planning are all, perhaps, no more than the requirements to plan well. This point is made because of the Department's own statement of its belief in policy analysis as an important component of planning.

19. There were also unspoken objectives and criteria, as perceived outside the DHSS. Planning would help to strengthen the Department's role in development, and the control of expenditure, and these were thought to be part of the reasons for installing the planning system.

20. These criteria may be regrouped into categories which are more relevant to evaluation:
   rationality: relate plans to objectives;
   comprehensivity: relate plans to all factors needed to match objectives;
   coherence: relate plans to surrounding areas and complementary services;
   participation: involve community, members, professions;
   flexibility: leave room for the unexpected;
   feasibility: relate plans to available means of achieving plans.
Between them, these criteria fall into groups, although with some overlapping as between the need to create an effective and efficient decision making system and the need to respect the behavioural patterns and needs of

the different working groups, including practitioners and clients involved in the NHS.

Regional Objectives

21. The criteria suggested by the DHSS are largely related to how planning as an activity should be conducted rather than the substantive issues with which planning is concerned. They established the modes rather than the content of the plans. At the regional level, the focus shifts to objectives, the aims of planning for the areas and districts (and regionally provided services). The region declares itself to be concerned with the *reordering of resources* among areas and among services, from hospital to primary care, from acute to chronic and long-stay. It is, at the same time, concerned with such continuing objectives as the *maintenance of teaching requirements* for health service professions and the *siting and maintenance* of future health care institutions.

22. Other objectives emerged from discussions with officers at different levels. At its most general level, planning is concerned with *establishing a working relationship between teams of officers* which will be based on agreement of targets of performance, allowing detailed management of operations to be delegated to the tier below. Planning is not only about the use of resources but about health service management in the wider sense. Planning as a way of *creating certainty* was a further objective specifically mentioned in the interviews. Once managers know what resources they may expect for the future and for what agreed purposes, they are able to act the more confidently.

Area and District Objectives

23. The broad objectives of planning, as seen by officers at district and area levels, do not dissent in spirit or substantive objectives from those of the region. Differences may be critical, however, in concerns about the relevance of particular objectives to more local situations, or about the achievement of objectives. The closer to the operational level one gets, focus shifts from "what should be done" to "how do we actually do it?" A different order of abstraction prevails, examining in greater detail the working of specific services in relation to practitioner and institutional patterns. The global problems become more limited in geographical, institutional and practitioner terms, and problems of application and implementation grow in significance. If DHSS and region are concerned with the rationality of planning (setting objectives), area and district are concerned with the participative and political pressures, with securing agreement and commitment to change. At area and district, strategic objectives set by the tiers above are more likely to come up against practitioner and public demands for service developments, and a point of stability might be harder to achieve because of its specificity. And within the general agreement about objectives, rational analysis of local needs may challenge regionally-set goals which become the "exceptions" to regional "rules". Flexibility and responsiveness to local needs are further criteria for objectives of planning brought in by districts and areas.

IV Issues Facing the Planning System

24. In meeting the objectives set by central government, region, area and district, those whom we interviewed encountered challenges in attempts to work towards the achievement of planning objectives within the existing patterns of service provision. These challenges are as follows:
   (a) meeting the substantive objectives of planning;
   (b) administrative and "real" time constraints;
   (c) relations between teams of officers:
      (i) flexibility and delegatory discretion;
      (ii) structure.
   (d) participation and other aspects of political process, both internal and external to the administration;
   (e) coherence, within health services and with other services;
   (f) predictability;
   (g) planning technology.

Meeting the Substantive Objectives of Planning

25. The identified problems which the region as a whole faced have already been discussed in paragraphs 5 to 15. The techniques of analysis used here were, put crudely, the levels of allocations the region could realistically expect to achieve over the next ten years, based on the trends already indicated by the national RAWP; and a re-examination of regional levels of service provision in comparison with national norms. From the interaction of these factors, the objectives of the strategic plan were derived.

26. A reasoned analysis of needs and resources by staff was insufficient on its own. Planning is more than an intellectual exercise and must also encompass the determination, to believe, first, that the future will be as predicted and, second, that remedial action is both necessary and possible. In so far as the region needed to convince areas of its determination to achieve reallocation based on analysis, its determination became an important component in achieving co-operation and providing a motive for planning at other team levels.

27. The regional planning system does not, of course, operate on its own. The region's operational plans, their selection and approval of capital schemes, their controls over some of the key establishments (with further modification made by the DHSS in the case of consultant and senior registrar establishments) and their attempts to move towards a more positive monitoring role through the issue of guidelines for individual areas, all help to reduce the danger that regional strategic planning will be abstractions divorced from working reality.

28. At area level the regional strategic plan takes on a different emphasis. There is no reason why an area authority should be primarily concerned with the way in which its services relate to those of other areas since that must be primarily the task of the region to resolve. But it will be concerned with other regional themes: the balance between hospital and community services; the vexing problem of how highly labour intensive and costly to maintain parts of the estate can be rationalised. Thus, the development of nucleus hospitals, the closure of redundant hospitals or their modification,

111

and the spending of capital resources so as to reduce revenue burdens are policies worked out in common between the region and the area; although there will be substantial differences as to the major details of rationalisation.

29. The area, too, has to make judgements as between the needs of the districts. In the area studied, the task was a daunting one because two of the districts contained one teaching hospital each which comprised not only a "centre of excellence" requiring, in the region and the area's views, differential bed and other allocations for teaching purposes, but also substantial investments as part of the main line acute national health service. As against those claims of the two teaching districts, there are, within those districts themselves, quite clamant needs for the improvement of community services in view of the ageing of the population in all three districts and the generally recognised need to improve services for the mentally ill, mentally handicapped and other home based groups. The area also has to take account of the particular problems of the non-teaching district, to attempt to redress imbalances of resources and needs, and to ensure sufficient collaboration among its districts so that area resources are used efficiently and in promotion of acceptable standards of care.

30. At the district level the nature of the problems shifts yet again as one gets closer to those who will have to pay the costs of planning: particular client groups (for example opposition to the closure of units, requirements that patients travel longer distances for services) and of practitioners (consultants who find their carefully developed specialties about to be "rationalised" in the interests of local economy, higher clinical standards and regional and area plans of redistributing resources to other parts).

31. At the three levels, identification and acceptance of overall objectives broadly exist. The problem in facing the implications of these objectives varies, however, and it is to the region (and indirectly the DHSS) that one looks for emphasis on rational and analytic inputs and to areas and districts for a greater emphasis on political skills to achieve working and workable achievements. These emphases are not mutually exclusive: the area will be analysing its own circumstances and those of its districts for variation from regional norms; and the region will be engaged in political (negotiating) activities to get agreements from among areas and among representatives of practitioner groups. Yet it does not seem untrue to say the major statement of objectives has come from region; areas and districts, once accepting the validity of these broad objectives, are faced with problems of evaluating them in relation to their own circumstances and to practitioner and community demands. The brokerage role of a planning team is more apparent at these levels than at region.

32. The region must also absorb the consequences of the DHSS decision to discontinue a more favourable element of costs for beds attributed to teaching purposes. An ad hoc formula which respects existing allocations between health service and teaching has been agreed through a working party on which the teaching hospitals are represented. It has been difficult to identify norms and there are proposals for an independent study which might lead to more definitive cost figures. There are inherent tensions between the needs of teaching and development of a community oriented

health service. The teaching hospitals feel that accommodation is not adequate for teaching purposes and that the location of teachers and students throughout a system of nucleus hospitals would be difficult and costly to arrange.

Administrative and "Real" Time Constraints

33. The determination of needs and the allocation of resources to meet them encounter the problem of differential time spans. The time spans are of two kinds: the administrative and accountability system time spans, and the technical time spans. The administrative time span problem is endemic throughout the public sector. Allocations of resources are made annually, theoretically so as to tie in with Parliamentary estimates cycles. In practice, and more particularly in recent years, the Treasury, the DHSS, the region and the areas have not been able to agree and authorise budgets within what any part of the system regards as a reasonable time. The district receives its annual allocation just before it is required to go into planning for next year so that next year's planning has to relate to guesses about the work that will have been completed within the current year. It is possible that decisions could be made earlier in spite of the inability of government to produce definite allocations in good time. The variation between each year is relatively marginal and it would not be too hazardous to make informed guesses upon which at least minimum allocations could be made and notified.

34. Other administrative time spans, three years for operational and ten years for strategic guidelines, are viewed differently by different participants. While most agree that a three year operational cycle is sensible, it was pointed out that capital developments needed to give effect to service plans often require a longer lead time than three years. The impact of this is to remove some of the flexibility attributed to a three year rolling programme and to create a four or five year time span for service plans.

35. Opinions vary as to the usefulness of ten years for the strategic plan. The commonsense criticism might be that thinking in 1968 hardly served as a useful predictive framework for the events being experienced by the health service now. But it is recognised in the DHSS document, and elsewhere, that the lead time for planning large scale health services, for commissioning buildings, and for putting them into operation, is rarely less than ten years. There is, therefore, no obvious "real" time series to which strategic planning can confidently relate and the arbitrary choice of ten years is likely to be as good as any.

36. The administrative burdens which the annual planning cycle impose are clearly thought to be formidable in terms of the effort to make the system operate. Respondents described problems in several ways. One was the danger of things "slipping through the net" because complexity and pressure of time meant that important problems were not adequately processed. The insistence on keeping to the timetable means that dissatisfactions with plans cannot be introduced during the current planning cycle, but must be carried forward to the next cycle and modified then. The tier above is faced with the need to undertake detailed assessment of several districts' or areas' plans within a matter of weeks before they must go to the authority

for approval. (In the first cycle, 10 days were all that were allotted for assessment of 200 capital schemes by the regional tier.)

37. These points all argue towards viewing planning as a continuous activity (a favourite phrase of respondents at all levels) as a means of coping with tight time demands. Yet the extent to which this may occur will depend in part on the managerial relations between tiers (discussed below in paragraphs 43 to 52).

38. The technical time spans have to be interwoven into administrative and public accountability time spans. The span ranges from changes in decisions which have to be made immediately—as when epidemics suddenly emerge, or sudden technological developments have to be taken up quickly, to political decisions which lead to a marked change of health service delivery systems. Other time spans have already been referred to. It is not only buildings that are a long term process but also the build up of the right mix of manpower within an operational service. Recruitment and training of people are less predictable than the building of physical facilities in which they will work. Different components of planning are not always easily matched. Thus, the training of nurses for a particular kind of service might require thought about the location of a training school or department so as to secure continuous recruitment and student nursing manpower. Yet providing nucleus hospitals, at the same time as the policy of teaching clinical medicine and surgery outside the confines of the main teaching hospitals is being developed, brings out conflicts of needs and interests between the teaching hospitals and the districts responsible for operational working. The teaching hospitals would prefer their own accommodation modules. The districts may feel that there are other priorities to be advanced.

39. The nucleus hospital concept (the first hospital so designed will open in the district under study in the early 1980s) is another example. This concept is in part an attempt to keep options for future development open. Few nucleus hospitals—designed as such—are as yet programmed. Yet the centring of a nucleus of hospital services in one or two locations, leaving the balance of service to be provided in a "federation" of other units is inherently more flexible than aiming to provide a large and specialised complex *ab initio*. As population and other factors change, the whole disrict service can be modified by modular planning in response to demands rather than as part of a globally determined scheme.

40. Each of the multiple activities of the health service has its own logical periodicity. Differential time spans need not conflict with the planning framework because whilst one, three and ten year periods are set, it is possible for a scheme to span different planning periods. Common time spans for choosing among priorities are needed. Otherwise, comparable merits are not considered on a comparable basis.

Relations Between Teams of Officers

(i) *Flexibility and Delegatory Discretion*
41. The question of timespan relates closely to widespread participation and flexibility. Planning intentionally pre-empts options inasmuch as it

seeks to create certainties among all concerned as to where the major resources will go, and when. But the opposite side of removal of uncertainty is the imposition of some inflexibility. Thus there are some experienced administrators who, whilst accepting the need for the annual, triennial and ten year planning cycles, would also look for shorter operational planning cycles of, perhaps, six months. This indicates, perhaps, the extent to which operational planning shades into day to day administration. Others, again, can produce cogent arguments for five and fifteen year cycles.

42. The preceding paragraphs have already referred to the way in which the planning process touches on inter-level decision making. Both the DHSS documents and stated regional policy referred to the intention to delegate to the districts. The districts, working within regional guidelines, make the first running in building up the operational plans and although they are not formally party to the strategic plan, the strategic plan is in a sense a summation of operational plans, although all have remarked on the difficulty of creating as yet a full blown strategy over the whole ten year period and for all of the services.

(ii) *Structure*

43. It is difficult, perhaps, to dissociate the difficulties of planning between levels from the more general structural problems of the multi-level health service. Thus, there is comment on all sides about the difficulties of getting informal joint thinking going as between the different levels. The complexity of the structure and the extensive consultative network impose a degree of formality on relations. The impact of such formality may be to encourage "positions" to be taken on issues which cuts out a stage of informal or free-ranging discussion. It is also pointed out, however, that even if informal relationships improved, that could not necessarily lead to consensus between the different perspectives. Always planning has to choose the workable rather than the ideal solution.

44. Planning is concerned with thinking about the future but where so many levels and parties at each level are involved, there is inevitably an emphasis on process rather than on product. Moreover, whilst it is recognised at all levels that operational planning pre-empts operational day to day decision making, and that this must be so, there is, too, some feeling at district and area levels that the overall logic of planning brings in too many variables to be handled in terms of working reality. It is difficult to steer a course which satisfies client groups and practitioners within the institutions delivering the services, at the same time as so many counter-indications have to be respected. In one area of developing policy, there are working parties at district, area and regional and departmental level. This may be as it should be, that is to say, there may well be different expertises and different perceptions to be brought in at all of the levels. If so, however, it must be necessary that multi-level thinking is brought together, so that those who have to both plan and run the service are able to weave their way through the different statements concerned with similar problems, and the danger of conflicting wasteful duplication of effort avoided. The DHSS is thought to be fully aware of this problem and is attempting to improve the system through a planning group at which all levels and different disciplines within the functions are represented.

115

45. "Planning is the one area of administrative work where there are no penalties for bad work." Not all would agree with this remark. Planning may be seen by some as an abstraction but it should lead to decisions that can be good or bad, effective or non-effective, as can any other form of decision making. The interviewee who remarked in this way was, however, referring to the fact that whilst a day to day decision can produce waste or difficulties that are immediately apparent, decisions on planning may invite the building up of euphoric, extravagant or weakly formulated proposals in the expectation that the level above will clean them up and that nothing is to be lost from spilling out the whole range of schemes that anybody with a voice in planning might produce. The term "devolution" is used within the region to express the intended relationships between the levels, but the sense of those interviewed is that a strongly *delegatory* system is needed so that responsibilities for planning decisions are more clearly identifiable. This would enable each tier to formulate its needs and demands, but within the discipline of priorities established by the tier above.

46. The guidelines issued by the DHSS, region and area to teams of officers directly below have been the subject of much comment. Guidelines are difficult to formulate: if left too broad and vague, no direction is given; if too specific, they cease to be guidelines within which discretion can be exercised. Importance was attached to participation in the formulation of guidelines so that particular problems identified as needing attention by a lower tier may be brought in; it was mentioned more than once how helpful guidelines backed by statutory authority may be in securing agreement at a lower level. An area officer summarised his criteria for guidelines as follows:

- (a) they must be sufficiently explicit and specific to give clear indications of the nature of plans acceptable;
- (b) they must be stated in quantifiable terms to indicate the order of performance acceptable;
- (c) they must be participative between the two tiers involved;
- (d) they must be supportive so that the tier below is assisted in getting acceptance for plans.

47. The delegatory theme is important because it generates an overt objective of planning. The region hopes that the operational managers, particularly at district level, will create their own performance targets and keep to them so that area and region can then take on a monitoring rather than a continuing strong managerial role. The theme came over in interviews, partly as liberal and participatory doctrine but also a necessary discipline.

48. Thus, it was observed in one interview in relation to capital schemes that if the districts were required not only to put up schemes but to employ cost consultants from their own funds to make a realistic capital and use cost calculation of the revenue consequences, the schemes would come forward in such a way that area and region would not have substantially to modify them. Yet, in the district being studied, the region's help was sought, and appreciated, in analysing the potential of a large hospital site that was to become part of a nucleus hospital.

49. The region has developed with the areas a method of enabling them to participate in the benefits of rationalisation. When an area can sell a part of its estate, it can keep the whole or the part of the money, according to the scale of the property being sold. It gives the area a direct incentive in considering what property it needs to hold and the benefits of getting rid of parts of it. The distribution of financial benefits has been a matter of dispute, but the regional intention* is that there will be in effect an incentive scheme, again, converting property which creates revenue costs into capital sums which can be used in other ways. So far, however, these benefits have not been felt by the district. (See case study on hospital closures.)

50. Officers at region see planning as becoming more effective when the disciplines and educational aspects of it become more firmly established. In this regard, it should be noted that the Department has held study days about the purposes and techniques of health service planning. It may be a question, however, as to whether the demands for more informal relationships between the levels, mentioned in paragraph 38 above, could not be taken up in terms of more systematic but informal educational events at which the larger issues can be considered outside the formal decision making process.

51. It would be wrong, however, to imply that difficulties are all likely to be solved over time as experience and confidence between the levels grow. There may well be legitimate grounds for conflict in recognition of the different perceptions of needs and pressures felt at different levels continue to impact on planning.

52. Moreover, the role of planners and of planning groups within the system is thought to need further clarification and recognition. Connections between planners at region, area and district also need further development. Second line officers need not be fully accepted by chief officers at other tiers, even if they have expertise to offer.

The Politics of Planning

53. Planning is a political process in which the multiple elements of a statutory system interact with each other and also are affected by many disparate interest groups seeking to affect decision making. In this case study, we have not been able to track through all of these interactions. If the political process can be considered in its external and internal aspects, the first point to note about the external political system is that the health service, more perhaps than any other area of public activity, has built in multiple political bases. It has brought together in one region groups that in local government might well be kept separate. For example, the area is required to consult the following bodies: community health councils, the Joint Consultative Committees, the statutory advisory committees, the family practitioner committees, representative medical committees, teaching hospitals and universities, MPs, local authorities and staff associations. The number of bodies consulted by the area is 32. The number of copies physically put together of the area operational plan is 1,000. We have already discussed

---

* Recently put into effect.

relationships between the tiers but obviously relationships among the various disciplines, and within the health authorities, also help to determine outcomes. In addition, as a public service which impacts on the well-being of individuals, other representatives and investigators on behalf of public opinion feel capable and obliged to pass judgement on operations and plans.

54. The bodies consulted each have their own characteristic constituents which affect their response to requests for comment on plans. The mechanisms through which responses are brought together before being forwarded to the area and regional authorities reflect the complexity of the whole planning process in different areas of consultation.

55. An elaborate system of consultation is formally observed by those responsible for planning. The statutory advisory committees see and comment on all of the district and area plans while local authorities and CHCs are consulted twice by district and area. For professional advisory bodies it may not be easy for them to do more than put in a collation of informed comments on those parts of the plans known to individual members. The more senior members of staff also, of course, have access to the discussion of planning issues through meetings which they attend as members of management or of working groups. The teaching hospitals, as has already been pointed out, have taken part in a working party on teaching hospital costs. They have members of, or access to, the regional and area authorities and the DMT. There is a regional–university liaison committee. The university, of which the teaching hospitals are constituent bodies, has access to the DHSS and UGC. The Staff Side is consulted on area but not on regional plans, and feels that it has better access to the area than to the regional planning system. A CHC refers district plans to a sub-committee for comments and then to a full council meeting, while consultation on area plans will involve a public meeting, inviting comments from the community. Consultation from local authorities will entail scrutiny of district and area plans by its social services committee (and possibly education and housing if necessary), policy and resources committee and approval by a full council meeting. It is worth noting that, of the 32 bodies consulted by the AHA, comments were received from 11.

56. If the formal system is there, there are obstacles to it operating in a meaningful way. The time limits imposed on the planners themselves are tight and this means that a participant body, with its large number of constituents to consult, might have three weeks in which to comment on extremely complex issues, although major individual issues such as hospital closures or change of use are subject to a fuller consultative procedure on a separate occasion. The comments sent to the area health authority, some of which the team has seen, show that in spite of the tightness of time, comments can be detailed and a lot of work is put into them by those concerned. Indeed, one group asked for the area to provide yet more detail. "Future area plans should detail how each planning proposal incorporates the (authority's stated) policy" which it felt had not happened in the document being discussed. The principal complaint was that information was not being made available to those consulted because the manpower implications of what was proposed had not been fully worked out in the document. Yet it is

118

perhaps inevitable that participants can never be sure what impact their views will have. It is also accepted that many of the more important developments are outside the control of the health authorities because they involve the co-operation and agreement of local authorities and general practitioners.

57. Whilst impact is uncertain, it is accepted that the system is "over-committed", and that it is "time and paper consuming". There thus seems to be no certain way in which the expression of varying demands can be brought together in such a way as to make sure that the system is at the same time responsive and authoritative in its decisions.

58. What effect do the external forces have on planning? In the end, no doubt, the full time professionals, analysing needs, enumerating resources, and matching them, have the dominant say. But there can be no doubt that the health service, at least as much as any other public service, has been required to be responsive to external political forces. Planning officers will find that their views, based on rational calculation, are countermanded by pressures exerted through the political system; a chairman of a health authority may be required to attend a public meeting and come back for a modification of the scheme for closure or for rationalisation. Demands for an expensive health centre in an area of virtually nil population have to be encountered, considered and at least in part met. Obviously, again, both members and officers use political pressure constructively. The planners, who are specialists in rationality, do not always find the ends-means type of argument the best way of securing what they consider to be the best policy. Moreover, the non-planners who are consulted do not always feel that rationality necessarily rests exclusively with the planners. Some of the groups consulted believe that they, too, are able to specify the objectives of the health service and suggest the appropriate means for reaching them.

59. Internal pressures present no fewer constraints. At district, certainly, the DMT has to reconcile the deeply felt needs of the different groups and put them together into some sort of consensual form. But it is at area that conflict and demands are heard at their loudest because it is at that point that both the functional needs of the different disciplinary areas and professions, and the geographical demands have to converge and be put into a meaningful time and priority sequence. AHAs contain representatives of the local authorities. They are the point of address of CHC representations. They are the first line of political authority within the system. The region is able to take a more detached and rational, ends-means, attitude although they, too, encounter, and in the area being studied, do not shirk, the pressures from both the internal and external political system.

60. The time allowed for consultation in the planning cycle is considerable (greater than that allowed for harmonising plans with received guidelines), but the value of it is under doubt. Deadlines are tight, and this tends to place those consulted under pressure and make consultation seem a formality rather than real participation; this is perhaps truer for those outside the NHS than for groups which are closer to the system. The results of consultation were questioned because they seemed to reflect the "parochial" views of the group, rather than contributing to a wider consensus. The very width of the consultation network, in the view of one respondent, meant that one or

two able advocates could dominate because so many were involved. There was criticism of blanket consultation, and a feeling that much more could be derived from a selective approach. Consultations may raise expectations which cannot be met.

61. Participation and consultation are thus seen as the centrifugal forces which challenge the rational basis of planning. A balance has to be struck between gaining acceptance and commitment whilst challenging unnecessary or wasteful development.

Coherence Within the Health Service and With Other Social Services

62. We have already alluded to the "political" difficulties of establishing a coherent set of priorities among the different practitioner groups and among the districts: a development by one may well entail a loss (or frustrations) by another. This is not assisted by what is seen to be the difficulties of the different practitioners and administrators working together on teams of officers or working groups. On the whole, such groups were thought to be fragmented in approach, more often than not medically dominated and more oriented towards practitioner wants than the analysed needs. Yet at the same time, it was recognised that practitioner perceptions were difficult to aggregate and may inherently be in tension with overall policies. It is also difficult to give adequate guidance early enough to planning groups, so that good results may be produced in time; if such groups are left to function "in a vacuum", it is not surprising that they put forwards the interests of practitioners.

63. It was often said that the tier below was parochial in its attitudes and outlook; it argued its case to be self-contained in service provision for its population and remained unconcerned with the needs of a wider population base. But it may be exactly the function of each authority to reconcile such claims. Given what is at stake, referral to a tier above having a wider view of needs and resources may be the only way of resolving such conflicts.

64. It is perhaps too much to expect that the complexities of establishing the planning system within the NHS would have allowed much effort to be turned to developing planning with other services besides health. Joint financing has not yet led to an adequate analysis of health and social services, reflecting the dominating position of the cost-intensive acute services. As with planning within the NHS, joint financing has claimed attention for its mechanisms rather than the conceptualisation of health and welfare needs. Joint planning, as opposed to joint funding, has yet to develop, and the problems of bringing together separate authorities, with their distinct systems of decision making and priorities, remain to be explored.

Predictability

65. A function of the planning system is, in the words of one respondent, to create certainty, to give an outline to the future so that managers and practitioners can develop services in a realistic manner. The determination of the region to produce a strategic plan and to institute rigorous examination of area plans in relation to strategy demonstrates the importance it attaches to this function.

66. The future, however, seems less certain to those at area and district. The impact of regional RAWP, for example, is not yet determined, and without this financial framework which will indicate expected resources, areas cannot be certain of how much they may hope to accomplish. Doubts about the reliability of information bases may reflect legitimate intellectual doubts and dissent as well as an unwillingness to accept unpalatable demands for change. These problems exist more forcibly at area than in the district studied, and perhaps relate to the anticipated improvements which the strategy objectives posit for health services within the district, whilst the area overall is having to contemplate rationalising facilities within its other two teaching districts. Uncertainties may also exist within the process because of factors beyond control, such as the development of complementary services by local authorities or of primary care services involving general practitioners.

Planning Technology

67. Some comment has already been made about the technical aspects of planning; the differences in time scales and the constraints on flexibility of response. Other aspects as well are seen to present problems. One is the difficulty of getting from strategic objectives, often phrased in quite general terms, to operational plans. This is in part a political problem, an unwillingness to be specific to avoid arousing controversy. But it is also technical, because of the complexity of factors involved and uncertainties of long-term developments. While capital developments have established various procedures for handling these problems, service development planning is much newer and less sure of itself and cannot, in its nature, be stated as clear objectives to be reached through predictable procedures. The roles of service planners are not clearly defined nor understood, and professional planners have much less experience and expertise to draw on.

68. Various criticisms have been put forward related to the information available for planning. These are summarised as follows:

(a) information is too frequently collected without reference to management needs;

(b) the distinction between routine information and that related to specific problems (and the different kinds of staff needed for these functions) is insufficiently recognised;

(c) information is too often collected on different bases, so it is not available for comparative purposes;

(d) most information comes from high levels such as demographic data or regional assumptions about services, rather than being picked up at the practitioner level;

(e) information often takes on too great an appearance of certainty to other tiers than it has to those who have presented it.

69. An additional point is that there is too much information and that demands for it can be an evasion of the need to identify problems and then collect information selectively for specific purposes. There is a need, it is said, for "horses for courses" and not for an unregulated data collection system. Not enough is known about the functioning and the impact of the

121

health care system to know what information is going to be useful until the problems are more closely identified.

70. Planning must start from what one interviewee called the needs-resources equation. But it is clear that not all such information yet exists, and that what does may well not be accepted because of the challenge it presents to individuals' judgements. The more general information relevant for planning purposes is used: demographic data; national norms; financial allocations using more sophisticated concepts as transferring revenue to capital to gain future revenue savings. The information felt most lacking is at the level of operational plans and implementation, precisely those points where political pressures are more strongly coming into the system.

V Evaluation

71. On our brief acquaintance with a region, area and district which have been quick to establish their planning systems we cannot, and do not, intend to evaluate the performance of that planning system. Our evaluation is concerned more to bring out the multiple considerations that the system reflects.

72. This section will be concerned with the following issues:
   (a) the extent to which the planning system focuses decision making towards long-term, future—oriented planning;
   (b) the extent to which participation, consultation and flexibility are thought to be present;
   (c) how far the assumed priorities of reorganisation are beginning to take effect because of the planning system.

73. Some respondents, administrators at the three levels and three interviewees at region in particular, commented on the gradual acceptance of planning as providing a framework within which arguments about resource allocations took place. But this view was challenged by those in planning posts and those at the area level. This division of opinion reflected two issues: how "political" the area tier was and the limited flexibility it possessed (RAWPing the region might hurt, but RAWPing the area hurt more); and the extent to which planning activities and community medicine in particular felt themselves unable to impact on the planning system. Planning as a "technology", a process of rationality, was not seen to have surmounted planning as an administrative or political exercise. Instances were quoted of decisions or developments being taken as one-off exercises, later to be regretted. It might be that more rigorous arguments are now needed to get extra allocations outside the planning system. But instances were also cited of how plans submitted by districts and areas were becoming more detailed and comprehensive in content, thus serving as a summation of the tier's thinking on immediate and long-term developments. The benefit of the planning cycle as focusing attention on planning was not denied; what was questioned was whether it was simply administration in a different form or whether it had come to be a different type of analysis. Different groups felt differently about this question.

74. The criterion of rationality came easiest to the regional tier where

shifts of resources and shifts of policy were undertaken on a broad enough scale to avoid the more immediate pain felt below. The regional strategic document presented considerable analysis of two main factors: regionally adopted national norms of facilities in relation to population; and likely trends in resources available. With these in mind, it could then propose the means to reach its stated ends, mainly the use of capital investment to achieve longer-term revenue savings, with reallocation following rationalisation. At area and district where strategic planning confronted more immediate realities, rationality seemed less relevant and more tempered by other demands: for example, the upgrading of operating theatres despite a foreseen change of use of the hospital; and keeping an accident and emergency department open despite the continued running of another one nearby, were responses to more immediately felt wants.

75. The political aspect of planning was an example of the multiple perceptions of rationality which exist. Practitioners may be more oriented towards a concept of rationality linking facilities to standards of care for patients, administrators and planning to equity of service provision and economic use of resources. Equally, it may be rational for those representing a community to argue for the best possible levels of service provision. Planning statements come to represent the balance found between different concepts of rationality. The economic criterion attempts to impose a hierarchy of values for decision making but unless the other, more practice-related criteria are introduced, the system may reach stalemate.

76. The planners within the region, area and district were conscious of the ideal planning approaches that might be contained in textbooks. The region, in particular, was prepared to forego attempts to reach the theoretical ideal in order to use planning systems as a mode of exercising authority in favour of distribution as between conflicting contenders and thus responding to their appreciation of both the health needs and the political demands placed upon the region. Hence their determination to "break into the planning system" which meant that they were more concerned with getting results than with establishing planning ideals. They therefore went ahead with the information that they were able to bring together even though they accepted, as did others throughout the system, that their appreciation of needs, of resources and of patterns of usage were essentially quantitative and global. The ideal planning system would include an assessment of need, of resources in terms of both physical plant and manpower, and an assessment of the care patterns and techniques available throughout the region and areas. It would have information about the way in which different building arrangements, including their sizes and potential flexible use, affected health care patterns. It would be knowledgeable about the best ways in which revenue could be converted into capital expenditures. It would have a clearer sense about the "production function" of health care, namely, the way in which differential use of health resources create differential results in terms of the health of the population. It would know more about the effects and ways of transferring care from hospital to the community and it would be able to make better cost analyses of capital schemes. We found those responsible fully aware of these planning ideals. But rather than allow the lack of knowledge about the qualitative results of decisions to stand in the way of action they operated

on what seemed to them to be gross data so as to get the system moving in what seemed to be approximately the right direction.

Participation

77. We have already discussed some of the problems encountered with consultation and participation by those operating the planning system. The views of those involved in consultation about its value and impact were mixed. Both chairmen of medical advisory committees felt the comments of their committees had been well received by the authorities, and the value of their contributions lay in the realism of medical practice and patients' need they were able to bring to proposed plans. On the whole, we have noted that professional advisory committees at both levels feel their views are taken into account by the health authorities although knowledge of the impact varies as between committees. Generally, however, the effort of organising committee meetings so that comments may be made in the time allowed is thought to be worth while. But it should be realised that this is a considerable effort, perhaps more so at the regional level as committee members are more widely located than at area. The RMAC, for example, in commenting on the first draft of the regional strategic plan, set up sub-committees which met eight times (approximately two hours per meeting) to put forward its views. Consultation was seen to be necessary to gain co-operation but when such detailed work must be done in a fortnight, the cost in terms of travel and disruption of normal work is considerable. On the medical side, a main benefit of consultation from the viewpoint of those being consulted was said to be the help given to the authority, rather than the value of participation to participants.

78. Consultation of bodies outside the advisory system seems to be felt as less satisfactory. In previous years, for example, the CHC of the district studied had thought its comments had been ignored by both the DMT and the AHA, although the health authority was always willing to meet with CHC members for discussion of plans. While both CHC and local authorities may in general have some knowledge of ideas being considered by the DMT, the district plan is the first occasion they have of seeing these ideas in specific proposals. From their viewpoint, consultation would have more meaning if a system of "early warnings" could be given at the beginning of the planning cycle, alerting the consulted bodies to the proposals being considered by a DMT. The staff side, too, felt that decisions made in response to particular financial and other crises affected the quality of planning and their involvement in it. Local authorities find it difficult to bring together views from their own complex committee system and also feel that they are consulted too late in the planning process for them to have a meaningful impact. This point takes on particular significance as health authorities seek to develop their community services in co-operation with local authorities.

79. If, as health officers say, planning should be a continuous activity, then it would be logical and helpful for consultation to be so too, so that views may be brought to bear on issues before they have been hardened into formal plans. There is psychologically a great difference between expressing a view about a fully worked out set of plans and about ideas to be further

124

developed. If a function of consultation on planning is to gain co-operation, then earlier and possibly less formalised consultation may achieve this co-operation more readily. It would also go some way towards meeting the pleas of almost every group consulted for allowing more time to consider plans.

80. Consultation is perhaps one of the more time-consuming aspects of the planning system. It is seen by both health service officers and participants as contributing comparatively little to planning, but this at area level more so than at the region. It may be that it is as difficult for the health service planners to absorb comments on formal plans as it is for those consulted to comment. Earlier and less formal consultation may be able to give more meaning to an activity the NHS is firmly committed to carrying out.

Priorities of Reorganisation

81. The majority of changes were still on paper; the region was in the middle of the implementation of the first planning cycle when attention was focussed more strongly on the process rather than the content. There was a strong need to "break into the planning cycle". One can say of the plans that they did take into account the priorities associated with reorganisation. There was an overall attempt to achieve a more efficient and effective use of resources, and, in terms of service policy, to build up better home based services for long-stay and chronic client groups, and of primary care in general. The intention was strong. The difficulties of identifying and causing change are, indeed, enormous. It takes particular pertinacity to work for large-scale changes which cannot become quickly visible and hence rewarding to those who have to defer present advantages for the sake of future gains.

Allocation of Responsibilities in Bio-medical Engineering: the Roles of Clinicians in Management

by Mary Henkel and Valerie Heyes

Introduction

1. This study is concerned with the processes through which a single district Area Health Authority arrived at a policy on the allocation of responsibilities between the Works and the Physics Departments in the field of bio-medical engineering. It was chosen for the following reasons: first, it throws into sharp focus the potential for conflict in the management and representative roles of clinical members of management teams. The problem of determining priorities between managerial and clinical interests and values was central: primary concern with the economic use of resources, with clear allocation of accountability in the system, and with managerial skills was set against focus on individual need, on clinical responsibility, and on academic and scientific knowledge and training. Secondly, it is a case which illustrates the complexity of decision making created by the recognition that an increasing range of disciplines have an important contribution to make to medical care. It promised to provide a good test of the adequacy of the reorganised structure both to take account of this contribution and to resolve the inevitable conflicts that would arise between representatives of the professional and interest groups involved. The incorporation of clinicians into management, the requirement of consensus decision making, the roles of the authority members, of the DHSS, and of the region, and finally the impact of structural changes upon power are all brought under scrutiny.

2. The main focus of the study is thus upon the capacity of the structure to promote good decision making. An attempt is made to use the particular problems faced on one issue by one authority to illustrate structural strengths and weaknesses, and to make explicit the criteria by which judgements on these are being made.

Method of Study

3. The subject of the study was suggested to us by the Area Administrator and one of his second in line staff. Preliminary discussion with this member of staff (Assistant Area Administrator (Planning)) made it possible to identify the scope of the study, the main documentation available, the key people involved, and some of the main issues. After an examination of the correspondence, minutes of meetings and reports, we interviewed nine people, namely, the Area Administrator, the Area Medical Officer, the two clinicians who were members of the AMT during the relevant time, the current consultant member of the AMT, the Area Works Officer, the Chief Physicist, the Chairman of the Medical Engineering Liaison Committee, and the Chairman of the Ad Hoc Committee set up by the AHA to make recommendations on the resolution of the problem. These interviews had two main purposes: to get an account of the events from each key participant, and to enlist their help in clarifying the main problems and issues by the use of a short questionnaire.

Background to the Study

4. One result of rapid growth and application of scientific and technological knowledge in diagnosis and treatment in health care has been the demand for skills and expertise in the electronics field to be readily available for the

maintenance of new and increasingly complex equipment. Development within this new area of bio-medical engineering could emerge from three potential sources, the firms supplying the equipment, the hospital Engineering department or the Physics department—the latter two possibilities being attempts to provide the necessary expertise within the health service itself. Both these departments could claim to be appropriate bases for the development of bio-medical engineering since this new specialism could be seen as a growth point from either of these accepted fields of expertise.

5. In this area the problem of deciding where to locate this required expertise had been under consideration since the late 1960s and therefore well before reorganisation. The particular debate at that time was the appropriate role of the Engineering department in maintenance work compared with that of the outside suppliers. The Group Engineer clearly saw himself as accountable for the safety and maintenance of all equipment, and in order to cope with the increasing maintenance problems arising from the use of more and more complex machinery was already employing and training technicians to carry out the work within his department. Additionally, he had recognised the need for further expansion. At the same time, the experience of the clinicians had made them sceptical about the capacity of the Engineering department to fulfil this role. They perceived medical technology as essentially requiring not only technical skill but also scientific understanding, and were beginning to use the Medical Physics Department as consultants on the adaptation and maintenance problems of equipment. They also thought that the involvement of the Engineering department was encroaching on their relationships with equipment suppliers. In the face of these complexities, a Medical Engineering Liaison Committee was established at the suggestion of the Group Engineer and held its first meeting in July 1973. The membership of that committee included a number of consultant users of the equipment, the Group Engineer, the Chief Physicist and the Group Secretary.

6. After consultation with the Regional Adviser for Scientific and Technical Services, the committee decided to consider the establishment of a Bio-Medical Engineering Department and to investigate its appropriate siting, namely in either the Physics or the Engineering department. The Regional Adviser was supportive to the venture and requested that there should be reporting back. He could offer no clear guidelines as a regional policy had not been developed. A new Chief Physicist was appointed to the Group in March 1974, and actually joined the committee in January 1974. He had experience and knowledge of bio-medical engineering.

7. Finally, and almost simultaneously with the creation of the new Area Health Authority under reorganisation, a policy statement supported by all members with the exception of the Group Engineer (who in the new structure, was later to become the Area Works Officer) was submitted by the committee to the Cogwheel Executive Committee. It was approved and forwarded to the AHA for consideration by the AMT. The statement was produced in May 1974 and its recommendations were as follows:

> *Area Works Officer to be responsible for*: (a) drawing up contracts with outside bodies for the maintenance of all mechanical/electrical and electronic equipment. These contracts would be drawn up by

the Area Works Officer in co-operation with the Heads of Department involved.
  (b) Safety in all equipment.
  (c) Maintenance of electrical and mechanical equipment and certain electronic equipment.
  Chief Physicist to be responsible for: (a) maintenance of all radio-therapy equipment, all nucleonic equipment and physiological measurement equipment.
  (b) Research and development work in bio-medical engineering.
Linked with the above recommendations was a suggestion that additional accommodation and facilities would need to be provided for the Medical Physics Department to undertake the nature of work required.

8. It appears that the key point of conflict concerned the responsibility for the maintenance of physiological measuring equipment. It was in this area that the Group Engineer considered that his staff possessed the expertise to provide necessary maintenance. The consultant users, however, wanted this to be in the control of a clinically oriented professional, as it was patient oriented equipment and sited in the hospital within which the Chief Physicist was situated (the largest hospital).

Summary of Events Following Reorganisation of the National Health Service

June 1974
9. The report was noted by the AMT. The AHA also noted the request for a minor capital scheme to improve Medical Physics on the lower ground floor of the largest hospital. Approval was not officially given as it was not expected that financial backing would be forthcoming. The AWO was not involved in AMT discussions as no appointment to this post had been made at that time.

July 1975
10. The matter was reopened as the capital plan to develop the Medical Physics Department was expected to receive the approval of the RHA, and the Assistant Area Administrator (Planning) wished to consider staffing implications and operational policies.

30 July 1975
11. A meeting was held with the relevant staff for this purpose.

1 August 1975
12. The Group Engineer, now in post as AWO, wrote to the AA requesting a discussion of the original decision. He was concerned about the waste of resources which would be involved in creating a department concerned with maintenance within Medical Physics. A meeting was arranged between the AMT, the AWO and the Chief Physicist. Before this meeting took place, a number of Consultant users wrote to protest that the original decision was being reconsidered.

30 October 1975
13. At this meeting the AWO argued that as under the policy of both the DHSS and the RHA he was clearly responsible for safety and maintenance, the allocation of the maintenance of physiological measurement equipment to

the Medical Physics department would entail unjustifiable duplication of resources. However, in view of the extent of disagreement, he proposed that there should be an independent investigation.

14. After negotiation with the AWO and Chief Physicist, a letter was sent by the AA to the Medical Engineering Liaison Committee suggesting a compromise, namely, that adaptation and/or amendment work should be the responsibility of the Chief Physicist while all other maintenance remained the responsibility of the AWO.

20 November 1975
15. In a joint meeting between the Medical Liaison Engineering Committee and the AMT, there was clear disagreement. The Medical Engineering Liaison Committee members stuck to their original statement and challenged the suggestion that the DHSS was in support of maintenance matters remaining entirely in the hands of the AWO. It was decided that further guidance should be sought from the DHSS.

December 1975
16. The DHSS commented that it was a matter for the authority to determine. In fact, it appeared that the position of the DHSS (and the region) had changed in the course of the events outlined. This statement had two predecessors: In August 1972, the Principal Assistant Senior Medical Officer at Region, after consultation with the Regional Engineer, made the categorical statement based on DHSS circulars, that "there is no doubt that the Group Engineer is responsible for the maintenance of all electronic and bio-medical engineering equipment to ensure . . . safety while the medical staff is responsible for its correct usage". However, in October 1973 a draft document was issued from the Chief Engineer of the DHSS which seems less certain. While it emphasised the importance of clear lines of responsibility to a professionally qualified engineer for the purpose of safety, it stated that division of responsibilities for maintenance may be allocated according to local circumstances, and responsibility for clinical performance and accuracy of calibration should be to a scientist.

1976
17. During the early months new problems were continually arising and the AWO and Chief Physicist were unable to resolve boundaries of responsibilities as there was no clear policy.

18. In February, the Assistant Regional O and M Work Study Officer was requested to analyse the work in order to give guidance as to the appropriate siting of different pieces of equipment.

30 June 1976
19. The AMT again gave the matter their consideration. The following day the AA wrote to the AWO stating that the conclusion reached was that the maintenance work as outlined by the Medical Engineering Liaison Committee should become the responsibility of the Chief Physicist. The response of the AWO was to agree to the change—suggesting 1 August as the date for the change over. However, he objected to the decision on the grounds he had already stated and complained that he had not been at the meeting when the decision took place. He cited 17 points of confusion which required

clarification. The response of the AA was to assure the AWO that the conclusion reached did not constitute a decision—it was the intention of the AMT to invite the AWO to meet them.

July/August 1976

20. The AMT met several times to discuss the matter again and eventually made a firm decision which reversed the original statement of the Medical Engineering Liaison Committee about physiological measurement equipment. They decided that:

    (a) There should be no change made in the present duties and responsibilities of the Chief Physicist and the AWO.

    (b) The Bio-medical engineering department should be established as soon as possible for purposes of research and development. It should be the responsibility of the Chief Physicist.

    (c) The Medical Engineering Liaison Committee should be reconvened for monitoring purposes.

21. It was agreed that this decision should be conveyed to the Chairman of the Scientific Services Division of the Cogwheel Executive Committee and that he should be informed that the AMT would not meet with the Medical Engineering Liaison Committee for further discussions. It appears that at this point the consultant member had become convinced of the arguments for the importance of management experience and clear accountability in the determination of the issue. The GP member was unable to attend some meetings as he was on holiday.

22. The response of medical staff was instant and active. The Chairman of the Medical Engineering Liaison Committee and the Scientific Services Division (at that time the same person) and individual consultant users wrote strong letters of protest to the AA, and Chairman and members of the AHA. At the Cogwheel Executive Committee, a vote of no confidence was passed on the Consultant member of the AMT and he subsequently resigned. This resolution of the Cogwheel Executive Committee was accepted by the Area Medical Committee.

17 August 1976

23. The AMT presented a report to the AHA outlining their decision and the reasons for it. The AHA decided to appoint an Ad Hoc Committee to consider the AMT decisions on the matter and to make recommendations to the Authority. This Ad Hoc Committee comprised five AHA members. They elected as their chairman a professor of engineering. The Assistant Area Administrator (Planning) acted as secretary to the committee.

24. The committee met on nine occasions. It received written and oral submissions from the parties concerned. It investigated other areas to find out how they handled their similar situation and it researched the guidance given by the Region and the DHSS. Its main conclusions were that a bio-medical engineer should be appointed to be responsible for a unit which would undertake the development and maintenance functions as broadly outlined in the original statement of the Medical Engineering Liaison Committee. It would be sited in the Medical Physics Department and the head of the unit would be directly accountable to the Chief Physicist. However, in

133

respect of planned preventative maintenance, safety and contracting procedures the bio-medical engineer should act as a contractor to the AWO who should be empowered to monitor these activities and provide the necessary administrative back up. Furthermore, an Advisory Committee on Medical Engineering should be established and it should report to the AMT and the Area Scientific Committee.

January 1977

25. With some minor amendments, this report was accepted by the AHA.

Analysis

The Roles of Clinician Members of Management Teams

26. The problem faced by this Area Management Team in the events outlined was one that could scarcely fail to test significantly the compatibility of the management and representative roles of clinician members and, indeed, to test the feasibility of consensus decision making. The problem had a protracted history, giving time for attitudes and beliefs about it to have become well established long before the AMT had first to confront it seriously in August 1975. The medical and administrative members of the team found themselves divided on the issue, and the clinicians knew that they were representing the strong and united views of their colleagues. They were also by now firmly established members of the AMT, consistent attenders at their thrice weekly meeting, and committed to the principle of consensus management. They, along with the other members of the team, set about the task of examining the extent and source of the differences between the AWO on the one hand and the Chief Physicist and consultant users on the other, with a view to finding a workable compromise, at the same time endeavouring to argue through differences among themselves. Eventually, when their attempts to reach a compromise acceptable to all parties failed, and when nearly twelve months after the matter was reopened, uncertainties about allocation of work, staffing policies and the potential effects of these upon standards of maintenance and relationships within the hospitals demanded that a decision be made, the matter had to be resolved. In the event, the consultant member was persuaded that the arguments for the importance of managerial experience in the organisation of the maintenance of equipment and for clear and undivided accountability for safety should prevail, and he changed his mind. The documentation on the timing of this change of mind is not entirely clear. It appears, however, that it occurred at the July meeting of the AMT in 1976 when the AMT reached its decision and subsequently reported it to the AHA. It was likely in this instance that the judgement of the consultant member would take precedence in the minds of his medical colleagues on the AMT, as he was the person closest to the consultant users. However, in point of fact, the GP representative was not present at this meeting as he was on holiday. It had been agreed by the clinical members of the AMT that both would not be absent at the same time, and that they would feel bound by decisions taken in their absence to which the other was party. We have here a clear instance where a clinical representative on the management team decided that he ought to exercise his discretion and to go against the known views of his constituents. In consequence, they passed a vote of no confidence in him and he resigned.

134

27. What is called into question by these events is the compatibility of the roles that clinician members of the AMT are required to fulfil, namely, as members of a management team operating on the principle of consensus decision making, and as elected representatives of equals. Could the outcome, the resignation of the consultant member, have been avoided or did his role contain within it such potential conflicts that it could not be sustained in a crunch issue? This question will be examined under three headings.

Clarity of Role

28. It was pointed out to us that the Grey Book contained an element of contradiction in its account of the role. It prescribes the relationship of the clinical members with their medical colleagues as follows: "They must enjoy the *confidence* of their colleagues, so that they can speak for clinicians not as mere delegates, unable to commit their peers without reference back, but as representatives using the discretion vested in them as a basis for action". (Paragraph 4.10.) However, in paragraph 2.55 we read the following, "When (clinical members) agree an AMT decision, they will in effect be judging that they have, or that it is reasonably likely that they will be able to obtain, the *support* of their colleagues". In the first quote, what is emphasised is the general confidence placed in the clinical member by his colleagues. In the second quote, there seems to be a more definite suggestion that the decision that the member makes will actually be endorsed in each case by his colleagues.

29. There is room, then, for differences in interpretation of the role. This is further suggested by the fact that a number of different views were put to us by those whom we interviewed. All of them perceived an element of conflict; their differences are on the question of whether and how it can be resolved. They reflect, in part, differences in priority between the representative and management role. The alternatives are as follows:

(a) the conflict is reconcilable by following the medical view when it is strongly expressed and coherent, but otherwise using one's own judgement. Priority is given to the representative role, on the assumption that the AHA, rather than the AMT, is the proper body to resolve disputes between management and the medical profession;

(b) the conflict is reconcilable through the exercise by the clinical member of his own judgement. Where this goes against that of his colleagues, it is his task to persuade them. If he cannot do so, he must stand by his judgement, on the grounds that it has been reached through the perspectives of management *and* clinicians, and based on a fuller appreciation of the range of factors involved. Stronger priority is given to the management role, and the assumption is that most problems must be resolved in the management team;

(c) the conflict is reconcilable but there is no general rule about the balance of loyalties and priorities. Thorough consultation of and communication with colleagues should always enable one of two outcomes: they persuade you or you persuade them;

135

(d) the conflict is reconcilable by following the medical view when it is strongly expressed and coherent. In the event of difference between this and the judgement formed by the clinical member, the clinical member must try to persuade his colleagues. If he fails, he must support their view in the AMT, on the grounds that any decision strongly opposed by the medical profession, but requiring their co-operation, cannot be implemented. If agreement cannot then be reached in the AMT, the issue must be referred to the AHA, but the same limitation will apply: there can be no final decision in matters centrally affecting the medical profession that does not command their support. The rationale of this stance is based not so much on the principle of representation as on that of feasibility —a management principle in fact;

(e) the conflict is irreconcilable. In a situation where no acceptable compromise between the perspectives of management and clinicians can be found, the clinician manager has two loyalties.

Particular Circumstances

30. In this case, the consultant member's standpoint is expressed in (b) above. However, it is quite clear from the account of the AMC meeting when his resignation was accepted, that it was at variance with his colleagues' interpretation of his role: their view is expressed partly by (a) and partly by (d). A major clash between the consultant representative and his constituents was perhaps inevitable.

31. There are two ways in which such a clash might have been avoided. Active communication with and consultation of his colleagues on the part of the consultant representative might have modified the perception of the problem on both sides, increased mutual understanding, and sustained the general confidence of the consultants in their representative. In the event, his conflict with them was exacerbated by what appeared to be a passive approach on his part to communication and consultation. He recognised this, but felt himself to be handicapped in elaborating the issues and arguments involved in Cogwheel or AMC meetings by the fact that the situation seemed to be constantly changing, and more fundamentally, by the demands of confidentiality, breaches of which, in his view, could have been very damaging at some stages in this particular issue. Time and geography were also against him. The time consumed by the fulfilment of the duties of a clinical member of the AMT was calculated by the GP representative to be two days a week. This commitment eroded the time which could be spent by the consultant member in informal meetings with his colleagues, the majority of whom were based at a different hospital from himself.

32. A second line was suggested in the report of the Ad Hoc Committee set up by the AHA to review the AMT decision of July 1976. They shared this consultant's interpretation of the role insofar as it gives priority to his management responsibilities, and considered that it should be accepted by his constituents, on the grounds that the AMT is not the ultimate decision making body. "The AHA have now demonstrated the possibility of varying an AMT decision by setting up a special committee".

33. In this latter respect, the views of the AHA Ad Hoc Committee and of the AMC are closely allied. Both bodies assert the authority of the AHA and advocate a stronger role in decision making for it than it had hitherto had in this area. But the difference between them is a basic one. It lies in their attitudes towards the importance of unanimity in the AMT, and the incorporation of clinicians as full members of the management teams. This brings us to the central point: the nature and validity of the purposes of electing clinicians to management teams.

Purposes of the Election of Clinicians onto Management Teams

34. The Grey Book made it clear that a major aim of the new structure was active medical participation in an integrated system of management: it "must be woven into the main design". (Paragraph 4.1.) The purpose of this was to ensure medical commitment to new developments, understanding by doctors of the needs of other parts of the service, and the incorporation of the ideas and perspectives of clinical practitioners into management decisions. (Paragraph 4.4.) Underlying this was the assumption that the medical profession has a central place in the health service, but that its aims and values can be and must be brought up against and reconciled with those of administrators and other groups.

35. The election of clinicians onto management teams can be seen as a key to the implementation of these ideas, and perhaps a further one, not explicit in the Grey Book. Clinicians bring a quality that is rare in any management group—level spanning. Their professional role requires them to move between caring for individual patients and organising systems within their own speciality. Becoming a manager compels them to go into a third kind of activity again, namely, the relation of needs and resources across the span of the health service within a prescribed locality. The opportunity to harness a perspective with this range and fluidity is an attractive one.

36. In our view, there is an argument for holding that an essential for the implementation of these ideas through the election of clinicians to management teams is the sustainment of tension, and perhaps even abrasion in the operation of the machinery. The incorporation of their representatives into a small management group, which must become cohesive if it is to be effective, is a powerful means of ensuring recognition by clinicians that the price of gaining some management power is serious consideration of the perspectives and demands of other groups in the health service. The other side of the coin is that the management group has within it two people who are daily brought face to face with the impact of the service on patient care, and whose interests therefore can be expected to remain closely identified with those of their colleagues. Both the field study and this particular case suggest that these interests are often far apart from those of management. If two further factors are added, namely the requirement that the management team reaches its decisions by consensus, and the concept of the management team as the front line body for the resolution of the differences between clinicians and others in the service, conditions for the creation of tension and abrasion are certainly set up. But it may be argued that what is also established is a potential for powerful, if subtle, mutual influence.

37. The question then is, can such machinery work and, in particular, can it work if the medical profession does not from the outset fully accept the aims as outlined? The key to this is the sustainment of clinicians' confidence in their representatives. It could be argued (and the argument is supported by this case) that good communication is even more vital for this than continuation by the representatives in full time clinical practice, provided that election to a management team is confined to a two or three year limit. Such communication would require one major forum for the discussion by clinicians of management team business, and thus the accordance of a central role to the AMC by all doctors. It would demand too that clinician managers have time and also preparatory training. For it to be achieved, they would need to cut down drastically their clinical practice, and to be paid enough for this to be possible. All this entails a further assumption that they are practitioners who have made their reputation in the profession. If, through these means, stronger communication were to be achieved, it might bring us *nearer* to the position outlined in (c) above under "clarity of role", wherein the conflict inherent in the clinician manager's role is found to be reconcilable because through good communication either he or his constituents will persuade the other parties of the rightness of their views. If this happened, the intolerable tension would be removed from the clinician manager without the loss of the creative tension in the management team, but it would be unrealistic to expect the system to work wholly smoothly.

38. Thus might run one set of arguments for an integrated system of management incorporating clinicians. They would certainly not be accepted by all. Two particular points might be set against them: the first is that it is not in the interest of the consumers of the health service that clinicians, dedicated to the view that they should strive for optimum medical care for their patients, should take more account of the scarcity of and conflicting demands upon resources. They should continue to insist upon their separate identity and values, and support a *contest* model of decision making. The risks of the absorption and submergence of their perspective are too great in an *integrated* system. This point is closely connected with the second one: that the system as outlined above entails an undesirable element of secrecy and elitism in a democratic society. Conflicts between clinicians and managers ought to be resolved not in the management team but by the governing body, where debate is public. In practice, this means that clinical representatives should not exercise their discretion to achieve consensus in the management team in the face of opposition by their colleagues, nor seek to influence their colleagues against their collective judgement, but rather ensure the referral of the issue to the AHA.

39. It is suggested that in this case the Authority had difficulty in operating the integrated model because of the problems of communication, time and conflicting perceptions of role, as described. That does not necessarily mean that it moved in principle towards adopting the contest model. It is unlikely that it, or indeed other authorities, has any fixed and final position on the continuum between these two models. Perhaps the major lesson to draw is that the concept of clinicians as members of management teams contains a wealth of often conflicting possibilities, not recognised in the Grey Book,

which remain to be explored and worked through in practice by those trying to operate the system.

Consensus Management and the Respective Roles of the AMT and the AHA

40. It is already clear that discussion of the role of the clinical representative cannot be divorced from concern with the principles of consensus decision making and with the respective roles of the AMT and the AHA. It is, we believe, possible to conclude in this case that the perception by the consultant representative of his responsibility and authority vis-à-vis those of his constituents was compounded by the perception by the AMT as a whole of the roles and responsibilities of themselves and the AHA. Both took upon themselves more than in the circumstances they could sustain. But there are general questions that arise from their particular approaches which might be put in the following form. Can the principle of consensus decision making be pursued too far? Can principles be laid down for deciding which issues should be resolved within the management team and which referred to the authority members?

41. Interviews with four of the members of the AMT suggest that throughout their deliberations they remained convinced that it was their duty to reach a decision rather than to refer it to the AHA and for two main reasons. First, they regarded failure to reach consensus as failure in the performance of the team. Secondly, they perceived the issue as one of management, and not policy, and indeed management in a highly technical, ill-understood field of work. At least one of them thought that referral to the AHA would inevitably mean that the decisions made would be lay or political rather than expert and rational. And although they knew that the conclusion they did reach was contentious, they issued it to the AHA as a report for ratification, not as a request for a decision.

42. A point frequently made in the Field Study was that the principle of consensus management may adversely affect the quality of decisions made. Conflicting points of view may not be clearly identified, arguments may not be pursued, or difficulties may be shelved. In this case, although there is some evidence that in the end at least one individual did put aside his own judgement in order to achieve a decision, there is no suggestion that the problem was not fully examined and pursued by the team members. With hindsight, their failure may be seen to have been in thinking that the level of disagreement within the authority on this issue was one that could be contained by management or indeed was their responsibility. This does not, however, suggest any need to abandon the principle of consensus decision making or to work less hard for it. A management team which strives for consensus, as is the case in this authority, is surely one whose failures to reach it can be important indicators of the primary issues requiring resolution by a health authority at any one time.

43. This leads directly to the second question. The problem of distinguishing in practice between management and policy is perhaps particularly well illustrated by this case. On the face of it, such a highly technical issue ought clearly to be a matter for expert decision. But it gradually emerged that there was no definitive solution based on expertise, and that the debate was not

simply about the best way to allocate responsibilities in order to provide the best service. It was also a matter of whose views should be given greatest weight. Management and policy, means and ends, were intermingled, and there was no simple formula for resolving the problem of who should decide.

44. Moreover, this problem had another twist in this case. The modes of decision making by the AMT and the AHA were not clearly contrastable in terms of emphasis on rationality and expertise in the AMT and on power and negotiation in the AHA. The device of appointing an Ad Hoc Committee took the process of decision making in the AHA out of the public political forum. And the committee, insofar as they collected information from other authorities on how they had resolved the problems, took the task of obtaining advice and information on which to base their decision further than had the AMT. For their part, the AMT, while admittedly in the end giving low priority to the criterion of acceptability, did nevertheless rely quite heavily on negotiation and search for compromise between the protagonists in their approach to the problem.

45. The need to clarify in practice the respective functions of management teams and authority members can be seen in both organisational and political terms. In a service in which the contribution of a widening range of people is recognised, inter-professional disputes are likely to increase. If, as in this case, the responsibility for resolving them is seen as primarily a management one, the management team becomes perhaps the major pressure point in the national health service. The amount of pressure that can be exerted on one group of people is a serious matter to consider, particularly in the context of a single district area. It was pointed out by one of the participants in the study that although single district areas provide simpler and more coherent administration, they also make heavier demands on management team members.

46. The question is, however, much wider than this. In a climate in which the value and the bases of authority are under question, and the status of knowledge is uncertain, almost every issue can be perceived as political. Immediately there is perhaps little likelihood of widespread acceptance of this view in the health service: the fear of the potential and in some cases actual impact of politics on the service was often expressed by respondents in the Field Study (although it is true that they were usually referring to party politics). But even if this fear were to subside and the assumption of the Grey Book about the "limited time" that authority members had to spend on the service were again challenged by reference to different assumptions within local government, a simple swing to the position where decisions of any significance are all referred to the Authority is not an adequate solution. It is an equal denial of the inextricability of the concepts of management and policy, and a rejection of the importance of the diffusion of responsibility throughout the service, strongly emphasised in the Field Study.

47. Clear formulae for the resolution of the problem may not only be unavailable but inappropriate. What may be more fruitful is, again, the concept of tension between management and politicians (or, in the terms of the previous discussion, integrated and contest models of governance), and also a flexibility, that enables authorities to evolve new principles and systems as

they encounter problems in the expectation that they in turn will need modification as different difficulties arise.

Structure, Culture and Influence: Did the Change in Structure Following Reorganisation Affect the Decisions Made in This Case?

48. Initially the change in structure appeared to have a direct impact on the decision making process. It may for example be significant that it was only after the Group Engineer was appointed Area Works Officer in the Authority (November 1974) that he asked for the policy of allocating to the Chief Physicist responsibility for the maintenance of physiological measuring equipment to be reconsidered (August 1975). In the reorganised structure the Area Works Officer is head of the Works Department in the area, and directly accountable to the Area Health Authority, not to the Area Management Team. Moreover, the head of his profession in the region, the Regional Works Officer, is a member of the Regional Team of Officers. The Engineering profession is thus given status and power in the national health service that it did not previously possess. In this case the Regional Works Officer gave his area colleague strong support in his stand and, given the newness of the change in status and power, it seems reasonable to accept the view put to us by some participants in this study that the question of responsibility for safety in bio-medical engineering was perceived as an important test of its reality.

49. There was no comparable change in status for the Chief Physicist in the new structure (already Area Physicist before reorganisation), and there is no member of his profession in a position at region that compares with that of the Regional Works Officer, as the Regional Physicist is not a member of the Regional Team of Officers.

50. The impact of the structural change on the position of the Area Works Officer in relation to the Area Management Team may have been reinforced by the factor of culture. The importance to him of the managerial element in his role is evidenced by both the style and substance of his communications with the authority. His arguments are put in terms of the economic use of resources, of the importance of clear and undivided accountability, and of manifest organisational structure, and additionally, they are set out in formal reports to management bodies, the HMC (pre-reorganisation), the AMT and the AHA. This contrasts noticeably with the style of the doctors and the Chief Physicist, whose communications with the management bodies are all in the form of letters. The Chief Physicist emerges from the story primarily as a professional scientist, and secondarily as a manager.

51. It could be concluded from this that structural changes, reinforced by cultural factors, did make a significant difference, in that they combined to increase the influence of the Area Works Officer on the Management Team, as well as apparently giving more general weight in the system to management efficiency.

52. However, in the end, the difference had, arguably, little significance at all. This was a crucial test case for the doctors too. Their confidence that their judgements would be given due weight in the reorganised system had at

141

this time been somewhat undermined, not only locally in the process of this dispute, where they felt that the case for transferring responsibilities to the Chief Physicist was uncontestable, but also in the direction taken by policies at central government level. In the event, although they failed to carry their case in the management system (AMT), they succeeded in getting a full hearing in the political system (AHA) and their confidence in the preparedness of the new authority to uphold their position was, at least partially, restored.

Roles of the DHSS and the Region

53. In a field of rapid development, where inevitably there exist *both* uncertainty about sources of knowledge and discipline boundaries *and* a high degree of specialisation, so that expertise is at a premium, what are the roles of the DHSS and the region?

54. In this case, one route to a resolution sought was appeal to a higher authority, exemplified in particular by the DHSS. For example, in November 1975 the AMT sought the advice of the DHSS. The arguments of the AWO throughout rested on his contention that his view was consistent first of all with DHSS policy in this field and, later on, as it emerged that there was no clear policy, with their guidelines on organisational structure and on accountability for safety. Finally, the Ad Hoc Committee of inquiry set up by the AHA again investigated the position of the DHSS and also the region in 1976.

55. There is evidence in the statements of the DHSS to which we had access, that as the field of bio-medical engineering became more complex, they moved away from clear central direction (1972) to a recommendation that this was a matter for determination by individual authorities (1975).

56. Those whom we interviewed were divided on the question whether the DHSS could or should have established a national policy on allocation of responsibilities in this new field. (They also differed in their perceptions of the DHSS as primarily a source of expert knowledge or a policy making body in a problem of this kind).

57. However, three people, including the Chairman of the Ad Hoc Committee, thought that the advice from DHSS Works and Scientific Divisions was contradictory, and that it was this rather than the lack of a national policy that created problems.

58. This feature of communication seems to have been reflected at regional level. The region gave no collective advice to the area, as their own working party had not finished its deliberations on bio-medical engineering. However, it seems that the AWO was given strong support in the dispute by the RWO, in his functional monitoring role.

59. In conclusion, it seems to us that in a field of rapid technological development the problems of establishing clear national policies are overwhelming. The thinking of central government must be informed and changed by developing experience of the specialists at work throughout the country. However, if individual authorities are to enable specialists to pursue such developments systematically, a crucial requirement would seem to be a strong and steady flow of information, and reponsibility for this in a

142

specialised field is surely an appropriate one to be assumed by the DHSS. It is arguable that one factor in the difficulties faced by this AMT in making a decision was inadequate information about possible alternative solutions. It is suggested that the DHSS might have played a stronger role in directing them towards obtaining such information, when they were not in a position to give them clear advice.

60. A wider issue of principle also seems to be raised by this discussion. The problems of distinguishing between mono-disciplinary and multi-disciplinary issues created by consensus management, and the element of conflict between the strengthening of a range of professional and occupational groups through the principle of functional management and the promotion of consensus and collaboration by multidisciplinary teams, have been mentioned in the Field Study. The events outlined in this case study suggest that these are difficulties experienced at the top of the organisation, at both DHSS and regional levels. If this is the case it would be interesting to know if and how they are being tackled by the DHSS. This, we feel, is crucial because on it depends the success of two central principles of reorganisation, corporate management and devolution of decision making.

Concluding Comments: Criteria for Decision Making

61. The analysis of this case has indicated that there are areas of ambiguity in the reorganised structure of the National Health Service, and that much work is required to achieve clarification in these. However, it has also suggested that ambiguities of structure often reflect ambiguities of aims, that do not admit to simple resolution. It has shown how concentration upon some aims, for example the achievement of corporate management in the AMT, can be detrimental to the achievement of others, such as representative and open government, but at the same time, a recurrent theme has been the desirability of the sustainment of tension between aims and principles rather than opting too soon for absolute priorities among them. Finally, it has highlighted some of the limitations of structure in affecting behaviour.

62. Some of the assumptions on which the analysis is based perhaps bear repetition. It is accepted that in society at large the values and bases of authority are under heavy challenge and the status of the knowledge of any one discipline or body of experts is uncertain. It is further assumed that the National Health Service is dependent upon contributions from a wide range of professions and occupations with conflicting prorities, that the claim of the medical profession to sole authority over either means or ends can in many circumstances not be upheld, and that the problems faced by the service are often such as to require the resolution of clashes of value and interest between various groups about aims as well as finding the resources and most efficient means to achieve them. It is felt that many of these factors are illustrated by this particular study.

63. Given these assumptions, criteria for good decision making that give priority to an oversimplified meaning of efficiency make little sense. The factor of *time*, for example, while it certainly cannot be dismissed as unimportant, has to be balanced against other considerations. *Rationality*, interpreted as the systematic and knowledge based building up of means to achieve ends,

has itself some limitations. For sometimes not only have conflicts between ends to be resolved, but also what might be the most efficient means of achieving ends are not politically practicable. The importance of the criterion of *acceptability* is illustrated by this case. Twice a policy was decided between the years 1972 and 1976, and twice it was reversed because of unacceptability. In each case it can be argued that the rejected decision was a rational one, but only in the eyes of particular groups of people. The judgement of the participants in this study that the decision of the Ad Hoc Committee was a good one can be seen in terms of it having found a satisfactory combination of speed, rationality, and acceptability. The test it has not yet completely passed is *feasibility*: nine months after the acceptance of the report it had not been fully implemented, because of delays over the appointment of the bio-medical engineer, although the requisite transfers of staff did take place at the agreed time.

64. If a balance between speed, rationality, acceptability and feasibility is taken as an embryonic formula for decision making, the dangers of according too great an importance to acceptability are very real, in particular as it begs a basic question, namely "acceptable to whom?" the answer to which in our present structure is clearly not weighted in favour of the consumer. Once again, the problem to be solved is one not so much of engineering as of values and aims.

Hospital Closures

By Nancy Korman and Helen Simons

Introduction

1. Hospital closures entail a decision making process which brings into play judgements of clinical practice, assessment of potential economic gains or losses, compliance with national standards of provision and community needs. These judgements are likely to be made by different groups who may arrive at quite different conclusions about the same situation. By taking two very different examples of hospital closures, one which was opposed (Poplar) and one which was not (Invalid and Crippled Children), this study describes the process of closure and, in particular, the interaction of judgements which are brought to decision making through consultative procedures. The cases are unique but the issues arising from them are of sufficient general interest to be relevant to other cases of closures.

2. Consultation, negotiation and participation have to some extent become "bandwagon" words in a society which is placing increasing demands on its institutions to be more open to public scrutiny. But it is not uncommon for different meanings to be attached to these terms by different people or for some to use them interchangeably. Frustration and misunderstanding may be generated by the lack of clarity of these terms. Consultation allows not only for group interests to be considered but for comments to be made on the quality of decision making. This study will, we hope, illustrate how consultation is perceived and practiced.

3. The study starts from two generally held assumptions:
   (a) that in a democratic society consultative procedures are necessary to respect individuals' rights to have their views represented, to be treated fairly and to be kept informed;
   (b) that total closure of health service institutions, removal of part of a service or temporary cessation of a service may be seen as a loss to a community (of a service, of employment, of tradition) and may evoke opposition unless some benefit can be demonstrated.

Method of Study

4. The study took place within one region only. Much of the data were taken from written sources: district, area and regional files. In addition, discussions with administrators, financial staff and the secretary of a CHC helped to illuminate critical decisions and action points and check the accuracy of reportage.

5. We first present a diary of events for both hospital closures, which describes in chronological order, the processes and events involved. These are then related to a thematic discussion of hospital closures and the impact of consultation.

History of Poplar Hospital

Poplar Hospital was built in 1855 to provide an easily accessible accident service for the East and West India docks and surrounding industry. Originally 20 beds, it had grown into a general hospital of 115 beds by the outbreak of the First World War to meet the greatly increased population and industry of the district. When it was taken over by the National Health Service in 1948 it had a complement of 120 beds. In 1955, the Chairman of the Bow Group HMC (to which Poplar belonged) requested that the RHB rebuild Poplar as it had sustained serious war damage. The RHB agreed only to minor repairs, because Poplar had no waiting list, and there was no justification for increasing the number of beds in Bow Group. Over the years, it had come to be known as the dockers' hospital while at the same time it was used by the local community as a service providing primary care. Both population and industrial activity began to decline after the Second World War.

The example of Poplar was chosen to illustrate two points: opposition to closure and its impact on closure procedures; and that difficulties over consultation have not necessarily been brought about by reorganisation.

Diary of Events—Poplar Hospital Closure

Date	Action by Authority	Reason	Date	Local Responses	Reason
			Nov 71	Inquiry by NUPE to Thames Group HMC Secretary about rumours and newspaper article about possible closure brings a reply that discussions are being held about distribution of hospital facilities in East London and assurance that closure procedures entail consultation.	
			Nov 71	Exchange of letters between MPs and RHB Sec. on local rumours of out-patients' clinics closing down. RHB has agreed to upgrading Accident/Emergency facilities at St. Andrews Hospital which will release existing Poplar casualty for new use. Promises consultation.	
			17.12.71	Local surgeon writes to SAMO, RHB, asking for investigation about rumours of closure.	Nursing staff think Poplar will close "within one year and hospital becoming demoralised".
			24.1.72	Secretary of Poplar League of Friends writes to RHB Sec. asking about possible closure.	Staff had approached them about Poplar closing "in 18 months".

149

Diary of Events—Poplar Hospital Closure—*continued*

Date	Action by Authority	Reason	Local Responses	Date	Reason
28.2.72	Chairman, Thames Group HMC informs RHB Sec that he is: (1) Discussing removal of acute services from Poplar with Town Clerk, MOH of Tower Hamlets, MP and staff at hospital. (2) Undertaking research into pattern of medical care in surrounding area. (3) Aware of local opposition to proposals; petitions by Resident Associations being prepared. (4) Suggesting meeting with local residents to explain (held on 26.4.72).	Part of informal consultation procedures.	Headline—*East London Advertiser* (ELA) "CASUALTY WARD CLOSURE RIDDLE".	3.3.72	(1) Local community MPs fighting closure of casualty ward. (2) Reporter heard from cleaner in hospital that staff offered alternative posts or redundancy and *closure* scheduled for 18 months' time. (3) HMC denies closure. (4) NE Met RHB says rationalisation under discussion. Could be up to 10 years.

Diary of Events—Poplar Hospital Closure—*continued*

Date	Action by Authority	Reason	Date	Local Responses	Reason
			10.3.72	ILEA asks for reconsideration of proposed transfer until alternative provision on Isle of Dogs.	
			24.3.72	Headline ELA "MPs Join Battle for Hospital".	
			27.3.72	RHB Sec. informs 2 MPs of reasons for proposed closure.	Sec. of State pressing for rationalisation of smaller hospitals, especially in E. London where there is more generous provision than in rest of country.
			14.4.72	Chairman, Thames Gp HMC meets with Tower Hamlets Council to inform of NHS plans and get informal views.	
			April 72	League of Friends writes to Sec. of State expressing concern over possible closure.	

Diary of Events—Poplar Hospital Closure—*continued*

Date	Action by Authority	Reason	Date	Local Responses	Reason
26.4.72	Chairman Thames Group HMC recommends to RHB Secretary that local residents not demanding indefinite retention but no closure until alternative provision is made RHB should make a public statement to allay rumours.		26.4.72	Chairman, Thames Group HMC meets with local residents.	Local opposition on the following grounds: planning study forecasts rise in population for the area; only 1 resident GP on Isle of Dogs; tradition of using hospitals for primary care; poor public transport to St. Andrews; no other hospital as far south as Poplar; not just Tower Hamlets—34% of patients from Newham; new DGH will not be ready until 1980; no major decision before reorganisation.
			18.5.72	Canning Town Labour Party writes to DHSS protesting closure of Poplar as a worsening of services to local area.	

152

Diary of Events—Poplar Hospital Closure—*continued*

Date	Action by Authority	Reason	Date	Local Responses	Reason
26.5.72	SAMO reports to RHB Secretary: (1) Tower Hamlets Joint Hospital Services Committee should be consulted on idea of Poplar's Health Centre. (2) Sec. of State be requested to agree to formal consultation on the closure of Poplar. (3) The Thames Group should be consulted on the possibility of concentrating surgical practice at St. Andrews.	NE Met is already committed to the upgrading of St. Andrews which will allow absorption of Poplar outpatients work and require Poplar in-patient surgery work to achieve full use of new resources. The problems of staffing, accommodation and equipment make it unreasonable to await completion of Newham DGH. But local views are not unreasonable.			
			7.6.72	Press release by Tower Hamlets Council agreeing to closure of Poplar emergency services because of upgrading of St. Andrews, but requesting such a service to Isle of Dogs when development plans are known.	
			15.6.72	*Newham Recorder.* Save Poplar Hospital Org. claim "Transfer Services Means a Total Shut-Down. "The Port"—article about campaign to prevent closure of Poplar A/E Department.	
			16.6.72	ELA "Poplar Hospital Closure Shock", "Giant Row Brewing", "Protest Petition 6,000". HMC denies closure intentions.	

Diary of Events—Poplar Hospital Closure—*continued*

Date	Action by Authority	Reason	Date	Local Responses	Reason
19.7.72	Meeting of Tower Hamlets Joint Hospital Services Committee agrees to idea of health centre and recommends closure of Poplar emergency services.		30.6.72	Chairman, Save Poplar Campaign, writes to *Express* (local paper) to ask HMC to reconsider transfer.	
8.8.72	RHB Sec. prepares draft Public statement seeking DHSS approval for formal consultations to start; sends to Chairman, Thames Group HMC for agreement.	Informal consultation has shown differing views on desirability of closure, so formal consultations must now be pursued.	21.7.72	Local vicar writes to RHB Sec. requesting no action until after reorganisation.	
24.8.72	Chairman, Thames HMC to RHB Sec.—draft statement should not be issued.	HMC initiated informal consultations but these showed that Poplar is meeting other health needs and should not be closed until alternative is available. Decision should be delayed until 1974 when new AHA may consider totality of health needs.	1.9.72	MOH Tower Hamlets indicates that if health centre on rota system can meet minor casualty need Poplar can close.	

154

Diary of Events—Poplar Hospital Closure—*continued*

Date	Action by Authority	Reason	Date	Local Responses	Reason
8.9.72	RHB Sec. to Chairman, Thames Group HMC. RHB Sec. replies to Chairman, Thames HMC: (1) Essential to get statement agreed with DHSS.	Controversy over informal consultation (first stage) so essential for RHB to request Sec. of State approval for second stage of formal consultation. Issue cannot just be dropped, in view of controversy aroused.			
	(2) Suggests informal meeting of HMC, ILEC, Tower Hamlets, Council, LMC and Joint Hospital Services Committee to get an agreed statement.	RHB cannot criticise other statutory bodies for inadequate service provision. Case for hospital closure must rest on factors affecting hospital services.	6.10.72	NUPE to Sec. Thames HMC asking for consultation but informed (by RHB Sec.) that approval for consultation had not yet been given.	
			12.10.72	*Newham Recorder* reports in last 6 months, 17,000 signatures on petition.	

Diary of Events—Poplar Hospital Closure—*continued*

Date	Action by Authority	Reason	Date	Local Responses	Reason
			5.11.72	Save Poplar Campaign to RHB Sec. protesting decision to close.	Poplar only 24 hour hospital available to local people. St. Andrews inconvenient to get to. Construction costs at St. Andrews are high. Petition with 20,000 signatures will be sent to local MP.
10.11.72	Meeting of statutory bodies to agree statement to be sent to Sec. of State (as from 3.9.72).	General acceptance that Poplar was not needed for hospital services, but doubt over adequacy of other medical services. Proposed meeting to consider adequacy of other services, as this is the reason why Poplar is opposed.			
30.11.72	Meeting to consider primary health services.	Agreed that patients by-passed GPs because hospital was there. SAMO showed that Poplar was over-doctored; GPs had shorter lists than in other London boroughs. Main problem was emergency services.	15.12.72	Tower Hamlets Town Clerk to RHB Sec.—no opposition to closure of emergency services.	Leave final decision to new AHA.

Diary of Events—Poplar Hospital Closure—*continued*

Date	Action by Authority	Reason	Date	Local Responses	Reason
5.1.73	RHB Sec. to DHSS, requesting permission for formal consultation on Poplar closure.	Uneconomic and inefficient to run; hard to staff; light work load; no waiting list; RHB satisfied that upgrading of St. Andrews will provide a better service.			
			16.1.73	Request from ILEC to RHB Sec. for more information to supply to local MP.	
5.2.73	DHSS to RHB Sec., requesting more information before going to Secretary of State.				
			27.3.73	Letters from 2 MPs, to RHB Sec. Poplar being deliberately run down for closure. Work on St. Andrews prejudiced decision on Poplar. Requests information on use of Poplar during weekends.	
			30.3.73	*East London Advertiser* "MPs join fight to save Hospital".	
6.4.73	Sec. of State agrees to formal consultation.		10.4.73	"The Port",—"Poplar Hospital to close".	
			13.4.73	Meeting of 3 MPs and RHB Secretary.	

Diary of Events—Poplar Hospital Closure—*continued*

Date	Action by Authority	Reason	Date	Local Responses	Reason
18.4.73	RHB issues public statement on consultation for closure of Poplar. Consultation to be completed by 31 May, from Newham and Tower Hamlets Councils; ILEC, LMB; Ambulance Service; NUPE; Labour Party; MPs.	Upgrading of St. Andrews; dockers moving downstream; new road facilities improve access to St. Andrews; ILEC agree general needs of population being met; age of Poplar makes it unsuitable for modern medicine; difficulty of staff recruitment.	30.4.73	Letters from local vicar to RHB Sec.	
			7.5.73	Save Poplar Campaign to RHB Sec. (also sent to Sec. of State).	
			11.5.73	Labour Party to RHB Sec.	
			May 73	2 local press articles, 8 letters from local people, hospital cleaner and doctor.	
			23.5.73	NUPE to RHB Sec. Ambulance Service and LMC reply.	
			May 73	Letters from 2 Labour Parties, 3 Unions, local housing association, 5 individuals, 2 local petitions.	
31.5.73	RHB extends consultation period to 30.6.73.		June 73	2 letters from Labour Party; 5 individuals, NUPE; Tower Hamlets Local Council; MPs; staff at Poplar; local councillor.	

158

Diary of Events—Poplar Hospital Closure—*continued*

Date	Action by Authority	Reason	Date	Local Responses	Reason
20.6.73	Finance and General Purposes Committee of RHB agree to meeting to discuss with local protestors.				
4.7.73	GNC inspectors decide to withdraw recognition of Poplar.	Too small; insufficient experience for training of enrolled nurses.			
25.7.73	Meeting at RHB—3 MPs, Tower Hamlets Council, Save Poplar Campaign, League of Friends, ILEC, HMC. RHB decision not yet taken.	Objections put forward: travel difficulties; use of Poplar on weekends and evenings; lack of late open pharmacy services; no difficulty of recruiting staff; poor GP services; need for Poplar during winter; shortage of beds.			
			July 73	Total of more than 40 letters from individuals received.	
19.9.73	RHB meeting refers decision to new Shadow authority.	New authority will have a wider view of health service provision.			
26.9.73	Public Statement issued.	RHB will seek views of City & East London AHA before deciding.	Oct/ Dec 73	2 consultants propose transfer of sessions from Poplar to St. Andrews.	SAMO thinks their requests are reasonable but cannot be allowed because it would pre-empt decision on Poplar.
1.11.73	DHSS agrees to delay.	Decision to close could not be implemented until new facilities at St. Andrews have been completed.			

Diary of Events—Poplar Hospital Closure—*continued*

Date	Action by Authority	Reason	Date	Local Responses	Reason
4.12.73	SAMO meets clinicians at Poplar.	Medical Unit considered unsafe and surgeon refused to continue work in isolation from other medical facilities.	1.12.73	Area Admin. briefs AHA Chairman on Poplar.	Immediate closure will cause political upheaval. St. Andrews not ready—present level of service should be maintained.
17.12.73	Meeting of St. Andrews and Poplar clinicians, RHB representatives of Royal College of Physicians. Recommend: (1) No new admissions to Poplar from 1.1.74 except for casualty. (2) All ambulances diverted from Poplar to St. Andrews. (3) Ward at St. Andrews converted to casualty receiving room.	Concern about medical standards, recent report thought some deaths were avoidable.			
17.12.73	Thames Group Medical Advisory Committee agrees to recommendations of meeting.				
19.12.73	HMC special meeting recommends that RHB authorise immediate employment of two hospital junior medical staff and defer action on closing Poplar until the end of winter.	Unsafe medical standards at Poplar. Shortage of hospital beds during the winter with consequences for the number of elderly patients; not possible to guarantee provision in other hospitals.			

Diary of Events—Poplar Hospital Closure—*continued*

Date	Action by Authority	Reason	Date	Local Responses	Reason
20.12.73	RHB meeting decision to close Poplar admissions from 31.12.73 outpatients to continue. All casualty and new admissions to St. Andrews.	Medical staff unwilling to accept clinical responsibility for patients treated in Poplar.			
27.12.73	RHB Sec. informs AHA Chairman of decision of 20.12.73.				
28.12.73	SAMO informs Thames HMC that Poplar can no longer be recognised by GMC for pre-registration training.		2.1.74	NUPE claims action is breach of RHB and shadow AHA agreement.	Staff not informed of RHB plans.
			4.1.74	NUPE informed that December decision restricting services endorsed by Thames Medical Advisory Committee but without prejudice to full consultation by AHA on future use.	
			4.1.74	EVENING STANDARD: 3 London MPs challenge closure of Poplar on Jan 1 on grounds it may be illegal.	
7.1.74	Meeting between Sec. of State, MPs and Save Poplar Campaign. Sec. of State asks RHB to consider two additional junior medical appointments.	RHB should restore service until decision on future of Poplar taken.			

Diary of Events—Poplar Hospital Closure—*continued*

Date	Action by Authority	Reason	Date	Local Responses	Reason
			8.1.74	Local primary school managers protest.	Undertaking to consult before deciding closure not being honoured.
			9.17.4	A consultant informs Chairman, Thames Med. Adv. Cttee that Poplar needs 2 additional junior medical posts.	
			9.17.4	Another consultant tells SAMO it is ethically wrong to take responsibility without support facilities.	
			1.41.74	EVENING STANDARD: Sir Keith decides Poplar can stay.	
			15.1.74	Headline—Local paper: Hospital Future Still in Balance.	
16.1.74	RHB decides Sec. of State request cannot be met.	Cannot provide safe service, basic problem remains. Willing to maintain outpatients clinics, day surgery.	16.1.74	Amalgamated Union of Eng & Foundry Workers urge Sec. of State to consider new DGH as matter of urgency.	
			19.1.74	TGWU complains about timing of closure, reconsider decision.	
11.2.74	Thames HMC meeting requests RHB to recommend to Sec. of State that no new admissions to Poplar, A/E Department kept closed; outpatient sessions continue; use of Poplar for non-acute.	Two additional medical posts will not improve situation. Poor quality of agency nurses			

Diary of Events—Poplar Hospital Closure—*continued*

Date	Action by Authority	Reason	Date	Local Responses	Reason
19.2.74	Shadow AHA decides to keep Poplar open in present form until 31.3.75, and to review all A/E facilities in Tower Hamlets.	Need for additional beds in winter, to complete up-grading of St. Andrews; and for comprehensive review of facilities rather than piecemeal.	Early March	Two consultants propose changing outpatient sessions from Poplar to St. Andrews.	Inefficient to work at one hospital and operate at another.
8.3.74	Poplar Hospital Secretary informs Thames HMC Sec. that consultants want to change, RHB will need to agree.	Consultants and GPs making little use of Poplar.			
11.3.74	DHSS informs AA that it cannot approach Sec. of State for approval on December action until it is known whether further action is needed.				
13.3.74	Chairman, Thames HMC informs RHB Sec. of his disapproval of consultants' change.	Change of outpatient sessions contravenes agreement not to close Poplar without consultation. But absence of Sec. of State's decision makes it impossible to move staff or to restart acute services. Point now passed when hospital could be re-opened.			
14.3.74 18.3.74	AA and SAMO contact local medical and administrative officers to ensure services at Poplar kept up.	Need to maintain staff morale and complete public consultation before making further changes.			

163

Diary of Events—Poplar Hospital Closure—*continued*

Date	Action by Authority	Reason	Date	Local Responses	Reason
			30.3.74	Another petition (1,074 signatures) to keep Poplar open.	
9.4.74	DMT/ATO meeting. Agree decision on future of Poplar after March 1975 must be taken by September 1974.	ATO want to close Poplar now but DMT protest that would increase resistance to closure and cause public outcry.			
19.4.74	DA informs AA that adverse publicity has made clinicians and public unwilling to use Poplar.				
26.4.74	AA asks DHSS for Sec. of State approval of February decision.	DMT reluctant to move staff without approval.			
			2.5.74	Chairman, AHA visits Poplar Hospital with Chairman, Save Poplar Campaign.	
13.5.74	Sec. of State meets 3 local MPs and asks Minister of Health to investigate.				
24.5.74	AMO asks DCP for suggestions on use of Poplar, ICC and Albert Docks.				
13.6.74	DHSS informs RHA that the Minister of Health will only approve February AHA statement if an overall plan for health service development for the area is submitted.	Local pressure about poor quality of health facilities. Minister wants to ensure a comprehensive examination so that deprived sections such as the elderly, are not neglected.			

Diary of Events—Poplar Hospital Closure—*continued*

Date	Action by Authority	Reason	Date	Local Responses	Reason
1.7.74	DMT report on Poplar situation for AHA.	Clinicians unwilling to use Poplar; declining morale of staff; declining number of nursing staff may cause sudden crisis.			
11.7.74	AHA meeting, decision to allow DMT to forbid admissions to Poplar if staffing situation degenerates.	Situation has degenerated more than expected, no longer possible to keep hospital open, need to keep staff and community informed.	July 74	DMT prepares contingency plan.	
5.8.74	AA supplies DHSS with information on area plans.		16.8.74 30.8.74	One ward closed at Poplar. Ward reopened.	Nursing staff crisis.
15.10.74	Report on A/E facilities in Tower Hamlets ready. Sent to RHA and DHSS on 1 November.				
15.11.74	AHA meeting. Official proposal to close Poplar made and consultation procedures instituted. AHA to recommend 12 hours casualty services in Poplar as outpost of St. Andrews. Savings of £400,000 p.a. if Poplar inpatient closed. Consultations finished by 16.12.74.		25.11.74	Save Poplar Campaign telegram protest to Sec. of State.	

Diary of Events—Poplar Hospital Closure—*continued*

Date	Action by Authority	Reason	Date	Local Responses	Reason
			25.11.74	Staff meeting at Poplar. Telegram to Sec. of State for investigation of December decision to close acute services. Asks for extension of consultation time.	
			26.11.74	Newham Council requests extension of consultation time.	
			27.11.74	Tower Hamlets Council requests extension of consultation time. Letter to Sec. of State from Poplar staff and Save Poplar Campaign.	
Nov/Dec 74	DHSS announces that Newham DGH chopped from list of capital projects to start next year.	Economic crisis forces cutbacks.			
Dec 74	AHA extends consultation time to 31 January 1975.		11.12.74	DMT meets with Poplar staff.	
			Dec 74	Article in *Tower Hamlets News* on Poplar closure.	
Feb 75	AHA meeting. No agreement possible on closing inpatients.	Supporting closure: AMAC; LMC; DMC; Newham Council. Against closure: Newham and Tower Hamlets CHCs; hospital staff; Tower Hamlets Council; 2 MPs; Area Inter-Union Committee.			
10.3.75	12 hour service agreed. AA and RA request Sec. of State decision.				

Diary of Events—**Poplar Hospital Closure**—*continued*

Date	Action by Authority	Reason	Date	Local Responses	Reason
19.3.75	Meeting between MPs, Borough Council representatives, Tower Hamlets and Newham CHC and AHA.	CHC protest about cutting of Newham DGH from capital programme and implication for Poplar closure.			
4.4.75	RHA recommends closure. Decision by Sec. of State.				
			25.4.75	Ministry of Health visits Poplar and other hospitals in the area.	Local pressure necessitated strong attention being paid to this decision.
			10.6.75	Meeting between Sec. of State and Save Poplar Campaign at House of Commons.	
31.7.75	Sec. of State announces closure and start of nucleus hospital.	Decision to upgrade St. Andrews pre-empted decision on Poplar.			
			2.8.75	Press statement by Save Poplar Campaign to show gains.	
1.9.75	AHA aim to close Poplar by November.				AHA planning improvement in primary health care; new DGH; health centre for Poplar.
18.11.75	POPLAR CLOSES.				

168

History of Invalid and Crippled Children's Hospital (ICC)

Originally a voluntary hospital, ICC was founded in 1894 as Canning Town Women's Settlement Hospital (a new hospital was built in 1905). In 1923 the hospital was transferred to the Invalid and Crippled Children's Society together with the Nurses' Home and equipment to be used entirely for children. It could accommodate 26 patients. In 1924 the beds increased to 28 and in 1932 a new outpatient department opened. In 1933 an open-air ward increased the complement to 36. At the time closure was first discussed it was functioning as 17 female orthopaedic beds and 16 children's ENT.

This study was chosen to illustrate closure procedures in the absence of opposition.

Diary of Events—Invalid and Crippled Children's Hospital Closure (ICC)

Date	Action by Authority	Reason	Date	Local Responses	Reason
18.10.73	Thames Group (Th. G.) HMC Secretary inquires about procedure for closure or change of use re ICC.	This is part of the policy of rationalising hospitals in East London.			
26.10.73	SAMO to Th. G. Sec., suggesting consideration of ICC as psycho-geriatric day hospital.	Shortage of such a facility in that area.			
3.5.74	RA to AA, outlining strategy for the region which includes rationalisation of hospital services, a list of hospitals in CEL Area considered candidates for closure given.				
20.5.74	RA to AA reminding him of informal consultation undertaken on possible closure prior to reorganisation.				
10.10.74	DA to AA informing of request by consultant at ICC for transfer of operating sessions to another hospital.	On medical grounds the request was considered reasonable. But if agreed would mean virtual closing of children's wards, leaving 17 beds on female long-stay orthopaedic ward. Consultant asked to defer transfer but refused. DMT cannot forbid because ICC not mentioned in his contract.			
9.12.74	DMT recommends AHA initiates closure and change of use procedures.				
31.12.74	AA requests approval of RA to start informal consultation.				

169

Diary of Events—Invalid and Crippled Children's Hospital Closure (ICC)—*continued*

Date	Action by Authority	Reason	Date	Local Responses	Reason
9.1.75	AHA recommends transfer of orthopaedic patients to another hospital; request RHA agreement to start informal consultations.	DMT and ATO agreed that ICC has no future use.			
17.1.75	AA to DA, indicating RHA will agree, and suggesting informal consultation should be started, and finished by 31 January.				
27.1.75	RHA agrees to informal consultation.				
7.2.75	DA to AA, notifying of no local objections to closure from CHC and staff.	All staff will be redeployed; children's ward already closed; better service for orthopaedic patients at another hospital, savings for the district.			
11.2.75	AA to DHSS, asking approval for formal consultation.				
25.2.75	DMT recommends that if hospital closes the building should be sold.	Investigation of alternative uses negative.			
27.2.75	DHSS informs AA of approval to start formal consultation.	Those to be consulted are: Borough Council, MPs, FPC, LMC, CHC, DMC, AMAC, ANMAC, RHA, staff, unions.			
21.3.75	Consultation process begins.				
			25.4.75	Letter from relatives and Friends of ICC patients objecting to closure.	
			3.5.75	Inter-Union Committee agree to closure if the site is used for development of local community.	Concern about rundown of services.

Diary of Events—Invalid and Crippled Children's Hospital Closure (ICC)—*continued*

Date	Action by Authority	Reason	Date	Local Responses	Reason
8.5.75	AHA agrees to closure.	No objections strong enough to challenge wide agreement of all consulted.			
12.5.75	AA notifies RA and DHSS of closure decision.				
16.5.75	Decision notified to those consulted.		17.6.75	NUPE claims it was not consulted.	NUPE had withdrawn from Inter-Union Committee in March because the IUC was not sufficiently militant over Poplar closure.
7.7.75	DA informs other hospitals of district that ICC will shortly close and cease admissions,	Reluctant to publicise cessation of admissions in light of NUPE challenge.	7.7.75	AA notes that NUPE informed Inter-Union Committee that it had withdrawn only at the end of June.	AHA reluctant to change union consultation procedures as these were currently under review.
			July 75 16.7.75	24 of 26 ICC staff join NUPE. NUPE meeting at ICC with relatives to discuss future of ICC.	
28.7.75	DA informs ICC staff that ICC will close by 22.9.75.				
7.8.75	AA informs RA that AHA decided to sell property.		15.8.75	Hospital Administrator meets with NUPE for consultation.	NUPE waits to ensure staff are not placed in another hospital which might close.
			19.8.75	Area Personnel Officer informs NUPE ICC decision taken and DMT will now implement.	

171

Diary of Events—Invalid and Crippled Children's Hospital Closure (ICC)—*continued*

Date	Action by Authority	Reason	Date	Local Responses	Reason
16.9.75	AHA decides 10.10.75 new closure date.		22.8.75	DA informs NUPE that closure postponed to October.	
			1.9.75	NUPE requests more information.	
			30.9.75	NUPE recommends AHA reconsider closure.	Formal consultation only a "token gesture". Decision should be taken in a wider context of district needs.
9.10.75	AHA endorses decision to close after review of NUPE objections.				
10.10.75	AA informs NUPE and assures of consultation over redeployment of staff.		5.12.75	Chief Executive, Newham suggests ICC as hospital for mentally handicapped.	Lack of facilities in borough.
6.1.76	DMT decision to await commissioned report on need for accommodation for mentally handicapped, ICC to close on 27.2.76.				
27.2.76	ICC CLOSES, TO BE DEMOLISHED BY END OF SEPTEMBER 1977.				

Discussion

Closure as Part of an Overall Strategy

1. Neither of these closures was a singular event: they took place as part of an overall plan. In the case of Poplar, the Regional Hospital Board (RHB) was reviewing hospital services in East London, which included the up-grading of accident and emergency facilities at St Andrew's. The Ministry of Health and later the Department of Health and Social Security were concerned to reduce the over-provision of beds within the RHB which was thus attempting to comply with national policy in considering hospital closures. In the case of Invalid and Crippled Children, a similar review was linked to a plan for overall health service provision in the AHA. The area as a whole had an over-provision of beds housed in buildings which were both small and old. Changes in medical practice required larger hospitals where a full range of medical specialties and back-up facilities could be provided. Modernisation of existing buildings, even if economic, would not have met medical standards.

2. There are some important differences in these two cases. For Poplar, closure threatened the loss of a service by a community geographically separated from access to other services. Because the hospital was used for primary care, evidence that the hospital's facilities were not needed was insufficient to satisfy local opinion. Although consultation with other statutory bodies revealed doubts about the degree to which the local area was receiving poor services (see Poplar entries dated 10.11.72 and 30.11.72) the local community certainly thought it was, and this was the basis of its opposition—no closure until alternative facilities were available. The indefinite retention of Poplar was not argued. This view was put in early discussions with the Thames Group Hospital Management Committee (HMC) Chairman, who conveyed his agreement with it to the RHB Secretary (see Poplar entry dated 26.4.72). The RHB, however, was not authorised to take such an overall view of health needs, and the absence of such authority became an argument for delaying the decision until after reorganisation. The importance of relating the total health needs of a population to overall health service provision was emphasised by the Minister of State for Health, who would not approve the emergency suspension of acute services at Poplar without receiving an overall plan for health services development from the new AHA (see Poplar entry dated 13.6.74).

3. For ICC, when closure procedures were started in December 1974, the first attempt at an area strategy for all health services was publicly known through the submission of information to the DHSS in August 1974 to achieve ministerial approval for the cut-back of services in Poplar (see Poplar entry 5.8.74).

Comment

4. The purpose of a strategy, from the viewpoint of the community, is that it creates some degree of assurance that actions are not piecemeal, but part of a plan to ensure adequate health service provision for the community. By being able to demonstrate that closure is part of a process of working towards redeployment of resources to provide a service which is better aligned

to recognised needs, the community may feel that it is not losing but gaining. Poplar shows one of the major justifications of reorganisation, the unification of different branches of the health service to provide and ensure a comprehensive policy.

Importance of External Events

5. Both hospital closures illustrate the extent to which external factors add pressure and influence the timing of consultation and decision making. One of the major external events in the Poplar closure was the imminence of reorganisation itself which was seen by the local community and the HMC Chairman as a reason for delaying a decision; a new Area Health Authority would have the means to consider the overall provision of health service needs rather than hospital services alone in the district. As early as April 1972 the local community cited reorganisation as one of their reasons for opposing closure (see Poplar entry 26.4.72). A local vicar protested on the same grounds in July of that year and in August the HMC Chairman suggested that the decision should be delayed until the new AHA took office. But the new authorities were not brought into existence until July 1973; before this, there was no AHA to which to refer the decision. When it met in September 1973, the RHA was for the first time able to consider referral of closure to the AHA, as one of its options. and this in fact was its decision.

6. A second important event was the consultants' withdrawal of acceptance of clinical responsibility for patients at Poplar in December 1973. This action was taken after the SAMO had consulted the HMC Group Medical Advisory Committee. This action, in effect, forced the RHB to act, temporarily closing down the acute services, and adding to the anger of the local community, who felt that they were being betrayed after promises of no decision without full consultation. (See Poplar entries, January 1974—Local Responses). The unions objected and, as reported in the *Evening Standard*, local MPs challenged the decision on the grounds that it might be illegal. To the local community, it seemed that the RHB should be in a position to insist that services be maintained. The Secretary of State in January, in fact, had asked the RHB to consider appointing two additional junior medical staff and to restore services until a decision had been taken. But the RHB had refused; even with two additional junior staff, it claimed, the basic problems were so unsurmountable that a safe service could not be provided.

7. Shortly after the consultants' withdrawal of clinics, the General Medical Council (GMC) withdrew recognition of Poplar hospital for training purposes. Five months earlier, the General Nursing Council (GNC) had withdrawn recognition for nursing training. The withdrawal of these recognitions meant that junior doctors and student enrolled nurses could no longer gain experience counting towards qualifications. So the hospital became more dependent on agency nurses and locum appointments. Continuity of care was threatened and staffing costs increased. The effect of these external events was not to delay, but to give weight to the arguments for closing Poplar.

8. The local MPs constituted another external force. Right from the outset they were formative in initiating and continuing a dialogue with the

RHB over proposals and decisions concerning Poplar. The fact that a Labour government was returned in February 1974 facilitated the influence they had, for it allowed three Labour MPs from traditional Labour areas to plead a special case with a Labour Secretary of State. This point emphasises the highly political nature of the question of Poplar closure.

9. External events did not affect the consultation and decision making procedures for the closure of ICC. But it may be assumed that the action of the consultant in transferring his outpatient sessions from ICC to another hospital made it necessary for the authority to act sooner rather than later. Although it is evident that ICC was already a candidate for closure, the particular timing of the start of consultation procedures seemed to come externally. (See entry dated 10.10.74).

Comment

10. Proposals to close both hospitals were clearly decisions by management. But management may not always have control over events concerning closure. External intervention was not a major factor in ICC but in Poplar external events certainly impinged on the conduct of consultation procedures. Decisions of December 1973 to suspend acute services were interpreted by those statutorily to be consulted as management promising one thing but doing another. Poplar was being closed "by the back door", as it were. The suspension of services at that particular time had two effects on consultation. First, it caused a delay in reaching a decision, since there was now the need to seek approval of the Secretary of State to temporary suspension of services. The new AHA when it came into being in April 1974, rather than being able to take a fresh look at the question of closure, was in the midst of negotiations with the DHSS about the suspension. Second, the sudden suspension of services caused community and other statutory bodies to think that decisions were being made without regard for their right to be consulted, and they had grounds for complaint. But the actions of the clinicians while within their sphere of competence to pass judgement, left management with no option but to legitimate decisions effectively taken elsewhere by others. The outsider view that management makes the decisions may not always reflect the reality of the situation. Other events (clinicians' later withdrawal of services and withdrawal of recognition by the GNC and GMC) related to the provision of a safe service. It is difficult to quarrel with the reason. But the timing of the action leading to suspension of acute services (in mid-winter of 1973) hardly seemed the most judicious time to some. It was this which aroused the local community's wrath and led to further delays in closure proceedings. The case of Poplar closure illustrates clearly how a situation may change *during* the consultation process, and the issue upon which consultation was based lies in the past.

Downward Spiral

11. At the beginning of the discussions on the closure of Poplar, informal consultation was taken by some hospital staff to mean closure (see entry 17.12.71). Nursing staff, it was said, thought that the hospital was closing in a year's time (i.e. five years earlier than it did). Rumour though this may have been, it had the effect of demoralising staff. Reactions to this rumour aroused a great deal of publicity, which with petitions, letters and press releases by

local groups, continued for the next three years and in fact right up until the hospital actually closed. Because of the adverse publicity, administrators found it difficult to get consultants and GPs to refer patients to Poplar. The lack of use of the hospital demoralised staff further and a staffing crisis developed which necessitated the temporary closing of a ward. (See Poplar entry 16.8.74). To the local community, it seemed as if the authority was attempting to run down services to prove that Poplar could not be maintained as a viable institution.

12. The shorter time needed for consideration of the proposed closure in ICC and the absence of opposition meant that it was not subject to the same pressures as Poplar. ICC also benefited, of course, from the lessons of Poplar. Management took deliberate steps to ensure that informal consultation was not publicised or proposals leaked to the press. It also operated a policy of personally informing lay groups of decisions taken wherever possible. Discouragement of discussion on alternative uses of the hospital while implementing decisions was also a deliberate policy on the explicit grounds that such discussions would only raise false hopes and thereby possibly damage staff morale.

Comment

13. Hospital morale is fragile; if staffs are not kept busy and the hospital sufficiently used, morale declines and the institution may find staff and referrals going elsewhere as the process of demoralisation feeds itself. When this occurs, it may be beyond the ability of management to reverse the process even when such a reversal is desired.

Dissent within an Authority

14. It is clear that in the case of Poplar, the HMC chairman was swayed by local arguments against immediate closure (see Poplar entry dated 26.4.72) and conveyed this to the RHB secretary. The necessity to issue a public statement and to seek permission to initiate formal consultations was delayed by four months until agreement could be reached on the grounds for closure. It meant that the RHB could not move as swiftly or decisively as it might have wanted; the delay in requesting permission of the DHSS for formal consultation gave a greater strength to the argument of postponing a decision until after reorganisation rather than allowing a "lame duck" authority to decide. The length of time these decisions took was seen to contribute to the decline in morale leading to staffing crises. In ICC, the Authority was able to approach consultation with unanimity of agreement on the need for closure.

Comment

15. There is an obvious advantage of an Authority being able to speak with one voice. When parts of the Authority adopt different stances on an issue, the consultation procedures become more difficult to operate and create uncertainty among those who are affected by proposed closure.

The Functions of Consultation

16. In both cases, the proposal to close a hospital was accepted. Because closure is an irreversible process, management would not have entered into

consultation without having been clear of its grounds. In its simplest meaning, consultation is seeking advice of others. But it may serve other purposes without being thought mere "window dressing".

(i) *consultation as participation and protection of group interests*: in both instances consultation gave professional and community groups, local councils and MPs an opportunity to express the views of their constituents. In Poplar, the wider health concerns of the community, local council and MPs caused delay in seeking authority for formal consultation from the DHSS and eventually led to these being taken into account in the final outcome. The opposition of the unions, staff, local councils, CHCs and MPs to the AHA proposal to close (see Poplar entry dated February 1975) at least ensured that these interests would be reconsidered at a higher level. In ICC the CHC was involved not only in commenting on the proposal to close but in visiting patients after transfer to another hospital, to make certain they were satisfied with the new provision;

(ii) *consultation as information*: for groups which are not necessarily part of the management structure, consultation provides an occasion when they may be kept informed of the thinking of the authority, both of immediate action and long-term plans. It provides information to those who may have a particular focus on the health service, perhaps helping to widen their views. Likewise, consultation can bring to the Authority information about the views of those outside the system, a point which was a key factor in Poplar;

(iii) *consultation as negotiation*: in Poplar, the actions of the Save Poplar Campaign and the involvement of the MPs on its behalf, took on a form of negotiation because of the strength of local feeling. Save Poplar Campaign had two meetings with the Secretary of State and a visit by the Minister of State for Health to the hospital. The Campaign refused to be pacified by anything which did not take its view of local needs into account, and without local opposition to closure the MPs would have had no basis for their own interest in Poplar. At the time when the decision by the Secretary of State was announced, the chairman of Save Poplar Campaign could publicly claim that the campaign had secured an early start to the new district hospital, a new health clinic for the area and considerable publicity concerning the area's deprivations (see Poplar entry dated 2.8.75);

(iv) *consultation as keeping a dialogue going*: the consulation of NUPE in ICC after the AHA had made its decision (see ICC entries starting 17.6.75) may be seen as a means of maintaining working relations with a body with whom the management system will be involved in the future. Its impact on the outcome was negligible but it allowed management to keep faith with the union;

(v) *consultation as a form of scrutiny*: by submitting a proposal for closure to other bodies, the judgement of the AHA becomes open to scrutiny; those who are consulted may go over the same reasoning process to ensure that sufficient weight has been given to factors important to them. Consultation acts as part of a review system; both instances of closure illustrate this function. The role of the

CHC is particularly important because it is the only body whose disagreement with an AHA decision on closure forces the decision making to another level for further independent scrutiny.

Differences in Perception of "Consultation"

17. As consultation serves different purposes, confusion may arise over what consultation may mean in a given circumstance:

    (i) the Authority must seek the views of others, but it need not accept them. One of the most difficult things for those giving advice to accept is that their advice may not be taken. Consultation then comes to be seen as a charade. The numerous meetings held by the RHB and AHA with the Save Poplar Campaign illustrate a willingness to provide opportunities when views may be expressed, although the authorities never actually altered their view on the necessity for closure. The same may be said for consultation with NUPE in ICC. Consultation is seen as negotiation;

    (ii) consultation may appear as a decision already taken. The early entries for Poplar show the extent to which "informal" consultation by the chairman of the HMC was interpreted by those consulted as meaning a decision had already been taken, and led to rumours of imminent closure. Consultation is perceived as giving information.

Consultation as part of Decision Making

18. The functions of consultation show ambiguity of the concept and the varied expectations which those being consulted bring to the process of consultation. Clearly consultation must imply a willingness to listen to the views of others; the question is how much more than this it entails.

19. The Field Interview Survey examined in general terms the extent to which CHC members feel frustrated in their role and uncertain of the degree of authority they have. It was evident that a number of CHC members thought CHCs ought to have a larger role in decision making, because their advice went unheeded or they were consulted too late. These attitudes were also manifest in interviews concerning hospital closures, and reflect different assumptions about decision making held by management and CHCs.

20. When an Authority consults other bodies, it has in effect made up its mind, at least tentatively, on an issue. Because closure procedure is complex, based on a detailed review of provision and needs, there is already a commitment to closure at the time an Authority recommends closure procedures be initiated. The Authority is still open to influence to the extent that it can be shown that the "decision" is unacceptable, based on inadequate information or misunderstandings. CHC members, however, see this as a "decision" already made, and the potential for influencing the "decision" as minimal. Consultation, from their viewpoint, ought to be based on two equally viable alternatives, to close a hospital, or not to close a hospital. It is difficult for CHCs to feel they have a real role in consultation if the decision seems to have been taken well in the past. CHCs thus think they should be given more information and consulted earlier in the decision making process.

21. Although CHCs are the only bodies which may require a decision on closure to be taken by the Secretary of State for Health and Social Security, if they disagree, they are not the only bodies with power. Poplar showed the extent to which other statutory bodies associated with health service provision or health service providers could also wield influence on decisions, especially in terms of maintaining acceptable standards. The actions of clinicians in exercising judgement about acceptable standards in December 1973 showed how the power of health service providers may force a change in consultative procedures. Likewise the agreement of the three medical advisory committees in February 1975 to closure was a support for the AHA's decisions. The withdrawal of recognition by the GMC and GNC may be seen as further evidence of the importance attached to professional judgements of standards. Consultation procedures involved judgements by local practitioners, but the stand taken by the GMC and GNC are instances of such judgements being exercised by national professional bodies and formed an additional constraint on the scope of decision making by management.

Consultation as a Source of Delay

22. It was frequently expressed during the Field Interview Survey that consultation was a serious source of delay in decision making, so it is important to examine in these two cases the extent to which delay may be attributed to consultation. The chart which follows gives a diary of consultative events.

Chart of Consultative Events

ICC

9.1.75	– AHA recommends to RHA that informal consultations begin.
21.1.75	– RHA agrees.
2.2.75	– District Administrator completes informal consultations.
11.2.75	– Area Administrator seeks DHSS approval for formal consultations.
27.2.75	– DHSS agrees.
21.3.75	– Formal consultations begin.
8.5.75	– AHA decision to close.
16.6.75	– NUPE objects to not having been consulted.
30.9.75	– NUPE submits its views on "proposed" closure.
9.10.75	– AHA endorses original decision to close.

ICC was first scheduled to close on 22.9.75 and finally closed on 27.2.76.

Poplar

Feb 72	– Chairman Thames Group HMC undertakes informal consultation.
Aug 72	– RHB ready to issue public statement and to seek DHSS approval for formal consultation but HMC Chairman objects because of local views.
Sept–Dec 72	– RHB Secretary meets with statutory bodies and local campaigners to determine the basis of claims by the local community of poor primary care services and the need for Poplar to be retained.
5.1.73	– RHB seeks DHSS approval for formal consultations.
6.4.73	– Secretary of State agrees to formal consultation. Formal consultation starts almost immediately, and is scheduled to end by 31 May, extended to 30 June.

19.9.73   – RHB decides to refer decision to new AHA.

19.2.74   – Shadow AHA decides to keep Poplar open until 31.3.75 and to review services in the area.

15.11.74 – AHA recommends closure. Formal consultations begin immediately, are scheduled to end by 16 December, extended to 31 January.

Feb 75   – AHA recommends closure to the Secretary of State.

31.7.75   – Minister of Health announces closure.

The hospital closed on 18.11.75.

23. Consultations may be said to have caused a delay of four months in ICC. Consultation with the local council over the use of ICC as a centre for the mentally handicapped (see entry 5.12.75) may have delayed the date of closure but in no way affected the decision to close. Formal consultations had ended by the time the enquiry was made. The DA referred the request to the area who rejected the idea on the grounds that structural alterations were necessary and the high revenue cost would be hard to meet. The area sought another opinion in the form of a clinician's review. Waiting for this report caused a slight delay in the date of closure. Although the clinician decided the hospital *was* viable with structural alterations, the DMT felt that they could meet neither the capital cost necessary nor the revenue costs of running the hospital.

24. For Poplar, there was also a four month delay, at the end of 1972; but a much longer delay was caused by reorganisation and the time needed by the new authority to establish its own priorities and review services. If reorganisation had not occurred, it is possible that the RHB on 19.9.73 would have decided on closure rather than this decision being made by the AHA in November 1974. Consultations then took a further two months, and the DHSS took five months to reach a decision. In theory, the decision might have been reached 18 months sooner.

25. It may be suggested that the time-consuming aspects of consultation are due to two factors. The first is found in the process of consultation itself; many of the groups to be consulted meet monthly at most, and some less frequency. A six week consultation period may be insufficient for these groups to become informed, consider issues and arrive at a submission to an Authority. For CHCs, which may be keen to gather additional views and information, this time period may be unrealistic, and contribute towards the attitude that consultation is just "window dressing". In Poplar, the consultation period was extended twice, after the RHB and AHA received complaints by local councils and hospital staff that insufficient time had been allowed.

26. Second, the Authority itself must absorb the views submitted to it by groups consulted; the more groups consulted and the greater the divergence of views, the more time this will take. Consultation generates information for an Authority and time must be allowed for it to be handled. For example, in Poplar the RHB needed four months to consider the relation of the claim of poor primary care services to the case for hospital closure (see Poplar entry dated 8.7.72). The DHSS took four months to process the information supporting the RHB case for initiating formal consultations and undertake investigations of its own (see Poplar entries dated 5.1.73, 5.2.73 and 6.4.73).

The first set of formal consultations on Poplar ended on 30 June 1973, but the RHB did not reach a decision until 19 September. Again, the AHA referred the decision for Poplar closure to the DHSS in February 1975 and the decision to close was announced on 31 July. Consideration of the results of consultation may take longer than the consultation process itself.

27. To say that consultation delays is to imply that decisions could have been made without consultation and that nothing was gained. Yet modification to a decision may not be the sole criterion for judging the importance of consultation. In ICC, a working relationship was maintained by allowing extra time for consultation. In Poplar, it allowed a decision to be made by a new authority able to consider a wider range of needs, so that the decision was thought to be more justifiable and in this sense may be said to have had an impact on the decision process. It also allowed time for strongly held views to be expressed and for a community to draw attention to its deprivations. In addition, it permitted people to adjust to a decision which initially was unacceptable. In both cases, consultation, particularly with community representatives, allowed the public to have a voice in deliberations.

Economic Costs

28. Savings which accrue from closures in relation to rising and changing costs are a complex issue. Estimates vary the longer the decision to close is delayed. Budgets are adjusted from year to year and if the hospital runs down, for whatever reason, while closure is under discussion, the amount saved in the end may be less than originally estimated. In the case of Poplar, for instance, the initial estimate of savings when the closure was first discussed in 1972/73 was approximately £500,000. The running costs in that year were £534,000; if there had been no change in the service the estimated running cost in 1975/76 (the year it closed) would have been of the order of £1,220,000. In fact in the year prior to closure the running costs were £410,000 and in the year of closure £400,000. The actual savings on Poplar Hospital which the Authority achieved were £370,000.

29. What happened to these savings? In the year following closure £250,000 was absorbed by RAWP, and overtime payments to junior doctors. The opening of two additional wards to absorb Poplar patients took the balance. If the closure had not been achieved it would have been necessary to reduce existing services to prevent over-spending.

30. In closing hospitals, there is often a period when some costs go on: rates and security costs are the main categories until the actual buildings are disposed of. These factors may eat into estimated savings.

31. The financial savings of approximately £30,000 achieved by the closure of the Invalid and Crippled Children's Hospital were on the General Services. Direct patient care costs, which included medical and nursing staff, were transferred with the patients to other hospitals in the district. The total running cost in the year prior to closure was £88,000.

32. Long-term savings may include capital from the sale of the site but in the short term, capital savings will not provide an argument for improving the quality of the service elsewhere in the district. No capital savings from

either closure has yet accrued to the district. Poplar which was valued at £50,000 was made over to the Supplementary Benefits Commission but the sale has been held up through lack of planning permission for use as a shelter for destitutes. ICC was sold to the GLC for £35,000 but again the transaction has been held up because planning permission has not been granted. The building has been demolished because the district has been concerned about the possible legal claim parents could make if children were injured while playing on the site.

Comment

33. The savings from closures are both real and notional. They are calculated at a particular point in time, yet accrue at another, and many factors may intervene to change estimates. The longer decisions take to be made, the greater the likelihood that the notion of savings will alter, usually downward because of the rundown of the hospital.

34. The concept of savings as a reason for closure is an attractively simple one; if less is spent on one service, then more ought to be available for others. But it may not always work out this way. If a district is under pressure to reduce costs, then savings on a closure may go towards preventing other services from being reduced; the savings are negative in that the financial situation is prevented from becoming as bad as it might have without the closure, rather than positive, actually having more resources to spend on services. If it is the policy not to have redundancies, the extent of savings is bound to be comparatively small as the major revenue cost is staffing.

35. What has not been costed are the costs of consultation itself—the amount of staff time devoted to liaising with outside bodies. In a case like Poplar, the additional meetings and correspondence might have come to a noticeable amount. For both closures, the time taken in interviewing and settling staff in new positions was considerable.

Concluding Comments

36. The hospital closures discussed above illustrate the tensions between participation and planning. Reorganisation attempted to bring both these concepts into play but these need not function together unanimously.

37. A planning system is based on a means–ends argument; decision making is to be rational. Participation, however, brings in those who do not see themselves as managers, responsible for the overall development of services. The "parochial" views of those being consulted may give different weightings to particular factors than would management and thus lead to different decisions. Participation may temper rationality, depending on circumstances and strength of opposition. Professional groups may, through local practitioner views of acceptable standards or through their national bodies, create constraints on management, limiting alternatives available. CHCs, because their opposition forces the decision on closure to the Secretary of State for Health and Social Services, are also able to insist that the rationality of a decision be scrutinised by those who up to that time have not been party to the decision. In the case of Poplar, while the AHA did not support the opposition, it may well have benefited from it in so far as opposition was

182

able through political channels to gain recognition for the general deprivation of the area and secure additional resources sooner than scheduled.

38. Consultation is often thought to be a source of delay, and this may at times be true. But it is a separate issue whether delay may not be beneficial and a better decision arrived at, in terms of acceptability. That consultation is extensive at least illustrates the importance attached to acceptability of decisions and the need at least to listen to the views of those affected by decisions. When consultation does delay decisions, for hospital closures this will have a cost attached to it. Anticipated savings may differ from real savings, and this may be one means of valuing the cost of acceptability.

Members' Committees of Inquiry in an Area Health Authority

by Barbara Goodwin

I Introduction

Background

1. This case study took place in a two district area in which the authority had set up fourteen internal committees of inquiry between June 1975 and June 1977. Seven of these were engendered automatically, as the second stage of the area's complaints process; seven were set up to investigate "unusual incidents". These were, essentially, inquiries into organisational errors, not into medical competence.

2. While a members' committee of inquiry is not itself a decision making, but a monitoring, process, it often constitutes a critical investigation of decisions taken at the operational level, and its report recommends decisions on policy and procedure, and so ultimately affects staff at the operational level. The reports are, in fact, an indirect method of making decisions of greater or less importance, which differs from routine decision making in that it is set in motion by some apparent deficiency in the service. The frequent use of such committees can thus be seen as a management device which strengthens the authority's control over the service.

3. Analysis of the inquiry process therefore gives a valuable insight into problems of structure, management, authority and responsibility in the re-organised NHS. The examination here of a number of committees of inquiry reveals the interplay of various parts of the organisation, in particular, the interrelations of:

   (a) the area health authority, area management team and district management teams;
   (b) the sector administrator, his district administrator and his hospital staff;
   (c) medical staff and administrators; and
   (d) lay members and professional staff.

In this area there is generally admitted to be some friction between area and district teams. In the absence of a regional tier, the DMT is con-stitutionally subordinate and responsible to the AMT, and has no direct contact with the AHA. In this particular area, too, there has been no delegation of specific powers to either AMT or DMT, and some role confusion has resulted. The case study reveals some of the consequent problems through an examination of the processes and attitudes generated by the inquiries. Also under scrutiny are the usefulness and the side effects of members' inquiries when used to monitor and manage the service as well as to investigate complaints.

Method

4. The approach adopted here has been to describe and analyse four selected inquiry processes, using records and interviews with those involved, in terms of the organisational issues revealed in each case (Section II). The more general comments made in the interviews on the role and repercussions of the committees of inquiry are presented thematically (Section III). The data are then analysed with respect to the internal logic of the inquiry process, the criticisms made by the inquiry and the organisational issues with which

187

the whole of this report is concerned (Section IV). Finally, the wider structural and policy issues manifested through this specific device are discussed and evaluated (Section V).

5. The study began with a thorough examination of four of the committees' reports (which are confidential), the surrounding correspondence, and the relevant minutes of the Authority and the teams involved. Interpretation of these documents provided the themes for the interviews, and the interviews themselves clarified the analysis further. Sixteen interviews were conducted. The interviewees' accounts and the resulting interpretations were then cross-checked and evaluated by reference to other material. Attendance at two meetings in the Area on management problems and the administrative structure provided further confirmation of the analysis.

6. The study focused on the inquiry *process* and its repercussions rather than the *content* of any inquiry. However, the content of the inquiry is of interest where the evidence taken by the committee, its discussions and its reports contain important revelations about, and comments on, the working of the National Health Service. "Process" is taken here to include the problems and debate which precede the inquiry, its repercussions at the time and afterwards, and the observations of those involved in or affected by the inquiry. Although only four inquiries were studied in depth, material from other inquiries has also been used to supplement these. The complaints inquiries do not differ substantially from unusual incident inquiries, except in origin, and this study does not distinguish between them, except in arguing that the incidence of the latter *is* indicative of the Authority's will to manage and monitor actively.

Committees of Inquiry

7. Soon after reorganisation, the area administrator devised a complaints procedure in line with the Davies Committee Report, which the authority adopted. Inquiries into complaints are automatically set up if the preliminary investigation, usually by district officers, fails to satisfy the complainant. This prevents unsatisfied complainants from having to go through a series of appeals to higher officers, but might, potentially, result in dissatisfied complainants bringing relatively minor matters to the members. Complaints of a very serious nature may be referred direct to area by the district administrator, or may be taken up by the authority because, for example, an MP has taken up the complaint. Only a tiny proportion of complaints (seven in two years) reaches this stage which suggests that officers deal satisfactorily with the vast majority. Only one complainant has subsequently gone to the Health Service Commissioner. Other matters for inquiry are generally referred to the AHA by the AMT, but members sometimes directly instigate inquiries into "unusual incidents", a term which has included suicides, union complaints and sexual allegations against nurses. There have also been a number of inquiries into financial matters, but since these are statutory, and so not a matter of choice for the authority, they have not been dealt with in this study. The decision to hold an unusual incident inquiry is generally taken by the chairman after consultation with the area officers, and endorsed at the AHA meetings. Between two and four members are nominated by the

chairman to constitute the inquiry, one designated chairman, and area officers are invited to nominate representatives to attend, as is the DMT who act as advisers. The area assistant general administrator organises the inquiry and acts as secretary, but the work of arranging a location and calling staff to interview is done by the DA. After one, or several, sessions in which evidence is taken and analytical discussions take place, the committee's report is presented to the AHA (with the AMT in attendance) which to date has invariably accepted its findings, sometimes adding comments. The report is distributed to the DMT which is required to implement its recommendations. Portions of the report may be disclosed to other staff for comment or implementation.

8. The area set up 14 inquiries as follows:
   3 in 1975 (June onwards)
   9 in 1976
   2 in 1977.

9. For the purpose of comparison, some figures on the use of such inquiries by comparable authorities are relevant:

Number of Inquiries Since Reorganisation	Number of Authorities
8 (2 complaints, 6 incidents)	1
4 (4 incidents)	1
3 (3 incidents; 2 incidents and 1 complaint)	2
2 (1 incident, 1 complaint in both cases)	2
1	–
–	1

("Incidents" is used here to include managerial and disciplinary matters as well as patient care matters.)

It appears prima facie that the area under study has made greater use of the inquiry format than other comparable areas, which may be significant, although, of course, it may simply have had more complaints and incidents. However, the definition of "unusual incident" is largely a matter of choice, and this authority has chosen to define it widely. It should be noted that a public inquiry into brutality at a psychiatric hospital just before reorganisation has made all the authorities in the country particularly cautious and vigilant in matters concerning psychiatric hospitals. One member of the AMT thought that interventionist management in the NHS dated from that event. Certainly, six out of seven of the unusual incident inquiries in this area were in psychiatric hospitals.

II Analysis of Four Committees of Inquiry

10. This section makes use of documentary evidence, and the additional information provided on particular cases by the interviews. The four inquiries were selected because each demonstrates points of particular interest; however, the interviews ranged over all the cases of which the interviewee had experience. Inquiries A and B took place in one district, C and D in the other.

189

11. This investigated the death of an 83 year old psychogeriatric patient who wandered off and was found drowned less than half a mile from the hospital 11 days later, after extensive searches. The DA submitted a routine report and documents on the event, but members thought it sufficiently unusual to investigate, being particularly concerned about search procedures, and security. Newspaper reports may have encouraged their involvement. This was the first inquiry in that district, which, unlike the other district, had not had a tradition of member inquiries in the time of the previous HMC administration, and the AHA's third inquiry, so procedures were still being created, and slightly uncertain. The inquiry was said, by the committee's secretary, to have been "an early one, very thorough and painful".

12. Although nursing staff were found to have acted properly, questioning revealed that the SA was not informed of Miss X's disappearance until the afternoon of the following day, and that his official notification did not reach the DA for another three days (although the DA had already been informed by a consultant and become involved in the organisation of the search). The DA issued a description to the press five days after the disappearance, and a large scale search with police and army personnel took place on and after the sixth day. The committee felt that an immediate notification of the administration (sector and district), and prompter action might have enabled a wide search to be instituted early enough to find Miss X before her death. In discussion it was said "The alertness did not come quick enough, high enough". The SA maintained that his lack of involvement was normal, missing patients being a nursing responsibility. One consultant said: "The responsibilities of doctors and consultants and various NOs and administrators are changing and the position is getting a bit blurred these days . . . it is not very sure how many people are supposed to 'carry the can' or what people have the authority to give orders". The report found "that the senior staff of the hospital were not involved at the crucial period". Recommendations on search organisation, co-ordination and the care of wandering patients were made, with an emphasis on written procedure.

13. No DMT representative was invited to attend the inquiry, although the DA was a witness. Subsequently the DMT was invited to comment on the draft report. It made 11 points, critical of the findings and conclusions, which, it was led to expect, would be considered alongside the report by the AHA, or incorporated. However, the committee felt that this would prejudice its impartiality, and the DMT's comments were not considered, but the DMT was asked to implement the recommendations. As a result of the DMT's and psychiatric division's protests against this treatment, a meeting took place three months later between their representatives and the reconvened committee to discuss their criticisms. These, in brief, criticised the committee's extension of its terms of reference and the consequent absence of some relevant witnesses, questioned the practicality or desirability of six of the recommendations and made two mitigating comments about the description of Miss X and the time scale of the search. From the record of the discussion, it is noticeable that the committee at no time explicitly withdrew any recommendation or conceded to the opinion of the local managers. Most of

its recommendations were in fact put into operation. An important organisational result was that the AHA agreed to a DMT representative attending future inquiries, with the right to join in discussion, though not, as it turned out, to question witnesses.

14. *One member* interviewed felt that the role of the SA was "diminished' by the revelations of the inquiry, partly because of the structure of the organisation. But the inquiry was conducted quickly and well, and was justified by what it revealed. *The SA* felt that the inquiry was unnecessary since wandering patients are common, and generally come to no harm. Two subsequent suicides had *not* been investigated. The inquiry had been a waste of time, revealing nothing that the hospital staff did not know, but it *had* given the hospital an incentive to formalise its unwritten search procedures, and the SA had been appointed search co-ordinator. *The DA* felt that the SA had been too *near* the situation to see the possible dangers and should have been informed more quickly. *At area* it was thought that the inquiry was valuable, revealing shortcomings in the organisation which were then eliminated. *The DMT* thought the recommendations impractical and useless others had already been under consideration by the DMT. Officers felt under criticism, especially those who were called as witnesses and questioned strictly. The DMT's subsequent pursuit of its right to comment had been a form of protest against this treatment (as Area perceived).

Interpretation

15. The "reduction to the ranks" of district officers in the inquiry process is significant, and their vigorous protests against exclusion from the process testify to the tensions between district and Area, and the unclarity of the district's role when the Authority intervenes in local matters. But the developmental nature of the institution is also evident, in that the DMT was able to establish a precedent of representation, albeit with difficulty. The vestigial role of the SA, at the end of a long administrative chain, and deprived of many "hospital secretary" duties by functional management, is also manifest.

Inquiry B

16. This concerned the death of a 16 year old voluntary patient, Miss Y, in a psychiatric hospital, who apparently committed suicide by throwing herself over the bannisters, and died a few hours later in the local general hospital. The Coroner recorded an open verdict. The local press reported this and the AHA set up an "unusual incident" inquiry three weeks later, partly because of concern about emergency facilities at the general hospital. There was also the question of whether this disturbed patient had been under adequate supervision, and some Red Cross workers present at the time had complained about this.

17. The committee at first sat at the area offices, summoning witnesses, which created tension among the nursing staff; later sessions were held at the psychiatric hospital. The written evidence suggests that the process was inquisitorial in tone, and that nursing staff in particular felt they were being criticised: the questioners certainly seemed anxious to find out details of hospital routine and infringements of the rule book irrespective of their

191

relevance. For example, the charge nurse who followed Miss Y to the stairs was asked if it was customary to leave the ward without informing another nurse. (The latter commented on the questioning to his DNO "The effect on me is to make me operate defensively".) A senior nurse in the emergency department who gave Miss X an X-ray when she arrived because no doctor was available was closely questioned about this assumption of a medical role. The report concluded that a senior professional member of staff who had earlier been informed of Miss Y's disturbed state had not conveyed "a sense of urgency" to other staff; that medical staffing levels in the general hospital emergency department were inadequate; that ward arrangements gave rise to nursing problems in the psychiatric hospital, and that other minor defects were apparent in this incident.

18. The inquiry took place in the same district as Inquiry A, three months after that committee had reported, and the relevant correspondence indicates increased disenchantment with the process among district officers. The precedent of attendance by a DMT representative had, by then, been established and the DA sat as an observer. Information was slow in reaching district through functional channels: one officer wrote to his area counterpart "I have heard it rumoured that a committee of inquiry has been set up to look into this incident. I would be grateful if you could let me know if this is the case". The DA was not informed of one of the committee's meetings, and the DNO found that his junior staff, for various organisational reasons, were supplied with copies of the report before he was. Later, the DA, replying to area's instruction to "implement the report as required", said that he had done so and added caustically concerning paragraph 7(b), an *area* responsibility, "Will you please confirm that action has been taken to implement this recommendation?"

Interpretation
19. As the SA said, Inquiry B "has left a 'nasty taste' in the mouth of every member of staff involved, and even now the reasoning behind the conclusion of the committee of inquiry is hard to understand". Inquiry B confirmed the hostility of district officers to an inquiry process in which they are inadequately informed and consulted, and relieved of all authority, yet retain the responsibility for arrangements and for implementation of the committee's recommendations. The memoranda and the interviews bear witness to this attitude, and the DMT minute of its discussion on the report, after pointing out that the team had frequently told the area of the need for better staffing in the emergency department, concludes "The team was also of the opinion that there was nothing in the Report of the Committee of Inquiry which had not been commented on repeatedly at district level and the views and conclusions of the Committee of Inquiry could have been obtained from district officers without the need for a Committee of Inquiry". A second aspect of the case is the bad effect on the morale of the nurses concerned. Thirdly, the case resulted in a protracted correspondence from the senior staff member who felt himself impugned in such a way that he could not vindicate himself, and sought assurances on the confidentiality of the report first from the district, then from area, which they could not give. He subsequently met members of the committee with his Professional Executive Committee and the wording of the report was amended very slightly. He twice resigned over

the matter, and was with difficulty persuaded to withdraw his resignation. This indicates the extreme sensitivity of professional staff to these committees whenever the report inpugns their behaviour even indirectly.

Inquiry C

20. This case arose out of a complaint by the brother of Mr. Z, a 62 year old man who suffered brain damage after a fall, and was inarticulate, incontinent and sometimes violent; his case was not susceptible to treatment. After seven months in an acute bed in the general hospital he was moved to a geriatric hospital, and moved the same day to a psychiatric hospital for treatment since he had become violent. After treatment he was returned to the geriatric hospital, but discharged the next day (a Saturday), the explanation given being that his own GP could then arrange for his admission to a psychiatric hospital. His brother and 90 year old mother looked after him for five days with great difficulty and with no help from supporting services before they could get him re-admitted to a psychiatric hospital. The brother complained in the strongest terms that both hospitals had been negligent in their treatment of Mr. Z.

21. The DA investigated this complaint in the normal way but could achieve little because no consultant would accept responsibility for Mr. Z, who fell into the "young chronic sick" category for which the area, like most areas, had no special provision. In interview, the DA felt that "there was a problem in distinguishing truth from emotion here", and an area officer commented "It's almost a tradition that our medical staff are resistent to questioning". (This comment should also be taken in the wider context of medical opposition nationally to the implementation of the Davies proposals on complaints procedures.) In this case, the DA passed the matter on to the AHA and himself suggested an inquiry, since he was unable to answer the complainant and felt the complaint to be serious; the chairman was willing to set up a committee, especially as the local MP had taken up the case.

22. The committee held four sessions and experienced some taciturnity on the part of the consultants who attended, but they were co-operative, especially by comparison with their behaviour in Inquiry D which was contemporaneous. The complexity of the organisation, some problems of liaison with social services and GPs, and the gap in the service through which Mr. Z slipped were clearly revealed. The report unequivocally condemned the fact and circumstances of Mr. Z's discharge, although the complainant's charge of negligence was rebutted; it felt that communications between the two hospitals had broken down, and that the geriatric hospital staff had not made adequate attempts to deal with the patient. It suggested the instituting of case conferences on difficult patients, and the development of a system whereby other hospitals could consult psychiatrically qualified staff. No particular consultant was named or blamed in the report, which used the generic term "the staff". Mr. Z's brother received an apology, and declared himself satisfied.

23. The report stirred up a hornet's nest among staff. An SNO at the geriatric hospital requested the DNO to have the report amended since "my staff and myself are put into a wrongful light"; they had in fact devoted

attention to Mr. Z to the exclusion of other patients during his stay, and had attempted to get psychiatric advice. The DNO argued that where "staff" were used, it should be made clear whether this was medical or nursing staff. The AHA instructed the AMO to invite the Medical Executive Committee's comments on the report and recommendations, with the implication that the consultants must collectively shoulder the responsibility for Mr. Z. The resulting indignant correspondence was continuing four months later, when this case study was conducted. To summarise the medical reaction, it was said that:

(a) the psychiatric division "expressed surprise that it had been found necessary to initiate an inquiry into a relatively trivial matter of this kind at area level rather than locally";

(b) the MEC could not adequately comment on the report unless it could see the written evidence, which was refused;

(c) the problem arose because of lack of suitable accommodation for Mr. Z which was an area responsibility, and the report should have stated this (a point at variance with (a) which views the case as relatively trivial and not an area matter);

(d) the committee "failed to elicit correct information, and the report would appear to be inaccurate as a result";

(e) a clinical psychologist should have attended the inquiry;

(f) formal case conferences would be time-consuming and fruitless since "the difficulty is usually one of inadequate facilities".

24. Other general points were that such inquiries had "witch-hunting tendencies" and that, if they were really necessary, the authority should find ways of supporting and boosting morale of its staff, as well as making "what may be fair criticism".

Interpretation

25. The defensive reaction of consultants to criticism of even their administrative actions by a lay committee is evident, and the MEC's comments to the AMO make a number of criticisms of the inquiry process which will be evaluated in Section IV. Medical prerogative was threatened and nursing staff also felt under attack. The DCP attended the inquiry for the DMT and felt that the local managers' views were adequately represented and that the report fairly reflected the evidence given.

Inquiry D

26. The cause of this inquiry was the cancellation in May and June 1976 of a number of operating sessions at the main general hospital; one member heard rumours of patients prepared for operations and then sent away, and he asked officers to investigate informally. District officers could only obtain partial and inconsistent information, but when the committee was set up it was also hamstrung by the refusal of consultants to attend, and it finally disbanded without making a report. The preliminaries are as significant as the inquiry itself, and dates are given to indicate how protracted the process was.

27. The cause of cancellation at first appeared to be a lack of operating department assistants; the DPO had sent a paper on policy for ODAs in

November 1975, receiving no comment, and the DNO and DMT had for some time put the appointment of ODAs at the top of their staffing priorities. After being informed by the DMT of some cancellations in May, the ANO and AMO visited the hospital and reported (15 June), as a result of which the AMT approved the appointment of two temporary orderlies. Area felt "It was not at all clear that the DMT had had an opportunity to examine and cater for the problem within existing resources", and so asked the DMT for an estimate of the staff needed for a permanent solution. Meanwhile the cancellations were raised by a member, and the AA requested the DA for precise information on the numbers and reasons. The DA replied (12 July) that there had only been one cancellation because of a sick ODA, and otherwise there was "rationalisation" of theatre use, i.e. using one instead of two. Annual leave and hot weather had caused problems. Meanwhile the DNO sent the ANO a memo on the need for ODAs, suggesting that their lack had caused cancellations, and an area community physician visiting the theatres for other reasons, reported that the lack of a registrar had caused one cancellation. The AA then withdrew his promised report before the AHA meeting and asked the DA (6 August) to redraft it "setting out the agreed reasons . . . so that there can be no further dispute about the accuracy of facts".

28. The DA's investigations were "bedevilled" by annual leave, short memories and the fact that some operations were cancelled without notification of the medical records office. The theatre supervisor would not allow a junior administrator to investigate confidential records. Some operations were apparently cancelled because of lack of anaesthetists. The DA's final report (14 October) contained several unaccounted for cancellations, and he concluded "As indicated previously, I am having increasing difficulty in obtaining co-operation from staff of all disciplines as a result of our constant inquiries regarding these lists". The amended report to the AHA (which did not mention ODAs at all) did not satisfy the members, and the Vice-Chairman stated that he did not regard the information as accurate. A committee was set up, and called, for convenience, a committee of inquiry.

29. The committee met three time (8 December 1976, 6 Janunary 1977 and 2 February 1977). The SA, in evidence, said that he had not known of cancellations since this was not his responsibility; likewise, the theatre team would not have thought it relevant to report them to the DA. The committee chairman found the administration's lack of information from medical staff "significant". The committee could not establish when an operating list becomes a list, some lists being formalised, others not. One registrar appeared to have cancelled five operations in one day but could not recall the reason. The chairman felt that there were reasons beyond the lack of ODAs known to district but not acted on. The final meeting could not proceed because of the refusal of two consultants to attend: they had been formally advised in the standard letter of invitation to consult the Medical Defence Union which advised them not to attend, although they expressed willingness to meet a sub-committee not entitled "committee of inquiry". In discussion of this deadlock, the chairman said he was still "convinced" that patients had been prepared for the theatre then cancelled, although no such patient had been identified. The committee disbanded without issuing a report.

30. In interview, the repercussions of this contentious case were widely commented on. One member said that the sector staff had been too weak to tackle the consultants and get information; another, that the DA had been wrong in sending junior staff to look at confidential records, and had not seemed very concerned about the problem. The committee chairman considered it a failure, and said he was still mystified about the true cause of the consultants' cancellations. An area officer felt this case illustrated the "desultory" attitude of the DMT which produced no information in four months of investigation. Other area officers blamed the inactivity of the district and the use of juniors where the officers should have acted personally; medical staff had been given a solid stick with which to beat the administration on the whole question of inquiries. The authority had virtually been provoked into holding the inquiry by the AA's report which made manifest the shortcomings of the information provided by district. Another officer thought that area officers had used the inquiry in lieu of management.

31. *At district*, it was felt that the DPO's report on ODAs, sent to the APO in 1975, could have prevented the problem, but *area officers* pointed out that new regulations on ODAs had superceded the report, making it impossible to implement. The extremely heavy workload in the busy general hospital sector had prevented staff from telling even the SA of the problem, so district had not been able to monitor it. The DA's attempt to get information routinely had met a "brickwall"; although consultants' professional competence was not in question, their administrative competence was impugned, which irked them. Nevertheless, the DA felt that if officers who knew the staff personally had investigated, they could have suceeeded. District officers still feel that the lack of ODAs was the root cause, and that the problem arose from area's inability to appreciate urgency until a crisis occurs. This point was supported by the MEC Chairman who thought that the inquiry, instead of abandoning its task, should have reported on the inadequacy of theatre staffing and the shortage of ODAs, both area responsibilities; but, he added, no committee makes recommendations which show up the defects of its own policies.

Interpretation
32. Although the difficulties in this case seemed to stem from the autonomy of consultants and the confidentiality of medical records, it clearly shows the disjunction between the clinical, operational and administrative levels, and the apparent powerlessness of officers, and ultimately the AHA, to control and monitor clinical activities. The problem of the ODAs highlights the lack of co-operation between area and district. According to their minutes, both teams had discussed the shortage of qualified ODAs over a long period, yet without formally collaborating on the problem. The APO did not inform the DPO that the policy document had been superseded by events, so the DMT merely presumed that the AMT had been inactive, and accused them of allowing a crisis to develop. The AMT felt that the DMT had not informed them of the problem adequately, although minutes show that they had done so, months before the cancellations. The importance of the lack of ODAs remains in dispute, for the inquiry's questioning and discussions scarcely mentioned them, and concentrated on the behaviour of consultants and anaesthetists.

33. As a result of these confusions, area officers were impatient at the failure of district officers to investigate vigorously, and provide the necessary information; hospital staff were obstructive, jealous of their confidential records, and angry at being repeatedly questioned about events which seemed to them insignificant or imperceptible, since a "cancellation" may have meant that the operating list was never compiled. Doubt is cast on the district officers' confidence in local inquiries by the problems they encountered in investigating. The authority felt that details were being withheld at some level, and that district officers had not acted properly. Consultants resented the authority's inquisition. No-one escaped untarnished.

III The Interviews

34. Interviewees were asked what they considered the *benefits* and *uses* of inquiries to be. They suggested that the outstanding disadvantage of the process is the damage it does to relationships, for example, between officers and members, and administrative and hospital staff, by the *usurpation* of staff functions, *intrusion* into professional matters, and general *lowering of morale*. Since the process is time-consuming and expensive (in terms of professional staff's time) and benefits cannot be guaranteed, because of the open-ended nature of the process, there must be justifying reasons for inquiries which are independent of the hoped-for benefits. Here, perceptions of the *role of the AHA and members* are important. Questions about the *necessity* of inquiries elicited accounts of preceding *failures and shortcomings* which caused members to intervene. The possible alternative, an *investigation by local officers* was also discussed. Other questions centred on the process of the committee, its procedures, its composition and the secrecy of its findings. The *relation of district to area*, and that of *officers to lay members* before, during and after an inquiry were seen as central by those interviewed.

35. Sixteen interviews were conducted, with members of area, district and sector officers and medical staff, all of whom were involved in one or other of the inquiries reported earlier. Since the variation in perspectives experienced in the field survey was also manifest here, comments made in interviews are grouped according to respondents' position in the structure.

General Views on the Inquiry Process

Authority's Role

36. Most *officers* felt that inquiries were a legitimate and proper function for the members, who are perceived as the managers and ultimately responsible, but a number said that members were over-zealous in setting up inquiries, and wanted involvement at too low a level, perhaps fearing whitewashing of mistakes at district level. Several felt that inquiries were indicative of slight distrust of officers and a *district officer* felt that the impossibility for 17 members of overseeing such a large organisation led to lack of confidence in the staff they did not know, and an apprehension of things going wrong, which they "monitored" by use of inquiries. Another said "Their activism is fundamental to our difficulties". Members were thought to enjoy inquiries, which give them status. A *sector administrator* felt they should use visits to achieve these ends, and a *consultant* was adamant that it is *not* the authority's

task to be involved in daily management, and that inquiries do not make it knowledgeable about the NHS. *Members* mentioned the need for eternal vigilance and for justice to be seen to be done: the enlarged number of local authority nominees might, they suggested, have increased the desire for public justice. Because of officers' vested interests, the authority must not take for granted what it is told, or merely rubber stamp officers' views. Members' first duty is patient care: since they can ultimately be criticised, they must also be in control. Inquiries teach them more about the service than visits, and allay fears of whitewashing.

Benefits

37. *Members* felt that inquiries alerted them to deficiencies in the service, showed up gaps and allowed them to operate as catalysts for change: they are a monitoring process, though not an ideal one because of their limited focus. Although it is impossible to monitor where recommendations about hospital routine have been implemented, at least the staff have been alerted to problems, and communications may have been improved. "Negative monitoring" can take place if the mistake recurs. A *consultant* felt that no benefits emerge, since the unusual incident itself alerts the staff, and the committee's recommendations are often operationally impractical. *Area and district officers* suggested a wide range of benefits and functions which inquiries can perform. In general, they highlight anomalies and problems hitherto unknown to local managers, and so help to improve methods and procedures: the case of Miss X was often cited, which stimulated sector and district to formalise search procedures, and the case of Mr Z re-emphasised they "grey area" of the young chronic sick, a longstanding gap in the service. Recurrent mistakes are prevented. They "keep staff on their toes", monitor the sector level, and usefully scrutinise the activities of professionals. "Staff can help management through enquiries". An independent body is useful in complaint cases, and is a good public relations device; also inquiries educate members on operational matters and, importantly, on the difficulties of running the service. But the critical orientation of the committees was condemned, and *district officers* had further reservations, maintaining that monitoring should occur *before* problems arise, and that members' recommendations reveal their lack of knowledge and are often impractical. For example, the suggestion that all 'phone calls to the emergency department must be booked in (Case B) is taking nurses away from clinical duties.

Effects on Staff

38. *Members*, on the whole, felt inquiries a necessary evil, possibly traumatic but justified. One argued that morale would be *raised* if staff were vindicated. Most knew of effects on morale only by hearsay. *Several area officers* felt the bad effect on morale was exaggerated by district officers in particular, to discourage interference. The area treasurer felt that claims about morale were used to prevent proper inquiry procedures, and that members leaned too heavily towards the staff on this matter, but the ANO thought the effect so "shattering" that feedback and reassurance were needed. Nursing morale was generally agreed to be worse affected, especially in psychiatric hospitals where most inquiries have taken place. (An independent study carried out in the area's psychiatric hospitals in summer 1977 bore out the view that inquiries had an adverse effect on nursing staff.)

Nurses may feel under scrutiny and criticism for doing their normal work properly, and they see no necessity for special inquiries into deaths which may seem to result from exceptional causes but which are, in psychiatric hospitals, routine. The dangers of a defensive reaction were noted several times, with a possible deterioration of patient care. A number of people emphasised that a suicide or death will itself lower morale. *One district officer* said that inquiries made district staff more embittered and entrenched; they were in an invidious position if called as witnesses, and might be questioned by junior staff. It was frequently suggested that the inquisitorial attitude of some committee members undermined morale. *An SA* felt his staff were embittered and uneasy after an inquiry into a cash loss, which had also involved the police (although police involvement is mandatory in cash cases). The effect on morale was also held to depend on the frequency of inquiries: one hospital had *two* within a couple of months, both concerning suicides, and staff were very distressed.

Attitudes to Medical Staff

39. *A consultant* argued that medical staff have no confidence in the use of inquiries and were unhappy about the way they have been employed. He suspected that area would be happier "if it had not had to deal with doctors". *Both members and officers* mentioned the generalised discontent of consultants and felt that committees of inquiry were "a natural battleground", a chance to express anti-administration sentiments. The DCP felt that consultants' lack of co-operation was not deliberate recalcitrance, however. Others agreed that inquiries were "disastrous" for professionals, but that consultants were perhaps over-sensitive and over-protective in their reactions. *A member* felt that the difficulties in Inquiry D raised the general question of whether inquiries could ever work properly when delicate matters of confidentiality and medical prerogative were involved.

Faults

Composition

40. There was criticism of lay membership. *District officers* felt strongly that members' lack of knowledge of local circumstances, and of medical expertise, marred their conclusions. One, however, felt that the presence of lay people was healthy, and that the professional representatives were too protective of their colleagues. A DA pointed out that a "trained, qualified experienced health service professional administrator" had not attended any inquiry. All felt the attendance of a DMT member crucial, to supply local expertise. The suppressed premise was that such a representative would also support their interests. *Area officers* (who have always had representatives in attendance) thought the professions adequately represented; a medical officer who regularly attends thought his role was to inform the members on technical details and sometimes to "mellow" their recommedations as the committees tended to come unanimously to "commonsense" conclusions. The *members* felt no imbalance in the composition of committees; one pointed out that attending experts are not *members* of the committee. Another thought that, with three medical members in the authority, most committees would have a medical representative (analysis of the committees in a later

section does not support this view). *One consultant* felt that the committee should have a lay chairman, but professional membership—otherwise crucial expertise is lacking.

Procedure

41. There was *general agreement* about the imperfection of current procedures, which were thought to be too formal and legalistic, antagonising staff and causing them to give defensive answers, though formality was also seen as a safeguard in an area of public concern where a public inquiry might be established later. In some inquiries the "prosecuting attitude" of some members had caused concern, as had the apparently fault-finding intention of some of the committees. *Area and district officers* who had been witnesses felt strongly that junior staff ought in future to withdraw when senior officers are questioned. Other complaints were made of the careless treatment of staff, the failure to call relevant witnesses, and the domination of the committees by particular members. The preliminaries had sometimes been conducted tactlessly, and the standard invitation to bring a union official or friend, though proper, made people wary. There were numerous constructive suggestions: committees should be more informal, and avoid harrassing witnesses, perhaps by having a character profile before they appeared so that inapposite questions would not be put. They should explain to staff what their purposes are. *Two members argued* that a system of rotating panels of members could, beneficially, ensure a more varied membership of the committees, and prevent domination by particular people.

Other Points

42. The secrecy or limited circulation, of reports was criticised by *some area and district officers* who felt that such reports should be seen in draft by those concerned, or even be openly circulated within the service. This is connected with the need to give staff positive feedback and reassurance whenever possible, and would facilitate the implementation of reports. Yet there would be legal risks in opening the evidence to anyone but the members themselves, and publication of reports could harm the good name of a hospital, so should be avoided. The Secretary to the committees felt that they were most successful when looking into specific abuses or incidents, but with general terms of reference and *one member* felt it essential that members should extend their terms of reference as necessary, if something seemed to be wrong. This was a point about which both the DMT and MEC had complained and in one case the committee's secretary was criticised for bringing forward other matters for investigation. Most people thought the members fair and open-minded, but a district officer argued that there was a presupposition that a mistake *had* occurred if an inquiry was set up, so prejudging took place in that sense. *District officers* felt that there had been too many unnecessary inquiries, but area officers noticed that the number was decreasing. The use of inquiries had been commonplace in one of the old HMCs. The ANO felt that members had a sense of proportion as to what merited an inquiry—District officers disagreed, feeling many matters could be dealt with locally. Several people felt the unwieldy size of the organisation made inquiries inevitable. *One member* thought inquiries should be limited to avoid loss of impact and lowering of morale. Almost everyone interviewed remarked on the extreme sensitivity of all health authorities in the country

since a local public inquiry had made shattering revelations about a psychiatric hospital: this explained members' caution especially where incidents in psychiatric hospitals are concerned. Another point frequently made was that inquiries had a critical orientation, and the service lacked a counterbalancing praise mechanism.

Officers' Inquiries

43. *Members* favoured restricting the scope of these to routine complaints while they felt that they should hold inquiries on serious matters themselves. There is a risk of whitewashing because of vested interests in a local inquiry, and the members are better satisfied if they procure the information themselves. Also, justice is more public if the members investigate. Inqiury C showed the members' committee had more muscle than an officers' inquiry. A DA commented that where "the employer" conducts the inquiry, it has a more salutary effect than an officers' inquiry. District investigations take longer—too long—and a members' inquiry can investigate before a problem festers. Although district officers are given "every opportunity to investigate" they may feel circumvented, usurped or even disciplined by the members' intervention. *Both members and area officers* felt that Inquiries C and D were necessitated by districts' failure to provide information. Area officers considered it convenient to have members undertake the time-consuming investigation process, and did not see this as usurpation. Only one area officer was "irritated" by the frequency of inquiries, and felt the authority's involvement was eroding the functions of the AMT, which he saw as having an executive role.

44. *District officers*, by contrast, were "extremely unhappy" about inquiries: they were not given time to investigate and were circumvented. Successful local inquiries were cited, and a DA and DNO strongly advocated officers' inquiries, perhaps with an impartial presiding member. Local managers have the relevant knowledge and in fact many of the committee's recommendations had previously been debated or advocated by the DMT. An SA thought that hospital-based inquiries with input from the DMT would be best. Both DAs mentioned the work load which an inquiry represents. It was generally felt that a members' inquiry could find out no more than local officers. But one DCP argued that since the district felt the area must ratify everything, it was unwilling to accept responsibility where it had no real authority to act. *A consultant* felt that informal procedures would usually be adequate, adding that, if officers were less busy with paper and meetings, there would be fewer problems to inquire into.

Relations of District and Area

45. Although this matter arose in the context of inquiries, the answers were more general. It must be remembered that the DMTs are directly responsible to the AMT and have no direct channel of communication with the authority, which they deplore since their views are modified or not transmitted to the AHA. *Almost every district officer* interviewed reiterated that "despite numerous requests" neither the AHA or AMT had prepared terms of reference for the DMTs, hence their unclarity of role. *One member* felt that inquiries would not be held if district managed satisfactorily, but that cover-ups take place, and the authority has to intervene. Another said that

Inquiry D raised the question: are district officers managing or just drifting? They must ultimately take responsibility, but DMTs should not comment on the draft report, as this would affect its impartiality. It was perceived that district officers might feel "tender" about their role, depending on the sensitivity of the case. *One area officer* suggested that the DMT's protests about the report of Inquiry A arose because it felt its organisation of the search had been criticised; the DMT also felt its function was usurped by Inquiry D. Another area officer felt that inquiries sometimes took place because the district had failed to monitor an arrangement properly, or to act vigorously.

46. *One district officer* stated that area gives no support or reinforcement; administrative staff received not recognition of their personal role in the search for Miss X, but implied criticism. Another said "Although the district manager is responsible, he should be given support". An anomaly of the inquiries is that their recommendations do not proceed to district direct, but are received via the area team as *instructions*. Both the procedures and results of inquiries are painful for the district, which feels that something in its care has gone wrong. Another officer, agreeing about the lack of support, said he felt isolated: although he was actively involved in the search for Miss X he could not be heard in the investigation. He felt that the districts have responsibility without authority.

47. *Officers in both districts* emphasised the importance of having a representative on the committees, although not all were satisfied with the results, since representatives had not been allowed to question witnesses (unlike area representatives). A DA felt that the AHA should take the views of local managers more into account. The DMT feels accountable for errors, and thought consulting area officers, should be allowed to decide whether or not to involve the authority. However, the members' expressed wish for involvement puts pressure on the DMT to refer up. If the DMTs had been detailed responsibilities, as recommended in the official guideline and requested by the DMTs repeatedly, their roles, and that of the AMT, would have been clearer and there would have been better understanding between managers and members. Now, it was said, everyone staggers from one "unusual incident" to the next, unsure who should investigate a problem. Another officer felt strongly that problems arise because area officers (many lacking recent hospital experience) do not see the urgency of the decisions needed at the operational level. The ODAs problem arose for this reason. Although the authority has the right to intervene if officers have not acted properly, it seems to feel the teams are an obstruction to its activities, and to enjoy intervening through inquiries. The committee's refusal to modify its report on Miss X in the light of the DMT's comments is indicative of the authority's will to impose its views on subordinate officers, and establish its managerial role.

48. *A consultant member of the DMT* criticised the inquiry process in the strongest terms, asserting that area uses inquiries to exculpate itself when it has failed to produce policies to solve problems. No report condemns policy deficiences. For example, the report on Mr Z did not mention the chronic lack of psychogeriatric facilities which are supposedly a current priority in the area. Area, unable to solve problems because of cash shortage, treats them as crises, and holds inquiries. Area officers have been too long away

202

from the operational level to understand grassroots problems. Asked whether "area" meant the AMT or authority, he said it made no difference since consultants had little contact with either, and the DMT can only communicate with the authority through the DMT.

Complaints

49. There was some agreement that a formal channel for grievances with an impartial lay element was reassuring for the public, although the risk of generating complaints by over-publicity was mentioned. From the complainants' viewpoint, although an apology may not be adequate compensation, the process shows that the authority does not cover up mistakes, but corrects them, and may restore confidence in the service. It was pointed out that the number of complaints investigated in this way form a tiny proportion of the considerable volume of complaints with which district officers deal successfully. In fact, the complaints procedure has been considered very successful by the Minister and is being recommended for adoption by other areas.

IV Analysis of the Material

Perspective

50. It can reasonably be assumed that committees of inquiry represent a predictable cost to the service in terms of time, extra workload for officers and work foregone by witnesses, leaving aside the possible costly effects on morale and staff relations. Inquiries must therefore, presumably, be justified by the special function which they perform which cannot be routinely performed by officers. Even if fourteen inquiries in two years seems to constitute a kind of normality, there is a prima facie case for regarding inquiries as abnormal processes and seeking reasons for these departures from normality. In the case of complaints, "due process" is the reason although it should be noted that the authority adopted a complaints procedure resting heavily on members' inquiries rather than on officer investigation. In the case of "unusual incidents" the reasons given for initiating inquiries by the members interviewed were general ones concerning their responsibility for the running of the service, their duty to safeguard the public and psychiatric patients in particular, their need to control and manage the service, to keep staff alert, to do justice publicly to complainants and "to see for themselves".

Criteria for Instituting Inquiries

51. The purposes of a committee of inquiry, stated in its terms of reference, may differ from its functions. Incidental and accidental functions were cited by members and officers as good reasons for holding inquiries, especially the education of members. More correctly, these are reasons for the members' willingness to contemplate the use of such committees as a managerial and monitoring process, or method of investigation. Although the monitoring function was mentioned by all the members interviewed, and appreciated by most officers, if not by consultants, the members' comments on why it was appropriate to monitor one incident and not another, were vague. An area

officer thought that there was "intuitive agreement" about what was suitable for investigation, but the district officers were often in disagreement about the need for investigation, although they felt that there were criteria such as "cruelty" in psychiatric hospitals which pointed to the need for imediate high level investigation. But one incident, such as a suicide, will be investigated while an apparently similar one is not. The criterion for instituting an inquiry in such circumstances has perhaps been the members' inclination to investigate rather than overwhelming pressure in the form of the intrinsic seriousness of the incident. This point is borne out by the investigation of three suicides, which medical and nursing staff deemed unnecessary, given that suicides are *not* unusual incidents in psychiatric hospitals.

52. Some prejudgement must occur in order to establish whether a case satisfies the criteria for setting up an inquiry, criteria such as serious breakdown of communications, or medical negligence. There is a clear contradiction in maintaining, as some interviewees did, that an inquiry only occurs when an incident is judged to be serious, yet saying, in answer to the question "Was this inquiry necessary?" "We could not know until we held it—that would have prejudged the issue". While it is no doubt true that additional information not in the records leads members to suppose that there may be mileage in one case and not another, this point supports the analysis of the last paragraph, namely that many inquiries into incidents are set up as an act of will, rather than because the event itself fulfils some criteria and objectively requires investigation. To this should be added the point made by many officers and at least one member, that particular members are especially interested in investigating, and often suggest inquiries. The table in the next section indicates that some members *are* particularly active in the inquiry process. Undoubtedly, the tenor of the authority's proceedings with regard to inquiries, and to other maters is largely determined by the personalities of its component individuals.

Membership of Committees

53. In view of the points made in interviews about the lack of qualifications and expertise of the members, an analysis of the membership of the committees is enlightening. Although the chairman determines the membership of committees, it seems that some members make themselves more available than others, which may be tantamount to self-selection. There is a great disparity in the number of inquiries which members have attended. Contrary to the suggestion that local authority members had increased the number of inquiries in their desire for public justice, it appears that they are not eager for public investigation to the point of participating extensively themselves. The infrequency of medical membership and chairmanship supports the complaints of a lack of medical expertise: only four committees have contained a medical member (although each has an area community physician in attendance.) Undoubtedly a few members play a dominant part in the inquiry process, and JPs have been particularly active, presumably because of their legal training. The chairman does not participate since a matter might have to be investigated by the full AHA with himself in the chair. 15 out of 17 members have participated at least once.

Composition of Committees of Inquiry

No of Inquiries Attended	No of Members	Relevant Professional Qualifications	Chairmanship
9	1	JP	8
6	1	JP	1
5	1	—	1
4	2	1 JP	
3	4	1 JP, 1 Dr, 2 Cllrs	Cllrs-chaired 3
2	1	1 SRN	—
1	5	Inc 3 Cllrs, 1 JP, 1 Dr	Dr chaired 1

Implications for the Role of the AHA

54. This analysis of the inquiry process confirms the authority's stated intention of interventionist management. Opinions vary on the virtues of this approach. In general, officers and other staff feel that the authority has misconstrued its task, according to official guidelines, and is managing at too low a level and not paying enough attention to policy: by contrast, the members feel that they are properly carrying out their managerial and monitoring duties in the only way possible, yet feel that they are still not adequately in control of the services. The number and frequency of the inquiries, reflects this attitude. Independent confirmation of this can be found in the authority's recent consultative document, which proposes to make the area into a single district area. The following passage summarises the authority's conception of its role:

> "The Health Authority has found that this description (the official role description which suggests that all functions which can be handled by officers should be delegated to them, to conserve the Authority's time) of its role does not match up to its own objectives and to the need which it sees to exercise a fuller managerial role with access at all stages to the information which it needs for this fuller role. In particular, its members have found that in order to carry out their task, they must concern themselves with day-to-day issues and ensure that their information is based on their own day-to-day experience. Whilst this approach is not entirely in accord with the official guidelines, the Authority considers that simplification of its management structures to take account of these factors will help it to exercise the policy making function to which the guideline refers."

Other passages speak of "months elapsing" between the authority's request for information and its receipt, and members' anxiety that they lack information and control of the service. In general, members felt their managerial role and public acountability keenly, and all referred to it in the interviews.

55. The criticisms which staff made of the inquiry process apply equally to this conception of the authority's role. The impropriety of an interventionist role for a policy making body was emphasised by one district officer who also pointed out that the reports of inquiries C and D were based on opposed covert policy assumptions: one suggested that consultants should *not* trans-

fer awkward patients such as Mr Z to achieve a better turn over of acute beds, while the operating sessions committee assumed quick turnover to be ideal. The implication was that members have no conscious or consistent policy convictions. An area officer commented that the members had no conception of policy making and so substituted intervention. Certainly the members' discussion of questions during the inquiries suggest that they have no overall policy goals or assumptions, and are motivated by the desire to use this opportunity to gather as much information as possible on all kinds of incidental issues. Likewise, at the management meetings, members showed great open-mindedness about policy, and were far more interested in practical details. The criticisms made particularly by professional officers and consultants, of intervention by a lay body in professional and technical matters, was extended by some interviewees to a critique of the principle of laymanship itself. Naturally, members saw no objections in principle to lay control, the authority's raison d'etre.

56. No judgement is implied in this analysis as to what role members should adopt, but the resulting effects of interventionism on officers and staff will be evaluated in 57–61 below. In brief, the officers are under no illusions about the authority's intentions, and these are tolerated by area officers, although some fear erosion of the team's function, but resented at district level and regarded as interference: "their activism is fundamental to our difficulties". In contra-distinction, the members feel that they can only "get to grassroots" through processes such as committees of inquiry, which temporarily assert their control over the unwieldy organisation. There is evidently a normal, regular lacuna of communication between the authority and the operational and district levels, institutionalised by the DMT's not being allowed to communicate with the authority except via the AMT. An inquiry can thus be seen as temporarily circumventing the AMT, and thus eliminating one filtration process. It enables members to question district officers and hospital staff directly, so that they receive unmediated information—which is what they want.

Effect on Area Officers

57. The consultant's suggestion that inquiries were, for area, a process of self-exculpation is worth consideration. Some district officers seemed to incline to a similar view, since it was often mentioned that the DMT had already discussed the problems highlighted by the reports, and brought them to the AMT's notice, but that nothing had been done. Arguably, area officers are a priori vindicated by the nature of an inquiry which usually investigates flaws in the operation of the system with which area officers are not concerned, rather than the policy behind it. Inquiries into the activities of area officers have been almost unknown, although some area witnesses have been given "a rough ride". But the inquiry process bypasses the AMT and is scarcely mentioned in its minutes, so area officers have different perceptions of the process from district officers. Although aware of the unusual extent to which committees are being used, they are satisfied with their rights to be represented at inquiries, and sometimes consider that inquiries ease their own workload. Also, in view of the AMT's strained relationship with the DMTs, it may not be unwilling to see members intervene

and monitor, or even reprimand, the district teams. Whereas the AMT is itself managerial by inclination, and intervenes extensively in day-to-day area matters, the inquiry process briefly brings into contact the polarised AHA and DMT, taking the pressure off the AMT. But the authority's attitude may also pose a threat to the AMT's autonomy.

Effect on District Officers

58. Although inquiries bring the DMT into direct contact with the Authority, its main complaint is that its proper tasks are circumvented by this intervention. Officers did not deny that some inquiries had had beneficial results, but objected to the principle, maintaining that identical results could have been achieved by less costly and intrusive methods, namely officers' inquiries. They anticipated the objection about whitewashing by suggesting a presiding member. A certain discrepancy appeared, however, in the district managers' opinion that they could have satisfactorily investigated the cancellation of operating sessions, this being the very case in which their failure to procure information had led to members' impatience and the inquiry. It bears repeating here that the format of an inquiry, set up to investigate an incident which district managers failed to prevent, and requiring the DMT to implement its proposals in a directly managerial way, is particularly hostile to any notion of district autonomy (to which members object in principle anyway) and threatening to the district officers' conception of their own roles which are, at best, unclear owing to the deliberate lack of delegation. Disparate but compatible comments such as "it is unclear who should investigate what" and "since everything must be ratified by area, there is no incentive to investigate locally" make the officers' problem, and alienation, clear. District officers do not distinguish clearly between the AMT and Authority, one intervening in routine matters, one through inquiries, but object generally to area interference although they are aware of tensions and differences between the area team and AHA.

59. Any analysis of the organisation of the NHS in this area must focus on the unhappy position of the two districts, and the sustained attempts of the authority and area team to erode their functions, of which no secret is made. The mutual accusations of area and district officers in the cancelled operation case show clearly the general uncertainty of roles and responsibilities, and the problems caused by lack of delegation. The committee of inquiry process, and the district's strong reaction to it, is symptomatic of this more general development. Several district officers expressed their problem as being accountable but without authority, and being held responsible for mistakes, but with no support from above. The "grilling" of district officers as witnesses in the inquiries, and the absence of consultation over the final report before submission, in an otherwise over-consultative system, typify the slights which district officers feel themselves to receive from their managers. Their persistent complaints about the lack of consultation on reports, and representation on committees of inquiry, in late 1975 and early 1976, signify a more general protest against this treatment of districts, but they also make the substantial point that they, the local managers, are more knowledgeable about local problems than members, and could usefully contribute to the final

recommendations. Consultation might also enable them to vindicate themselves from the criticisms of their actions which have appeared in some reports. Some of the teams' unsolicited comments were directed to this end: for example, on a report which had suggested that the officers' investigation had been tardy, and inaccuracies had resulted. The team's comments emphasised the DMT's and the DA's heavy workload and commented that all possible efforts were made, and they felt that the criticism was unjustified. It is worth noting that this particular DMT's officers are located in a very popular sector, and that complaint of overwork may well be justified; some of the area's problems spring from a great disparity in size between the districts.

60. There have been developments in the inquiry process and format which are to the district's advantage, and make their position with respect to the inquiries more tolerable: namely, the participation of the DMT's representative, and the now automatic presentation of the DMT's comments on reports to the authority. However, the continuing distaste of district officers for inquiries are a reaction to being placed under additional stress in a situation which is already stressful, because of the unsatisfactory structure.

The Role of the Sector Administrator

61. In most cases where inquiries took evidence from SAs, the outstanding revelation was that these administrators are virtually powerless, and not informed or consulted by nurses and doctors about what is happening clinically (Cases A and D). Although this seems to be true generally in this area it is emphasised because SAs here are at the end of a long administrative chain down which no powers have been developed; their impotence is, as it were, directly derived from that of the DMT, and indirectly from that of the AMT. Nevertheless, they too clearly felt that the inquiries had intruded on their proper managerial functions, and should have been made by District officers. The consultative document on the single district area implies that the abolition of districts would be followed by the strengthening of sectors, but some interviewees were sceptical that this would in fact follow, there being no tradition of delegation. The other reason for the weak position of the SA was functional management and the division of responsibilities which were once the hospital secretary's between nursing and medical staff, as in the example of the search for the wandering patient, Miss X. But the SA's position is basically a reflection of the problems of the DMT.

Medical–Administrative Relations

62. As both members and officers suggested, the clinicians' objections to committees of inquiry are almost certainly part of a general hostility to the administrative structure, which predated reorganisation but has recently been reinforced by problems about pay and changing status, and difficulties caused by the increased complexity of the reorganised service. Consultants discourage intervention, even by their own medical officers, and are especially opposed to what appears to them as an inquisitorial intervention by unqualified members into medical matters. The tension between professional expertise and lay control is, of course, not new. It gains a dimension in the

208

inquiry situation, where consultants suspect that a scapegoat is being sought —they, ultimately, are responsible for the well-being of the patients and therefore vulnerable—and that they may be blamed for the malfunctioning of a system which is impossible to operate because of policy defects. Certainly, the consultants' reactions to Inquiries C and D were self-protective, but this might have been because other circumstances put them into a defensive mood. However, it is noticeable that the only inquiries against which the consultants reacted strongly were those few where they were criticised and that they seemed to co-operate with other inquiries happily, and accept their reports. The fate of the abandoned inquiry D is a clear measure of the entrenched power of the consultants and the extent to which they can defy their officers and authority if they so wish, rendering useless efforts at monitoring and control. The preceding confrontation, and this revelation made Inquiry D a traumatic process for all those embroiled in it, and the repercussions continue. The authority's methods of inquiring into such delicate matters will no doubt be modified as a result. The consultants too have conceded that an informal group, or the committee under a different name, would procure their co-operation. One further point is that the consultants' resistance to inquiries may be an application of their opposition to the consultative plan for a national complaints procedure on Davies lines, and so may disappear when negotiations on this are completed. An area officer felt that their attitude would be modified if their professional representatives were members of the AMT (instead of the DMT) and had access to the AHA i.e. in a single district area.

Content Analysis of the Reports

63. The twelve reports available were analysed in terms of the problems raised. With such a small number, a quantitative analysis would not be appropriate, but it can be seen that some kinds of recommendations and criticisms occur more frequently than others. Each report makes a number of recommendations of different kinds, some particular, some general. Here we need only note that a large number of these contain criticisms of staff, but some contain exonerations or praise. The analysis of defects strongly emphasises *procedure*: ignorance of procedure, lack of procedure or procedures put into operation too slowly. Breakdown of communication is the other common fault highlighted. Recommendations mainly dwell on area policy and some working suggestions for nurses. The Appendix contains a content analysis of all the available reports.

Merits and Demerits of the Inquiry Process

64. These were, of course, asserted or called into question throughout the interviews, and varied with the perspective of the speaker. Each perspective has its own validity, and it would be invidious to judge between them here, but an objective assessment of the merits and demerits will be attempted, first on the basis of the date already given, and secondly, through the content analysis of all the available reports of committees, to see how far they bear out the claims made for and against them.

Merits

Monitoring Role

65. This is certainly effective, since the members receive co-operation and usually, it appears, full information, but this relates to only a small part of the service in each case; there should surely be wider and more routine monitoring devices. The suspect nature of the "unusual incident" again obtrudes itself here: the authority can only inquire into the rare cases in which human error had fatal results, while other instances of carelessness or malfunctioning remain uninvestigated. Inquiries certainly reveal some unexpected gaps in the service as a member claimed, but because of their limitations in scope and time it is doubtful if they can do all that is claimed for them. The deterrent effect which some mentioned can be at most marginal because of the limited circulation of the report, although those involved in the incident are already doubly deterred by the event and the inquiry process.

Side Effects

66. The desirability of the function which inquiries perform in informing and educating the members and fulfilling their desire for involvment may be evidenced by the large number of inquiries held.

Members' Inquiries

67. These undoubtedly have more authority than officers' investigations and keep staff alert. Everyone interviewed in the case study was keenly aware that the members are "the managers" and "the employers", so the abrasive monitoring device of an inquiry undoubtedly has a powerful effect. The problem lies in deciding when the ultimate weapon is appropriate, which sometimes seems to have been misjudged.

The Fate of the Committee's Recommendations

68. This might be the clearest measure of their usefulness, but the researcher was in no better position to monitor this than the members, since most affect hospital routine. But those interviewed mainly agreed that the recommendations are implemented wherever practicable: the AMT's chasing-up function and the DMT's responsibility to report back within a few months guarantee this. A member's claim that "however painful for staff, committees of inquiry induce improvements in the service" seems accurate.

Public Accountability

69. All members interviewed saw the inquiries primarily as both an acknowledgement and an assertion of their public accountability, and justified them on these grounds. Most officers concurred unambiguously that the AHA is publicly accountable, and therefore has the right to know and hence to investigate.

Demerits

The Morale of Staff

70. This could not be tested at first hand since to interview reputedly upset members of staff would have seemed like further interrogation. Analysis of the reports (Appendix) suggests that hospital staff are rarely overtly criticised. However, the assertions by the ANO, DNOs and other district officers that nurses are worried, and feel threatened and criticised, by

inquiries, is borne out by the transcripts of the evidence, in which they sometimes appear to have been questioned with unnecessary rigour on seemingly unconnected matters, about which they knew little. The claim of some area officers, that inquiries do not lower morale much, is, in the circumstances, baseless. The aftermath of Inquiry B for the senior professional staff shows how seriously such matters are taken. The effect on the morale and functioning of district officers is undoubtedly bad, but area staff are virtually unaffected. Consultants are affronted rather than upset, and are ultimately impervious to criticism by administrators, though vulnerable to criticism by their colleagues. What a cost benefit analysis of the inquiry process would need to estimate is how deep and permanent its effect on morale may be, and what damage it may thereby do to the future goodwill of staff.

Insensitivity
71. Insensitivity to feelings of staff is obvious in the tenor of some of the proceedings and the summary memoranda requesting attendance. This aspect could be ameliorated without difficulty, and is incidental to the main problem. Progress has been made—one chairman sent out letters of thanks to witnesses and some reports include praise for staff.

Cost in Time and Effort
72. There is an area officer, the AAGA, partly occupied in servicing the committees, acting as secretary, and collecting documents for the members. Otherwise, the cost of inquiries falls heavily on the district staff who have to furnish the AAGA with the relevant documents and information, and arrange locations and witnesses. One DA pointed out that, apart from the memos on file, he may have spent the equivalent of two days on the 'phone over one enquiry. Inquiries are prodigal with the time of paid staff, whereas a system of thorough monitoring visits would use the unpaid time of members.

The Critical Orientation
73. The critical orientation which such inquiries appear inevitably to have signifies a general problem in the NHS, in this area and elsewhere; the monitoring relationships seem to operate negatively, and there is little encouragement or positive reinforcement for staff. This lack is particularly detrimental to the intermediate staff who have neither the feelings of achievement associated with patient care, nor the satisfaction of high level management—in this area, the district and sector staff. It may be that each level of the service perceives its superiors as being thankless, for one DNO said that his subordinates had taken to sending him copies of letters of thanks received, as counterweights to the criticisms of inquiries or managers. A consultant felt that there should be committees of approbation as well as inquiry, and the problem was mentioned in various guises by many interviewees. Since monitoring and correction must take place, it can only be concluded that it should be done as pleasantly as possible, to avoid giving the service a negative slant from the authority downwards: the problem is more extensive than that of morale, and may affect the mode of working of the whole service.

74. Policy recommendations to the Authority itself are made in a number of cases, while the only three comments on medical policy are couched as *requests* to the Psychiatric Division to examine problems. Most recom-

mendations suggest the institution of administrative procedures to avoid future errors; these are basically the commonsense suggestions which a lay body might appropriately make. Contrary to consultants' complaints, there is little evidence that the recommendations tread on medical toes, or that lay members are interfering in professional practice, although doctors may regard the suggested procedures as cumbersome.

75. The reports are constructive in tone and most recommendations seem to be reasonable attempts to close gaps revealed by the inquiry. The DMT's charge that committees generalise from one instance and try to build a system on it may be true, given their emphasis on the introduction of written procedures to eliminate every possible error. The reports are perhaps unselfcritical, but it is hard to see where self-criticism would be appropriate, except in the general matter of shortage of staff and facilities. Communication and liaison between various bodies are shown by the reports to be the Achilles' heel of the organisation, but these are a matter of procedure rather than policy.

76. In conclusion, it appears that administrative officers, especially at district and sector, bear the brunt of criticism in these reports. Although some area officers appear as witnesses, it is rare for area staff to be criticised, while the criticism of medical and nursing staff is usually veiled or absent. The comments about morale should be reviewed in this light.

V Concluding Evaluation

Members

77. This case study illustrates what must have been a perennial problem in the NHS, namely, the separation of the lay members from the clinical organisation, and their problems in understanding and controlling the service as a whole. Comments from members and staff identified this as a problem, and most favoured the pre-1974 organisation which, they thought, promoted greater contact and control between members, officers and hospital staff. The extensive use of committees of inquiry is, in effect, an attempt by the lay authority to establish a sporadic control over small parts of an over-large and bureaucratic organisation. Several of those interviewed remarked on a correlation between the increased size of the organisation with the need for formal inquiries. The committees are also a useful intrument whereby the authority expresses its intention of active management. The involvement of many members in local politics, it was said, had produced a politicisation of health issues which harmed the service. The interventionist attitude of the Authority is, at least in part, a result of this local phenomenon, and has had repercussions on the functioning of the reorganised NHS here.

78. The criticisms made of committees of inquiry on the grounds that members are too remote to understand local conditions, and not properly qualified to make judgements on medical and other operational matters, exemplify both the problem of size and that of laymanship. Indeed, laymanship could be seen as an anomalous element in a highly professional service. The new emphasis on multidisciplinarity is arguably contrary to the spirit of lay management, and the tension between the two institutional principles is

reflected in the comments on the composition of the committees of inquiry, with each profession and level wanting representation of its own expertise and interests. The lay authority, although it has two medical members and an SRN among its numbers, cannot claim to be a professional body; consequently its management is inevitably subject to criticism by professionals, and the more interventionist it is, the more strongly it is criticised, as this study has shown.

79. Through meeting the members individually and seeing them operate collectively in an authority meeting on the single district area proposal, it became clear that they are more or less oblivious to the administrative problems which the service has and are almost exclusively interested in the operational level. They would no doubt justify this orientation on the grounds that they are responsible to the public for *patient care*, a point which members made repeatedly, and sincerely. But in discussion many members seemed unaware of the tension between area and district. In fact, they appeared to perceive the AMT and DMTs as much of a muchness, and view both with some suspicion, lest a cover-up of administrative inefficiency should take place. Members are also more or less ignorant of the "constitution" of their service as set out in the ministerial guidelines and do not know, for example, the significance of "coterminosity". Indeed, they had so few preconceptions about the administrative organisation of the service that they discussed apparently impartially numerous alternatives to the single district area at this meeting, including the unconstitutional suggestion of splitting the area. (The above comments do not apply to the chairman, who is extremely competent and well informed). This lack of interest in the administrative process, coupled with genuine concern with and involvement in patient care matters is significant. It gives rise to officers' claims that members are not interested in policy making. Evidently, they are particularly uninterested in administrative policy, seeing this as a diversion from the true business of the service. As a consequence, the authority has not provided direction for the administrators, or delegated specific powers to each level, and the resulting vacuum has engendered specific administrative problems. Another consequence of the lay members' lack of knowledge is that the AMT is very influential, especially since the DMTs have no access to the members.

Administrators

80. The committees of inquiry also illustrate the uncomfortable and ill-defined position of professional administrators at all levels of the reorganised service. Analysis of the reports shows that they are most often criticised by the committees, and most exactingly questioned by the members. Although they are in no way recognised as chairmen or leaders of the management teams, they appear, in the inquiries, sometimes to have been held accountable for what were team decisions, or for decisions taken by their professional colleagues of which they had not been informed because the role of co-ordinator is largely nominal. The inquiry process itself, being an administrative matter, adds to their work but professional administrators have no representatives in attendance on the committees to explain the administrative viewpoint. The DAs enjoyed solidarity with and support from their DMT colleagues, perhaps because all felt under siege from area, but the SAs as per-

haps the AA seemed to be in isolated positions, and somewhat at the mercy of their medical colleagues. Their co-ordinating role did not always mean that they were well informed, and did not give them authority over their professional colleagues or functional managers.

District–Area Relations

81. Problems of liaison, co-operation and communication between district and area are demonstrated in the operation of the investigation and inquiry processes. Communication problems occur, for example, when the ANO decides to distribute information through the administrator rather than down the functional nursing hierarchy, causing a temporary lacuna of information for his DNOs. Such small irritations are magnified in a generally unsatisfactory situation. But the main problem highlighted is the position of the DMTs which are accountable without having authority. Responsibility has been delegated downwards while authority, power and functions are not devolved beyond area due to the managerial attitude of the authority and the "executive attitude" imputed to some area officers. One member of the AMT emphasised that the NHS structure here had "'strengthened the executive role of the AMT''. The considerable weakening of the role of the DMTs is the consequence. Another area officer said that inquiries illustrated "what a cumbersome administrative apparatus district and area together constitute". The current situation has all the properties of a vicious circle and is bound to deteriorate because, as district officers freely admitted, they are taking a defensive line and refusing to take decisions, referring to area any decision which is problematic or might involve them in reprimand. This naturally reinforces the authority's and the AMT's view of the usefulness of a district level. A proper division of labour might make the system operable, but the AMT favours the alternative of simplifying the structure by creating a single-district area.

Perspectives in the Service

82. Once again, the multiplicity of perspectives within the service was revealed in this study. Members were earnestly convinced of the necessity of their investigative role, whatever its effects on morale or the functioning of staff, while district officers were convinced of their own competence to handle most problems, and wanted the opportunity to do so. The double perspective was ubiquitous: what members required as "control", officers invariably regarded as "involvement at too low a level". Comments received from members and staff on the first draft of this study reinforced the researcher's impression that there is mutual incomprehension between district staff (and those at hospital level) and area staff (and members). Some of those who commented continued to express doubts about each others' viewpoints, and to demonstrate that these did not accord with the facts. But opinions and sentiments not according with the "facts" indisputably affect morale and modes of behaviour, and so they have been recorded here as expressed. The important revelation is that the service is being run here (and no doubt elsewhere) by teams and individuals who are expected to co-operate but who constantly question each others' working assumptions and doubt the validity of each others' perspectives. The stratification of the service

has made differences of perspective inevitable, but this manifestly obstructs its smooth running.

83. The authority uses committees of inquiry to (1) fulfil its public accountability duty; (2) manage at the operational level; (3) inform itself about the operational level; (4) serve a public relations purpose, and (5) institute change both in policies and working processes. By contrast, the district sees such committees as (1) performing the managerial function in an inappropriate context and unnecessarily; (2) being a defence of area against criticism, and (3) constituting the inquisition into District's own activities, and those at hospital level. The irreconcilability of these views, and their validity in their own perspective, illustrates the disarticulation of the organisation, parts of which are set in opposition to, or alienated from, each other, and the confused relationships which result from the structure.

Structural and Operational Problems

84. In this area, both the system of structure, and the way in which it has been operated, appear to be to blame for the unsatisfactory functioning of the administrative side of the service. The interventionist and actively managerial attitude of the authority and the malfunctioning of the area–district relationship, with resulting antagonisms, are striking features of the service here, but may not be untypical. Although these are two separate phenomena, the authority's approach further weakens the districts' roles and increases the district officers' dislike of area intervention, and their reluctance to act managerially lest their actions be questioned. The structure of the service in this country has produced a potentially executive AMT by making the DMTs directly responsible to the area team, while in this particular area, the operation of the system (especially the lack of delegation of specific powers to the DMTs, and area officers' executive attitudes) has reinforced the tendency of the structure to enhance the AMT's powers and reduce the DMTs to subordinates and intermediaries. The authority's managerial approach is consequently in part an endeavour to control the activities of the powerful AMT. Members in interviews and meetings showed a desire to scrutinise the AMT's proposals (hence the wish to "see for themselves") but it is probably true that the nature of the system makes it impossible for them to control their area officers to any extent. Since the individuals operating the system can influence it greatly, it should be added that although the AMT members are evidently executively minded, the authority chairman has a powerful personality, and exercises a strong controlling function over the team by virtue of this.

85. While the DMTs see a solution to their unsatisfactory situation in the strengthening of their own powers, the AMT favours the abolition of the district level altogether. The AA argued that the need for multidisciplinarity would be catered for by a team at just one level in the service, the area, and that to maintain the principle at district and sector levels was cumbersome. The polarity of attitudes on the matter was made clear in the responses to the consultative document mentioned earlier, on the single district area. Those consulted unanimously agreed that the present system was working unsatisfactorily but, while area and other staff gave the proposal qualified or total approval, district staff (and unions) were totally opposed to it. This can

215

justly be described as an impasse. What originated as a structural problem—the difficult relations between the teams—will apparently be given a structural solution, but this may not solve the second problem, the relation between officers and the authority.

Personnel Problems

86. The formal subordination of district to area also causes difficulties in the relationships between staff. DMT members are skilled and highly paid officers, many of whom were used to taking major decisions in the old HMCs; they now find themselves unable to take decisions of substance, and subordinate to AMT members whom they consider not to be conversant with operational problems. They also find themselves by implication subordinate to second in line area officers who are, in institutional terms, not their equals. A DA objected to being questioned in an inquiry by a second in line ANO(P), and a DNO objected to being sent to meet assistant administrators over a problem which he wished to discuss with the AMT. But these anomalies are endemic in the new structure here, the implementation of which constituted a demotion for district officers who had enjoyed authority and independence in the HMCs.

Inquiries

87. As for the committee of inquiry process itself, it can be argued that in a public service where deficiencies or negligence may pose a direct threat to the health or lives of patients, it is fitting that complaints and unusual incidents should be investigated swiftly and thoroughly by the highest authority which can scrutinise the operation of both the clinical and administrative sectors of the NHS. It is also desirable that a complainant should not have to proceed through several administrative layers before getting satisfaction. These inquiries have been largely successful in satisfying complainants, and also function as a useful managerial device. From an objective viewpoint, inquiries may have some of the virtues claimed for them, but the countervailing costs are underestimated. The process can imbue individuals and the organisation with negative and critical attitudes, and defensiveness and non-co-operation may result, which will in the long run detract from patient care. By definition, inquiries investigate failures, not successes and everyone concerned feels under scrutiny. There should be limited use of them, and the authority might give more consideration to incentives and mechanisms for encouragement. Committees of inquiry, like unpleasant medicines, can only be taken in small doses.

Conclusion

88. Needless to say, the use of members' inquiries is an experimental and developmental process, as is the operation of the reorganised NHS itself. In this area, the extensive use of the device is indicative of an imbalance of powers and responsibilities at all levels of the service. A new report* on the

---

* First Report from the Select Committee on the Parliamentary Commissioner for Administration: Independent Review of Hospital Complaints in the NHS. (Cmnd Paper 45, HMSO, December 1977.)

Health Service commissioner suggests that authorities should *not* set up ad hoc inquiries, but should pass complaints to the HSC if an investigation by the DA does not satisfy the complainant. If implemented, this will presumably change this authority's modus operandi. In any case, the number of inquiries in this area is diminishing, and so it would be wrong to draw hard and fast conclusions about the working of the inquiry system over a longer period. But through an analysis of the inquiry process this study has suggested ways in which the new organisation in this area falls short of an ideal administrative and managerial form.

Appendix

Content Analysis of the Reports
and the Committees of Inquiry

The analysis shows that in complaints cases staff are generally exonerated, while criticism is often made in unusual incidents cases. The emphasis on procedure (including good communication) in the recommendations is also noteworthy.

1. *Criticism*

Nurses

A NO "did not take sufficient action to become informed".

Doctors

Two reports blamed psychiatrists for not making the dangers of patients' suicides clear to nurses.

Another blamed a qualified professional for failing to convey a sense of urgency about Miss Y's condition.

"Staff"

Hospital staff (i.e. nurses and doctors) made inadequate attempts to cope with Mr Z and should not have discharged him. (COMPLAINT INQUIRY.)

Officers

One DA (by implication) issued inadequate description of Miss X.

In the case of a nurse suspended after serious allegations, the District and Area officers did not act with sufficient urgency, the DMT "failed to realise the seriousness and urgency of the case at the outset" and Area officers were too worried about the legal implications, albeit they were *protecting the Authority*. District officers should have investigated the case sooner.

"Senior Hospital Staff" (i.e. the SA) should have been involved in a search earlier, and arranged a large-scale search sooner.

An SA should have informed staff on procedure for handling cash.

Other

Complainant blamed by implication for not telling hospital staff of her husband's deteriorating condition. (COMPLAINT INQUIRY.)

2. *Exoneration*

Doctors in emergency department exonerated. (COMPLAINT INQUIRY.)

Ambulance crew vindicated of complaint of undue delay. (COMPLAINT INQUIRY.)

"No medical negligence" in another complaint case. (COMPLAINT INQUIRY.)

3. *Praise*

Nursing care "as impressive and effective as possible" in suicide case.

Ward staff's search for Miss X properly carried out.

218

4. Disciplinary Recommendations

A nurse reinstated with written reprimand.
A nurse removed to a different post.

5. Analysis of Defects

Communications Breakdown
In two cases, in communication between nurses.
Between the "staff" of two hospitals over Mr Z.
Between hospital and GP of Mr Z.
Between psychiatrists and nurses in two cases.
Between nurses and medical staff in one case.
Between hospital or District Officers and police in two cases where more information or co-ordination needed.

Ignorance of Existing Procedures
Staff need training on Mental Health Act.

Lack of Procedure
No written procedure for cross-matching blood.
Elaborate written search procedure needed.
Kardex system should identify potential suicides.
Procedure needed to record which anaesthetic given.
Need to keep record of drugs given by psychiatric patients on holiday.
Need for system of booking 'phone calls in accident department.

Staffing Problems
Shortage of psychiatric nurses revealed in suicide case.
Two reports mention short staffing in emergency department.

System Operated Too Slowly
Medical advice should have been taken more quickly over allegations against nurse.
Search procedures should have been activated sooner.
In *three* cases, the committees felt that investigations should have taken place sooner so that staff were interviewed when events were remembered. (By implications, officers were tardy.)

6. Recommendations

Area Policy
Personnel Department should prepare guidelines on procedures for staff accused of crimes.
Authority to develop policy on "lending out" of psychiatric qualified staff.
Authority to develop mechanism to deal with "grey area" patients such as Mr Z.
AMO to report on staffing in emergency department.
Authority to arrange greater liaison with community before discharge of disabled patients.
New unit for mentally handicapped children to be reviewed.

Medical Policy

Psychiatric Division to examine categories for special supervision, as a result of two cases, and also to examine ward arrangements in one hospital.

Working Suggestions for Nurses

Nurses should be able to call on extra doctors in emergency department.
SNO should pay longer visits to scrutinise patients on holiday.
Potential suicides should not be left in wards on their own.

PART IV

Conclusions, Recommendations and Summary

1. This report has recorded the views expressed by over 500 interviewees concerned with the running of the National Health Service. At the end of each section of the Field Interview Survey and of the Case Studies we have summarised the main findings and it would be tedious and unnecessary to repeat them at this point. Instead, in this final section we select those points which reflect on the nature of decision making, and the structures created for it, in the reorganised National Health Service and which lead to particular recommendations to the Royal Commission. We begin with general interpretative comments before coming to particular major consequences.

I Some Interpretative Points

2. For the most part, the aims of reorganisation have not been achieved three or four years after it, and where they have been achieved it has been costly in terms of additional work, uncertainty and frustration. The *overload* of both administrative and of the participative machinery has affected all concerned with the running of the service. This has happened at the same time as *clinicians* have been suffering a *loss of status*, a feeling of *lack of identity* with the reformulated institutions for which they work, and have been upset by what seem to them to be organisational proliferation and wastefulness at the same time as resource growth in the health service has decelerated. These views have been voiced by those concerned with the management of the health service, as well as by clinicians.

3. Much of the difficulty has turned on the failure of the reorganised system to make an effective balance between *potentially conflicting objectives*. In particular, individual practitioners, and the institutions where they do their work, have been, or feel that they have been, demoted in favour of the more abstract considerations that constituted the justification for reorganisation: the need for a rational, allocative, equitable, accountable and participative system. These seem to many to be liberal vogue ideals which are *collective assumptions* and are justified in their own right but which are in tension with the *individualistic assumptions* associated with good health care and medicine. There is too much hope put into the unitary fallacy, the belief that conflicts of objectives will be resolved by bringing all together into a single system. To some extent the aims are potentially reconcilable but, all the same, choices have to be made between them. It may be that some of the aims are only superficially compatible.

Structure and Functions

4. Apart from the question of whether different roles and values can be accommodated within one system, there is the issue as to whether *structure* is related to *function*. Different levels, structures and different time scales are needed for different kinds of work and the decisions deriving from work. So the machinery may not be able to cope with the wide range of demands made and problems placed on it. Some of the problems arising from what might be inevitable differences between functions and the structures created for them are discussed below.

5. The NHS is a large and complex system. It must be controlled and decisions framed on resource allocations that take account of the com-

plexities. There are thus problems of how control and authority will be exercised in a complex system, which include the control of the work of specific groups such as doctors, and of a large bureaucratic organisation. To a large extent the NHS has been left to find its own way although so much of the power is external and national. These points are brought out in the case study of members' inquiries which raises questions of how members assert control over a complex administrative system, the study of hospital closures which shows how national policies relate to local decision making and pressures, and the study of the planning system. The machinery developed to meet the problem of multiple types of control is that of consensus management, of multidisciplinary decision making and consultation. But our report has recorded how those specific attempts to meet the problems of control and authority are difficult to implement.

6. A further similar problem concerns conflicts of aims and values. The NHS has to accommodate several points of view at once. Major decisions must take into account national policies, both political and administrative, the varying beliefs of authority members at both regional and area levels, local authority and other community interests, practitioner interests, and the administrative ethic of those concerned with management, of running a service efficiently and equitably.

7. The conflicts of aims and values are particularly exemplified in the study of planning which shows how planning and participation are inseparable as they operate but are exceedingly difficult to reconcile in terms of machinery and efficient working.

Role Uncertainty

8. It is not surprising, given these tensions in health service objectives, and the over-elaborate organisation that has resulted, that many working within the service are uncertain of their role.

9. The central departments do not appear to be certain as to whether they should manage the field authorities, or monitor them, or simply hold the ring within which the real decision making in the field can struggle on. They are clear about their responsibility for resource allocations and on their need to lead on planning, but the boundaries and textures of the resulting relationships are not clear. The same uncertainty occurs in other key managerial roles, and particularly those of the professional administrators whose authority to co-ordinate, let alone monitor, on behalf of the authorities, is uncertain. Although it was never all that clear in the pre-reorganisation hospital service the relationship between consensual and participative decision making and getting things done efficiently is now much less clear. Nor are the CHCs clear about their role. Are they expected to get close to, or in to the system? If they become an effective counter system, providing counter analysis, will they become too much a bureaucratised system of their own? Practitioners involved in management try to reconcile the feelings of their colleagues with managerial decision making. This point is fully explored in the case study on bio-medical engineering decision making. Uncertainty, too, surrounds the health authorities as they face the daunting planning tasks exemplified in our first case study. They have to shift re-

224

sources and close some of their systems down, so as to release resources for use elsewhere. In taking on this planning and allocative responsibility they start from entirely defensible base lines. But they can never be sure whether the rational considerations are acceptable to the client groups whom they seek to serve, or the practitioners who do the work. "Getting decisions right" is difficult enough. The reorganised service is also seeking to make them acceptable through participative and consultative models. It is doubtful whether it is ever possible to get decisions both right and acceptable, if indeed there is ever a right decision.

Consequences

10. What policy consequences flow from the difficulty of achieving good machinery for the performance of the ascribed functions of the NHS? In our view, much of the difficulty arises from a failure to recognise that it is not possible for any one part of the public service to carry all of the political idealism of the late 1960s with equal devotion and at the same time to work efficiently. Participation and consultation lead to elaboration in decision making. The effort put into them, and the attention paid to them, have to be balanced with the need to plan and operate the system effectively.

II Decision Making

Criteria

11. There has to be recognition, therefore, that there are criteria of good decision making, but that not all can be taken into account simultaneously. The research team could paraphrase the main criteria derived from our study as follows:

Accountability
Responsiveness to publicly determined policies (as exemplified in the relationships between officers and authority members, the case study on members' inquiries and certain aspects of the planning case study).

Acceptability
Management of conflict and ensuring commitment (as exemplified in the arrangements for multi-disciplinary and consensual and consultative decision making and staff consultative machinery).

Participation
Of both employees and the public (as exemplified in the community health councils and statutory advisory machinery).

Delegation
Diffusion of responsibility and relating it to implementation at the points nearest service delivery (not easily exemplified in current arrangements).

Efficiency
Economy of resource use. The cases of hospital closures and planning exemplify this.

225

Coherence

The bringing together of policies and practices which lead to coverage (as exemplified by the officer team structures, the planning systems and the joint consultative machinery).

Comprehensibility

Clear communication of decisions.

Certainty

Knowing who is making what decision and how they will be implemented (as exemplified by the line relationships, by decisions made authoritatively within the planning systems. Not thought to be a good feature of the reorganised NHS).

Rationality and Feasibility

Relation of means to ends (as exemplified by the planning system).

12. It should be noted that these criteria are consistent with those stated by the DHSS in their "The NHS Planning System", June 1976 (paragraph 13) but that we have reformulated them to meet the criteria emerging more directly from our studies.

Characteristics Affecting Decision Making

13. These general conclusions lead to policy proposals. We need to be clear first as to what characteristics affect decision making for good or ill. With the criteria stated in paragraph 11 we might ask which aspects of working are intrinsic to a UK health service and the environment in which it is likely to work as against those which are changeable and, if necessary, corrigible.

14. There are features deriving from health service tasks which can be improved not by changing the structure but by accepting that there are inherent tensions and ambiguities and that choices have to be made where no perfect solution can be found. Thus the prescribing role of the individual practitioner and his right and duty to act according to his perception of individual patient needs are fundamental and unchanging assumptions. But, as we have observed several times throughout this study, there is tension between individual discretion and institutional development on the one hand, and the administration of allocative justice and accountable systems on the other. This fundamental cleavage leads to role ambiguity amongst senior practitioners who have to be both representative of practitioners and parts of managerial teams. On the same theme, the health service needs prime institutions—hospitals, health centres, patterns of family practice, residential care settings—which are strong, and confident about the work they do. But institutional discretion and creativity have to be fitted into a system using vast resources and coping with needs going beyond the individual clinicians, firms or hospital. The case studies show the mind boggling complexity of the system in which these dual criteria have to be met.

15. A further desirable and unavoidable aspect of the system is its participative and consultative nature. Participation is intended to meet the demand for a service to be *democratic* (but our comments on Community

Health Councils, the advisory systems and on authority members, demonstrate that there is uncertainty about the democratic base of participation). It is also, however, compatible with *rational* planning. Information and values are derived from clienteles and from those working within the service. The participative mode, however, is costly of resources. It can also cost a lot in terms of administrative confidence. That cost of being participative must be weighed against the dangers of the service being unreflective as to what people need.

16. More generally, the health service has to bring together a wide range of caring professions, working in different settings, such as patients' homes, and acute hospitals, and it is likely, therefore, that the system will not work easily as a unified whole. There will not be a "right" policy for the most part, but only policies that are seen to be the result of careful thought and reasonable process, and acknowledged as such. It is difficult to see how any of this can be changed by administrative or structural reorganisation. It may be a well-meaning but fallacious optimism to assume that the redefinition of the boundaries of health care can be made other than through professional interaction.

17. The NHS reflects movements of social change. Reorganisation encouraged aspirations, particularly among staff in the community sector, which it has so far proved difficult to realise. For staff at all levels, the uncertainties of reorganisation have been compounded by financial restrictions. Uncertainties, too, stem from changes in the political and social climate of the NHS. Emerging professions and trade unions are challenging traditional statuses, a process which, to some extent, gained encouragement from the reorganised structures. Many feel that values of service have been eroded by self-interest.

18. The NHS is going through an extremely difficult period. The reorganisation had traumatic effects on many individuals who found themselves forced to apply for their own jobs, to settle into new roles, to understand a new and apparently overwhelmingly complex organisation. The advantages of reorganisation, such as rational planning; the establishment of consensual and participative methods of working; the building up of systematic as well as of detailed practitioner relationships between different parts of hitherto divided health and other services; the marking out of a place for client views in the provision of health services; and the resulting need for changed behaviour on both sides; are all long-term processes.

19. Reorganisation is an example of government attempting to pack a wide range of objectives into one system. It was intended to produce a system that could make calculations about total need and allocate resources whilst allowing local patterns of practice and decision making to emerge. Yet we found too strong a *sense of inevitability* about the system. When asked, few would desire another wholesale reorganisation. But there seems to be no reason why each health authority should not be allowed to adjust, if only at the margin, their existing organisation. We now briefly summarise some of the main points relevant to potential change.

Integration

20. The main objective of the service, integration, was generally thought to be achieved by management teams and there was some evidence that the integration of hospital and former local authority services had improved. The strength, however, of the hospital as the most powerful prime institution remained as a problem perceived by those concerned with community services. Yet those working within them sometimes felt that the hospital had been somewhat demoted as a result of integration. The continued separation, however, of family practitioner services, was a most serious issue, exemplified by the difficulty of dealing with the type of health patterns exemplified in our case studies on the planning system. The solution did not lie in changes in structure, to judge from the examples of Northern Ireland and Scotland where the integration of the family practitioner services within an area health authority did not lead to reports of better integration of planning and practice. Independent contractual status, so highly prized by doctors, remains as a primary obstacle to full integration since there are no rewards or sanctions for better or worse working together. The motives and incentives for change lie elsewhere than in organisational change. *No clear recommendation on this issue can be made therefore, which does not include a radical change of concepts and values.*

21. It may well be that full integration will never be possible because of the sheer complexity of health services and the wide range of professions in a wide range of working contexts. Technical and working assumptions are different in hospitals and in the home or school, or community services. Yet if full integration is not possible then working together and overall planning must be achieved. So far, the teams of officers work to bring together hospital and community services and policies. Health care planning teams should be carrying the procedure further by connecting services for particular client groups. At the operational level, indeed, we found reports of good working, but not all in any way related to reorganisation. *Once the overall system is better established integration, or working together at the operational level, needs to be pursued more strongly.* Changes in structure do not necessarily affect behaviour if there is no motivational inducement.

Structure

22. There was a widespread feeling that there are too many administrative levels in the service. In England the major problem was identified as being located at the area and sub-area levels. These difficulties are fewer and less marked in single than in multi-district areas. The problem of competing autonomous teams at two levels responsible to the same authority, as well as the absence of any managerial relationship between the officers of different teams, created what many participants, in both SDAs and MDAs, saw as the major difficulty of the reorganised structure. Many interviewees advocated the creation of more SDAs as a solution to this problem and this may well be advantageous in some authorities, although not possible or even desirable everywhere. *The research team does recommend, however, that each region and area should review its structure with a view to simplification.* Such a review should not require that the principle of co-terminosity be adhered to if

228

it conflicts with health service considerations in the determination of boundaries. It may well be that, in view of the pressures on senior NHS officers and to aid acceptability of any proposals for change, *the reviews should be carried out by independent research teams which should be at pains to respect local conditions and wishes and not to propose pre-constructed solutions derived from theory or current management studies rhetoric.*

Consensus Management

23. There was general support for the principle of consensus management because team members should gain a better understanding of the NHS as a whole and because commitment to team decisions should be enhanced by this mode of decision making. Some problems were noted. Decisions were thought to be slower, and more prone to "weak" decisions. Individual and sometimes trivial issues might be referred for team resolution, when its attention should be focussed only on the major interdisciplinary issues.

24. A major problem of consensus management was the extent to which teams felt unable to accept failure to agree. A failure to agree on occasion is inevitable in teams of chief officers (and clinicians in DMTs and AMTs), from different professional disciplines. Recognition of this would have two main benefits. It would enable clinician members of teams to reconcile their conflicting roles as managers and representatives (see the case study on bio-medical engineering) more easily by leaving the final decision to the AHA where consensus is not possible. In addition it would provide a more meaningful role for AHA members who find that the unanimity of consensus decision making pre-empts an effective role for them within the managerial system. *Here the changes to be made are not structural but behavioural.*

Relations with Local Authorities

25. The arrangements for the reorganised NHS accorded a high priority to the establishment (or maintenance) of good relations with local authorities in order to encourage liaison with their relevant welfare services. Participants believed that co-terminosity could confer some benefits but its imposition almost everywhere produced boundaries which in some cases did not relate to well established health care links. *Co-terminosity should not be regarded as sacrosanct if it provides an obstacle to the simplification of the administrative structure advocated in paragraph 22.*

26. Both the integration and the co-terminosity issue threw doubt on the extent to which complex systems can work together by virtue of organisational change. The particular case of health and social services in Northern Ireland, which is the strongest example of a determination to achieve integration by structural change, shows how important it is not to be misled by the "organisational" fallacy, the assumption that institutional change will, of itself, cause good working together of professional groups with different expertise, social values and traditions of relations with clients.

Advisory Committees

27. The place of advisory committees within the NHS decision making process presents one of the major problems of the new structure. The principle was widely accepted and extensive consultation increased the acceptability of decisions. But the need to consult with so many people on

so many issues delayed decision making and created extra work. In some areas the need to over-consult, as some participants put it, was seen as the major problem facing the NHS today. *The recommendation of the research team is that the review of the administrative structure, advocated in paragraph 22, should be accompanied by a close look at the advisory system with a view to establishing which committees should form part of the consultative process.* Experience may show that certain committees are no longer required while others may be needed for professional purposes but may not need to relate to the management system. Here, as elsewhere, the objective should be a greater simplification of an over-elaborate structure.

Authorities

28. The major issue concerning members was the extent to which they have impact on NHS policy making. Unlike the local authorities there is no system of standing committees to enable members to be directly involved in managing the system. Members were to make policy and allocate resources while officers were to manage the service remaining accountable to the authority. The research team believes that the distinction between management and policy, plausible enough in theory, cannot easily be made in practice. Effective policy making arises more readily from a sound knowledge of the management of the service. The potential isolation of members from effective policy making is aggravated by the consensus mode of decision making employed by officer teams. The unanimity of a multi-professional officer team is hard to challenge and effectively pre-empts a serious role for members. For authorities to participate adequately in policy making they must be offered genuine policy options and not simply be presented with worked through solutions. In addition, teams should be more open about their internal differences and hence allow the AHA or RHA to be the final arbiter where officer disagreement exists. But, our case study on the use of members' inquiries also demonstrates the difficulties caused by determined attempts by members to manage the system. *Again, no structural changes seem necessary although further learning of how to relate roles together is needed.*

Community Health Councils

29. The principle of a consumer representative body was generally accepted although there were reservations about both the ways in which some of the CHCs interpreted their role and the receptiveness of health authorities to this form of critique. Much of the criticism related to the lack of a responsible approach by some CHCs to criticisms concerning aspects of the NHS in their district. *More carefully worked out processes of ascertaining, evaluating and publishing facts are needed* if the CHCs are to develop their full role and to work in a more appropriate relationship with the service. None of these changes would derogate from the fact that CHCs are part of the legitimate politics of health. One of our case studies shows how planning is, and should be, responsive both to the evaluation of data and of practitioner feelings by "the system" and of the perceived needs and wants of clients.

The Decision Making Process

30. The overwhelming impression of both participants and the research team is that of a top-heavy and over-elaborate management system. There are too many levels of administration and too much duplication of functions

230

at the different levels. Any reduction in this number of levels must simplify decision making if only by a reduction in the communication and co-ordination inevitably required where authority is located in many centres. *Along with a simplification of the structure there should be greater delegation of authority to the hospital or field work centre.* More issues can and should be settled by administrators and professionals at the institutional level. The emphasis on functional management needs to be brought into perspective with the need to delegate. *The consultative process should be streamlined so that decision making can be made more speedily and effectively.* The process of involving everybody is in the end harmful to everybody. The balance between efficiency and acceptability is weighted too much against efficiency. The balance must be restored.

General Conclusions

31. Within the present structure it is unlikely that decision making can be efficient. It is even less likely that morale can be high. We emphasise that many of the sources of low morale have nothing to do with reorganisation. It is a bad time to be a public servant. Management faces virtually incessant bombardment from employees wanting changes of status as well as of conditions and salaries, from clients who want a voice in the management of the system, from members who are under far more political pressure than used to be the case within the former hospital service. The authorities face demands from the centre to reallocate resources, and have to cope with both the vagaries of demographic change and with all but impervious and immovable resources. But we have to record a great deal of anger and frustration at what many regard as a seriously over-elaborate system of government, administration and decision making. The multiplicity of levels, the over-elaboration of consultative machinery, the inability to get decision making completed nearer the point of delivery of services, and what some describe as unacceptably wasteful use of manpower resources were recurrent themes in most of the areas where we worked. On one point, indeed, the Royal Commission can allay public disquiet. It was not our task to evaluate people and performance, but it was the unanimous feeling of the research team that most of the people we met were committed, able and concerned. Most accepted the main objectives of reorganisation. Few were over-enchanted by the previous system (and has there ever been a time when the hospital service was thought to be working well?). The service is not full of bureaucrats who enjoy over-elaboration and bureaucracy for their own sake. Too many are unhappy about the *corrigible* aspects of a structure whose main fault is over-elaboration. *Our principal recommendation is; therefore, that health authorities should begin to make a careful, slow and reflective attempt to enhance delegation, to remove levels of administration, many of which are known to fail to contribute towards efficient working.* This will certainly involve some shedding of the ideals associated with reorganisation. There is, indeed, a values overload which shows itself in the form of organisational over-elaboration.

32. The research team wishes to record the splendid co-operation received from the members of the NHS with whom we have worked. We also feel,

however, that that co-operation would not have been forthcoming so readily if there were not important messages to impart.

Department of Government
Brunel University
January 1978

APPENDIX
List of Sources Consulted

General Sources

Brown, R. S. G., *The Changing National Health Service*, Routledge & Kegan Paul, 1973.

Brown, R. S. G. (*et al*), *Humberside Reorganisation Project*, Institute for Health Studies, University of Hull, 1972–75.

Draper, P., and Smart, A., *Value Judgements in Health Planning*, Community Medicine, 2 February 1973.

Draper, P., and Smart, A., *The Future of our Health Care*, Department of Community Medicine, Guy's Hospital Medical School, 1972.

Howie, W. B., *Problems of Area Planning*, Health Bulletin, May 1976.

Klein, R., *NHS Reorganisation: The Politics of the Second Best*, Lancet, 26 August 1972.

Nuffield Centre for Health Services Studies, *Issues and Prospects*, University of Leeds, 1974.

Office of Health Economics, *The NHS Reorganisation*, 1974.

Queens University of Belfast, Department of Business Studies, *The Reorganisation of Health and Personal Social Services in Northern Ireland*, August 1974. (J. A. Bates, J. S. E. Maynard, P. E. McCready).

Official Documents

Booz, Allen and Hamilton, *"An Integrated Service: The Reorganisation of Health and Personal Social Services in Northern Ireland"*, February 1972.

Common Service Agency, "Building Division", (Leaflet).
    "Building Division", *Management Structure*, September 1974.
    Common Service Agency for the Scottish Health Service, July 1977 (Unpublished).

Department of Health and Social Security, *Management Arrangements for the Reorganised Health Service*, HMSO, 1972.
    National Health Service Reorganisation: England, Cmnd 5055, HMSO, 1972. (White Paper on Reorganisation).
    Guide to Planning in the National Health Service (Draft), March 1975.
    The NHS Planning System, June 1976.

Ministry of Health and Social Services, *Summary of a Report on "An Integrated Service: The Reorganisation of Health and Personal Social Services in Northern Ireland"*, May 1972.
    Guide to the Central Services Agency for Health and Personal Social Services, March 1973.
    Guide to the New Structure for Health and Personal Social Services, November 1972.

Oxford Regional Health Authority, Review Committee for the Oxford Region, *Report on the Management Functions of the Regional and Area Health Authorities*, Discussion Document, January 1977.

Scottish Home and Health Department, *The Medical Advisory Structure Within Health Boards in Scotland*, A Review, April 1977 (Unpublished).
    Working Party on Relationships Between Health Boards and Local Authorities—Report, 1977.
    Health Service Reorganisation, Scotland, *CSA: Building Division*, September 1973 (HSR (73) M.1).

Scottish Health Building Code Part I, *Procedure for the Preparation and Approval of Individual Projects,* July 1976.

Scottish Health Building Code Part II, *Cost Control,* July 1977.

Select Committee on the Parliamentary Commissioner for Administration, First Report, *Independent Review of Hospital Complaints in the NHS,* Cmnd 45, HMSO, December 1977.

Welsh Office, *Management Arrangements for the Reorganised National Health Service in Wales,* HMSO, 1972.

Documents Relevant to the Planning Case Study

The City and East London Area Health Authority (Teaching), *Are~ Pl~* 1978/79.

  City and Hackney Health District Plan, 1978/79.
  Area Strategic Plan, March 1977.
  Newham Health District Plan, 1978/79.
  Tower Hamlets Health District Plan, 1978/79.

North East Thames Regional Health Authority, *Regional Guidelines 1977/80,* July 1976.

  Regional Operational Planning Guidelines, 1978/81.
  Regional Resource Allocation Working Party, Interim Report, September 1976.
  Regional Strategic Plan, Revised Draft, December 1976.

Printed in England for Her Majesty's Stationery Office by Oyez Press Limited

Dd587102   K24 5/78